INTENSIVE BASIC

Intensive Basic Latin: A Grammar and Workbook comprises a dynamic reference grammar and related exercises in a single volume. The book presents forty individual grammar points, covering the core material which students would expect to encounter in their first year of learning Latin. Grammar points are followed by contextualized examples and exercises which allow students to reinforce and consolidate their learning.

There is a particular emphasis throughout on familiarizing students with real, unadulterated Latin and the task of teasing information from the Latin via translations. To this end, there are matching exercises with unedited Latin excerpts and rough English translations in the chapters, encouraging students to take a hands-on approach in their learning. In addition to this, a short reading relating to the adventures of Hercules is presented at the end of almost every chapter; these readings, which become progressively more complex, give the course a strong sense of narrative cohesion and interest and provide students with opportunities to develop their comprehension and translation skills.

Key features include:

- Clear, accessible format and jargon-free explanations of grammar
- Many useful language examples
- Abundant and varied exercises with full answer key
- Controlled usage of vocabulary throughout, allowing students to concentrate on building up their grammatical knowledge
- Review sections at intervals throughout the text, providing exercises specially designed to consolidate knowledge of language points covered
- Useful English–Latin and Latin–English dictionaries at the back of the book.

Written by an experienced instructor, *Intensive Basic Latin: A Grammar and Workbook* is an ideal resource for beginning students of Latin. It can be used as a textbook, grammar reference and practice resource and is suitable both for class use and independent study.

Jean-François R. Mondon is Assistant Professor of Foreign Languages at Minot State University, USA.

Other titles available in the Grammar Workbooks series are:

Basic Arabic

Basic Cantonese
Intermediate Cantonese

Basic Chinese
Intermediate Chinese

Basic German
Intermediate German

Basic Irish
Intermediate Irish

Basic Italian

Basic Japanese
Intermediate Japanese

Basic Korean
Intermediate Korean

Basic Persian

Basic Polish
Intermediate Polish

Basic Portuguese

Basic Russian
Intermediate Russian

Basic Spanish
Intermediate Spanish

Basic Welsh
Intermediate Welsh

Basic Yiddish

INTENSIVE BASIC LATIN: A GRAMMAR AND WORKBOOK

Jean-François R. Mondon

 Routledge
Taylor & Francis Group

LONDON AND NEW YORK

First published 2015
by Routledge
2 Park Square, Milton Park, Abingdon, Oxon OX14 4RN

and by Routledge
711 Third Avenue, New York, NY 10017

Routledge is an imprint of the Taylor & Francis Group, an informa business

© 2015 Jean-François R. Mondon

British Library Cataloguing in Publication Data
A catalogue record for this book is available from the British Library

Library of Congress Cataloging in Publication Data
Mondon, Jean-François R., author.
  Intensive basic Latin : a grammar and workbook / Jean-François R. Mondon.
    pages cm
  1. Latin language–Grammar.   2. Latin language–Textbooks.   I. Title.
  PA2087.5.M58 2015
  478.2421–dc23

                                                      2014021733

ISBN: 978-0-415-72362-6 (hbk)
ISBN: 978-0-415-72364-0 (pbk)
ISBN: 978-1-315-74022-5 (ebk)

Typeset in Times New Roman
by Graphicraft Limited, Hong Kong

For *mémé* and *pépé*.

CONTENTS

INTRODUCTION

This book is intended as a synopsis of every major grammatical point usually taught in a first semester college Latin course. Since the central focus of this book is grammatical structure, the vocabulary used throughout the Latin-to-English and English-to-Latin exercises is kept constant and repeated often, allowing the reader to focus solely on the grammar and not on acquiring new words every unit, as most conventional books do. The pool of words which are used in the fabricated sentences throughout the book is largely confined to those words that are used in the exercises of units in which grammar unique to specific lexical items is introduced; namely, Units 2 (1st, 2nd, 4th conjugations), 3 (3rd conjugation), 4 (1st declension), 5 (2nd declension), 6 (1st–2nd declension adjectives), 15 (3rd declension), 16 (3rd declension *i*-stems), 17 (3rd declension adjectives), and 36 (4th and 5th declensions). Aside from the focus on grammar, this book also aims to acquaint students with the task of dealing with real, unadulterated Latin and teasing information from the Latin via a translation. To this end, starting in Unit 2 and running until the end of the book, each unit contains a matching exercise with unedited Latin excerpts and rough English translations. Additionally, in order to give more cohesion to the book and to give students the sense of completion not to mention some enjoyment, the story of Hercules is presented from Units 5 through 39. Naturally, the Latin used in each snippet becomes progressively more complex. Unit 40 ends with the opening lines of Caesar's *Gallic Wars*, syntactically parsed along the lines of my *Caesar's Dē Bellō Gallicō: A Syntactically Parsed Reader* which is also available from Routledge. These reading excerpts may be shorter than some instructors would like but it is believed at this stage of language acquisition that the student must focus on truly acquiring the forms, something which is oftentimes lost when the task becomes translating large passages with unknown vocabulary. I have therefore opted for quality over quantity. In order to get longer passages, however, an instructor could hold off on reading the various Hercules excerpts until the relevant units have been covered. So for instance, rather than read the first part of Hercules' battle with the Amazons in Unit 27, the class could hold off and read it along with the second and concluding part of the story after Unit 28.

Seven review sections are littered throughout the book, roughly divided along thematic lines. The order of grammar topics is gradient and builds upon earlier units, though someone wishing to use this book for review could certainly skip around as the units are largely self-contained. I think most instructors will find nothing crazy about the ordering of units though it may strike some as odd to present adverbs near the end of the book. I concede that this is unusual but since the grammar of adverbs is rather simple and nothing is lost by not introducing them earlier, I have decided to hold them off until comparatives and superlatives have been introduced, so that all aspects of adverbs can be presented in one fell swoop. An answer key is provided at the end of the book, though translations of the reading excerpts and answers for the seven review sections are absent. Latin to English and English to Latin dictionaries close out the book.

As stated above this book is intended as a first semester college Latin course (it could certainly be used in high schools too). The 40 units can be covered in a single semester for those courses which meet four or five hours a week. For those courses which meet three hours a week, working through the first 28 units is reasonable. The second volume of this series, *Intensive Intermediate Latin*, has as its focus the subjunctive, subordinate clauses, and longer reading passages. The two volumes together form a complete collegiate Latin sequence, preparing students for higher level Latin prose or poetry courses.

A book such as this is not written in a bubble but bears the imprint of many people I would be remiss if I did not formally thank here. To begin with this book would probably have never seen the light of the day had I not been forced to take two years of Latin back in high school. I'd like to thank Larry Iezzi, my first Latin teacher, whose enthusiasm for this amazing language was palpable and contagious. George Beöthy, whether he knew it or not, helped kindle my growing interest in languages through our many conversations about all things linguistics-related. Additionally, along with Fr. Richard Wyzykiewicz, Sch.P, he helped get me permission to base the Hercules excerpts used here on *Roma Aeterna: A Second-Year Latin Book* by the late polyglot Fr. Ladislaus Magyar, Sch.P. Aside from my professors in college from whom I learned the beauty of giving short 7-minute quizzes to my own students (Aislinn Melchior), the reality of spoken Latin (Shane Butler), and its rich and intricate history (Don Ringe, George Cardona), I absolutely owe a great debt of gratitude to my bosses, past and present, Jeffrey Lyons and Linda Olson. The former took a chance on a recent college graduate and entrusted him with three classes of Latin at Notre Dame High School in East Stroudsburg, PA. Besides having had the good fortune to acquire tidbits of pedagogical advice from fantastic senior colleagues, it was there that I first had the opportunity to begin to put Latin grammatical notes together. I cannot thank enough my students from those three memorable classes (Latin I, II, and AP Latin (where we happily read more Catullus than Vergil)) who not only taught me how not to teach but reminded me that this profession is pretty awesome. Linda Olson invited me with open arms out to Minot State University where she not only has given me free rein to start a

Latin concentration but has been unimaginably encouraging of all of my endeavors and whose exceptionally positive comportment is truly admirable. It is here at Minot State that my grammatical notes became the full-fledged units which comprise this book. This work has benefited tremendously from my students here who dealt with my random asides into Classical Armenian, Celtic linguistics, and the Amish and were always happy to point out typos. In particular I would like to express my gratitude to Megan Alley, Kortney Arnold, Kaylee Dockter, Deb Kinzell, David Lavergne, Ashley McGonigle, Steven Merkel, Misty Neumiller, and Matthew Volk. This book has benefited greatly from three anonymous reviewers. While I could not incorporate all of their feedback, those comments which have been included have made this book that much better. I would like to thank Mary Dalton who had the unenviable task of reading through an early manuscript and making sense of erratic sentences. Additionally, I express my gratitude to proofreader Claire Trocmé who worked through all the exercises and who not only caught many oversights but provided a much needed user perspective to the work. Finally, Andrea Hartill and Isabelle Cheng at Routledge have made this task so unimaginably easy. I thank them for always being positive and immediately responsive to my questions and in particular thank Andrea for allowing this book to become a reality.

Maximās grātiās vōbīs omnibus agō!

LATIN SOURCES

The abbreviations follow those used by the Perseus Digital Library (www. perseus.tufts.edu).

Apuleius *Met.* — *Metamorphoses*
Caesar *Civ.* — *The Civil War*
Caesar *Gal.* — *The Gallic War*
Catullus — *Carmina*
Cicero *ad Brut.* — *Letters to and from Brutus*
Cicero *Agr.* — *On the Agrarian Law*
Cicero *Amic.* — *On Friendship*
Cicero *Att.* — *Letters to Atticus*
Cicero *Brut.* — *Brutus*
Cicero *Caec.* — *For Aulus Caecina*
Cicero *Cael.* — *For Marcus Caelius*
Cicero *Catil.* — *Against Catiline*
Cicero *Clu.* — *For Aulus Cluentius*
Cicero *de Orat.* — *Dē Ōrātōre*
Cicero *Deiot.* — *For King Deiotarius*
Cicero *Div. Caec.* — *Dīvīnātiō against Q. Caecilius*
Cicero *Dom.* — *On his House*
Cicero *Fam.* — *Epistulae ad Familiārēs*

Cicero *Fin.* — *Dē Fīnibus Bonōrum et Malōrum*
Cicero *Flac.* — *For Flaccus*
Cicero *Font.* — *For Marcus Fonteius*
Cicero *Har.* — *On the Responses of the Haruspices*
Cicero *Marc.* — *For Marcellus*
Cicero *Mil.* — *For Milo*
Cicero *Mur.* — *For Lucius Murena*
Cicero *Off.* — *Dē Officiīs*
Cicero *Orat.* — *Ōrātor*
Cicero *Parad.* — *Paradoxa Stōicōrum ad M. Brūtum*
Cicero *Phil.* — *Philippics*
Cicero *Pis.* — *Against Piso*
Cicero *Planc.* — *For Plancius*
Cicero *Q. fr.* — *Letters to and from Quintus*
Cicero *Red. Pop.* — *To the Citizens after his Return*
Cicero *S. Rosc.* — *For Sextus Roscius of Ameria*

Cicero *Sen.*	*Dē Senectūte*	Pliny the Elder	*The Natural History*
Cicero *Sul.*	*For Sulla*		
Cicero *Top.*	*Topica*	Pliny the Younger	*Letters*
Cicero *Tusc.*	*Tusculānae Disputātiōnēs*	Q. Tullius Cicero	*Essay on Running for Consul*
Cicero *Vat.*	*Against Vatinius*	Quintilian *Inst.*	*Īnstitūtiō Ōrātōria*
Cicero *Ver.*	*Against Verres*		
Gellius	*Attic Nights*	Sallust *Cat.*	*The Catilinarian Conspiracy*
Horace *Ars*	*The Art of Poetry*		
Horace *Od.*	*Carmina*	Sallust *Jug.*	*The Jugurthine War*
Horace *S.*	*Satyrārum Librī*		
Josephus *Ap.*	*Against Apion*	Seneca *Ben.*	*Dē Beneficiīs*
Livy	*The History of Rome*	Seneca *Cl.*	*Dē Clēmentia*
		Seneca *Ep.*	*Moral Letters to Lucilius*
Lucretius	*On the Nature of Things*	Seneca *Her. O.*	*Herculēs Oetaeus*
Martial	*Epigrams*		
Nepos *Them.*	*Themistocles*	Seneca *Phaed.*	*Phaedra*
Ovid *Am.*	*Art of Love*	Servius Honoratus	*Commentary on the Georgics of Vergil*
Ovid *Ep.*	*Epistles*		
Ovid *Met.*	*Metamorphoses*		
Ovid *Tr.*	*Tristia*	Statius *Silv.*	*Silvae*
Petronius	*Satyricon*	St Jerome	*Vulgate Bible*
Phaedrus	*Aesop's Fables*	Suetonius *Aug.*	*Dīvus Augustus*
Plautus *Am.*	*Amphitruo*	Suetonius *Cal.*	*Caligula*
Plautus *As.*	*Asinaria*	Suetonius *Dom.*	*Domitiānus*
Plautus *Capt.*	*Captīvī*	Suetonius *Gal.*	*Galba*
Plautus *Cas.*	*Casina*	Suetonius *Jul.*	*Dīvus Iūlius*
Plautus *Cist.*	*Cistellāria*	Suetonius *Nero*	*Nerō*
Plautus *Cur.*	*Curculio*	Suetonius *Tib.*	*Tiberius*
Plautus *Epid.*	*Epidicus*	Suetonius *Ves.*	*Vespasiānus*
Plautus *Men.*	*Menaechmī*	Suetonius *Vit.*	*Vitellius*
Plautus *Mer.*	*Mercātor*	Tacitus *Ann.*	*Annālēs*
Plautus *Mil.*	*Mīles Glōriōsus*	Tacitus *Hist.*	*Historiae*
Plautus *Mos.*	*Mostellāria*	Terence *Ad.*	*Adelphī*
Plautus *Per.*	*Persa*	Terence *Eu.*	*Eunuchus*
Plautus *Poen.*	*Poenulus*	Terence *Ph.*	*Phormiō*
Plautus *Ps.*	*Pseudolus*	Valerius Flaccus	*Argonautica*
Plautus *Rud.*	*Rudēns*	Vergil *Aeneid*	*Aeneid*
Plautus *St.*	*Stichus*	Vergil *Ecl.*	*Eclogues*
Plautus *Trin.*	*Trinummus*	Vergil *G.*	*Georgicon*
Plautus *Truc.*	*Truculentus*	Vitruvius	*On Architecture*

UNIT 1
Pronunciation and stress

I. Pronunciation

Background

Knowing how a word is pronounced in Latin is much easier than in English since the spelling system is so regular. One letter equals one sound. Nothing like English *read* exists in Latin, where the same word can be pronounced two different ways each with different meanings: *You read it now.* vs. *You read it yesterday.*

There are two ways to pronounce Latin:

- classical pronunciation

  - The way the language actually sounded in the first century BCE

- Church pronunciation

  - This is very similar to Italian, differing from classical pronunciation in a few key spots. It reflects the pronunciation of Latin after the Roman Empire (*c.* 500 CE) and is the standard used today by the Vatican.

In what follows classical pronunciation is presented alongside a transcription into the international phonetic alphabet for those readers who may be familiar with it. Unique developments of church pronunciation are indicated after each section.

Vowels

The pronunciation of the models reflects a northeastern American accent.

Latin			*International Phonetic Alphabet*
a	*a* in *ago*	[ə]	
ā	*a* in *father*	[a]	
e	*e* in *bet*	[ɛ]	
ē	*a* in *made*	[e]	NB: this is not an exact correspondent since the *a* in English *made* is a diphthong (see below)
i	*i* in *in*	[ɪ]	
ī	*ee* in *meet*	[i]	
o	*o* in *bought*	[ɔ]	NB: many English dialects lack this vowel, using [a] instead
ō	*o* in *most*	[o]	NB: this is not an exact correspondent since the *o* in English *most* is a diphthong (see below)
u	*oo* in *took*	[ʊ]	
ū	*oo* in *moon*	[u]	

Diphthongs

The movement of the tongue in the pronunciation of a single vowel is a diphthong. Some diphthongs in English occur in *I, my, die, how, mount, tone, show, doe, bay, mate, boy, toil.*

The principal diphthongs of Latin are:

ae	*y* in *my*	[aɪ]	oe	*oy* in *boy*	[ɔɪ]
au	*ow* in *how*	[aʊ]	ui	*wea* in *weak*	[wi]

Church pronunciation

ae	*a* in *save*	[e]
oe	*a* in *save*	[e]

Consonants

Those consonants for which nothing follows are pronounced as in English.

Latin		*International Phonetic Alphabet*
b		[b]
c	always as a hard *c*, like the *c* in *cook*	[k]
d		[d]
f		[f]
g	always as a hard *g*, like the *g* in *gate*	[g]
h		[h]
i	like the *y* in *yes*	[j]
l		[l]
m		[m]
n		[n]
p		[p]
qu		[kw]
r	trilled as in Spanish *rojo*	[r]
s		[s]
t		[t]
v	like *w* in *wet*	[w]
x	like *x* in *ax*	[ks]

Note that *i* may be used to write both a vowel and a consonant.
  As a rule of thumb *i* is a consonant when it occurs first in a root:

- this corresponds to the start of a word:

  - **iubeō** *I command*   has 3 syllables: **iu-be-ō**

- this also corresponds to a root which follows a prefix such as **con-**

  - **coniūrātiō** *conspiracy*   has 5 syllables: **con-iū-rā-ti-ō**

As you learn more Latin, you will get a feel for the recurring prefixes of the language.

Church pronunciation

c is like the *ch* in *church* when

- it is followed by: *e, ē, i, ī, ae, oe*   [tʃ]

g is like the *j* in *judge* when

- it is followed by: *e, ē, i, ī, ae, oe*   [dʒ]

v is like English *v*	[v]
ti before a vowel is pronounced like *ts* in *cats*	[ts]

II. Stress

Fundamentals

One syllable in every word bears the stress in Latin. This is similar to English. However, the two languages differ in whether the location of the stressed syllable in a word is predictable or not.

- In English, which syllable bears the stress is unpredictable. Speakers of English simply need to memorize that the word *fundamental* bears stress on the third syllable, *American* on the second, *record* [the thing placed on a turntable] on the first, and *record* [the act of copying something to a CD or DVD] on the second.
- In Latin, on the other hand, which syllable carries the stress is perfectly predictable according to a simple algorithm.

Algorithm for determining stress

Stress in Latin may only occur on one of the last three syllables of the word, which are called:

ultima	the final syllable	[from Latin **ultima** *final*]
penult	the second to last syllable	[from **paene ultima** *almost final*]
antepenult	the third to last syllable	[from **ante paene ultima** *before the almost final*]

Stress is placed on the *ultima* if the word only has one syllable.

- Remember that **qu** counts as a single consonant and not as a consonant + vowel.

  - **quis** *who* has only one syllable

Stress is placed on the *penult* if one of the following three conditions holds:

1 the word only has two syllables
2 the penult has a long vowel (**ā, ē, ī, ō, ū**) or a diphthong (**ae, au, oe, ui**)

3 the vowel of the penult is followed by two consonants or **x**

- **x** counts as two consonants since it is pronounced as *ks*
- **qu** counts as a single consonant

Stress is placed on the *antepenult* when:

- the penult does not fit any of the above 3 conditions

Exercise 1

Each of the following words is stressed on the ultima or penult. In the case of the latter, indicate which of the three conditions it satisfies. It may satisfy more than one.

1 nauta *sailor*	8 imperātōre *by the emperor*
2 poēta *poet*	9 rēx *king*
3 nātūra *nature*	10 lībertās *freedom*
4 via *road*	11 mīles *soldier*
5 vīta *life*	12 senātus *senate*
6 pugna *fight*	13 quibus *to whom*
7 adulēscentis *of a young man*	14 quisque *each one*

Exercise 2

Determine whether the *ultima, penult,* or *antepenult* bears the stress in the following words and why.

1 haec *this*	11 equitātuum *of the cavalries*
2 tempestātem *storm*	12 quem *whom*
3 ambulāvissem *I would have walked*	13 aliquis *someone*
4 hiemis *of winter*	14 speciēs *appearance*
5 negōtium *task*	15 passūs *of the pace*
6 īnsidiae *ambush*	16 vallēs *valley*
7 īnsidiārum *of an ambush*	17 removeō *I remove*
8 proelium *battle*	18 rīdeō *I laugh*
9 amantium *of the loving ones*	19 Rōmānus *Roman*
10 pāx *peace*	20 interficiō *I kill*

UNIT 2
Present tense: conjugations I, II, IV

Background

The present tense conveys an action which is in the process of occurring. English has three ways of expressing this:

He walks.
He is walking.
He does walk.

The first two verbal forms differ with respect to aspect.

- *Walks* indicates that the action is habitual or commonplace, but does not imply that the action is necessarily taking place right now. It is termed *simple aspect.*
- *Is walking* emphasizes that the action is still currently in progress, hence it is termed *progressive aspect.*
- *Does walk* is used to respond affirmatively to a statement or question negating the sentence, for instance *He doesn't walk* or *He doesn't walk, does he?*

English hardly possesses any traces of personal endings in the present tense. In the 1st person (*I, we*), 2nd person (*you*), and 3rd person plural (*they*) forms, no ending is added: *I walk, we walk, you walk, they walk.* Only in the 3rd person singular (*he, she, it*) is an ending added: *s/he walks.*

Verbs in English are also grouped into classes termed *conjugations*, though the large majority fall into the *regular conjugation* (historically called *weak verbs*).

In listing the forms of a verb in English, one states the *verbal root*, the *past tense*, and the *past participle*. These are the three forms of a verb (termed the *principal parts*) needed to form every tense and aspect of the verb. For instance:

- The *verbal root* is used to form the present tense (*I walk, he walks*) and the present participle (*walking*)
- The *past tense* is used to form the simple past tense (*I walked, he walked*)

- The *past participle* is used to form the perfect tenses (*I have walked, I had walked*) and the passive voice (*The dog was walked, the dog has been walked*).

	Regular conjugation/Weak verbs	
Root	*Past tense*	*Past participle*
walk	walked	walked
look	looked	looked
wave	waved	waved

A minority of verbs are irregular and belong to other conjugations which are formed in English usually by changing the vowel of the root. These verbs are historically called strong verbs. While accounting for only a small percentage of English verbs, these irregular verbs are highly frequent.

	Irregular/Strong verbs	
Root	*Past tense*	*Past participle*
begin	began	begun
sing	sang	sung
swim	swam	swum
wake	woke	woken
speak	spoke	spoken
steal	stole	stolen

Latin structure

Latin only possesses one present tense form. The three different types of English present are all translated by the same Latin form.

Latin has *four conjugations*, with very meagre traces of a 5th which is termed the *3rd-iō conjugation*. As opposed to English all four of the Latin conjugations have many members.

A Latin verb possesses four principal parts, each of which must be memorized when learning a new verb, since they will each be used to form specific tenses and moods. For instance:

1st conjugation:	**amō**	**amāre**	**amāvī**	**amātus**	*to love*
2nd conjugation:	**videō**	**vidēre**	**vīdī**	**vīsus**	*to see*
3rd conjugation:	**dūcō**	**dūcere**	**dūxī**	**ductus**	*to lead*
3rd -iō conjugation:	**capiō**	**capere**	**cēpī**	**captus**	*to seize*
4th conjugation:	**sentiō**	**sentīre**	**sēnsī**	**sēnsus**	*to feel*

The four conjugations are differentiated by their *infinitives* which is the 2nd principal part (**amāre, vidēre, dūcere, capere, sentīre**).

- The *infinitive* in English is the '*to*-form' of the verb and is the dictionary form. All Latin verbs in this book will be glossed by their English infinitives.
- The principal parts of 1st conjugation verbs are predictable, always taking the endings -**ō**, -**āre**, -**āvī**, -**ātus**. Because of this 1st conjugation verbs are simply followed by (**1**) in dictionaries rather than having all their forms written out.

The 1st, 2nd and 4th conjugations all share the feature of having an infinitive with a long vowel followed by the ending -**re**. This vowel before the -**re** which marks the conjugation class of a verb is called a *thematic vowel*.

Conjugation	Infinitive	Examples
I	-ā-re	**amāre** 'to love'
II	-ē-re	**vidēre** 'to see'
IV	-ī-re	**sentīre** 'to feel'

These three conjugations form the present tense identically:

- Go to the infinitive and chop off the -**re**:

amāre	→	**amā-**
vidēre	→	**vidē-**
sentīre	→	**sentī-**

- Add the following endings:

	Singular	Plural
1	-ō	-mus
2	-s	-tis
3	-t	-nt

- Perform the following 4 alterations to the vowel before the ending:

  - Drop -ā- before the ending -ō in 1ˢᵗ conjugation verbs

    ○ **amō** and *not* *****amāō**

  - Shorten a long vowel before another vowel

    ○ **videō** and **sentiō** and not *****vidēō** or *****sentīō**

  - Shorten a long vowel before a word final -t and -nt

    ○ **amat** and **amant** rather than *****amāt** or *****amānt**.

  - Add a **-u-** before the **-nt-** in 4ᵗʰ conjugation verbs.

    ○ **sentiunt** and not *****sentint**

- The second and third alterations are general rules of Latin which are true throughout the language.

The result is:

	I	II	IV
1sg.	**amō** I love	**videō** I see	**sentiō** I feel
2	**amās** you love	**vidēs** you see	**sentīs** you feel
3	**amat** s/he loves	**videt** s/he sees	**sentit** s/he feels
1pl.	**amāmus** we love	**vidēmus** we see	**sentīmus** we feel
2	**amātis** you love	**vidētis** you see	**sentītis** you feel
3	**amant** they love	**vident** they see	**sentiunt** they feel

Note The 1ˢᵗ principal part of the verb is the 1ˢᵗ sg. of the present tense; that is, it is the *I* form of the verb.

Advanced topics

- Despite having an infinitive in **-are** rather than expected **-āre**, the verb **dō, dare, dedī, datus** *to give* is conjugated like any other 1ˢᵗ conjugation verb (**dō, dās, dat, dāmus, dātis, dant**). The same goes for **stare** *to stand.*
- The present can be used to express a past action in order to make the action more lively:

cohortīs paulātim incēdere *iubet*   he ordered (literally: orders) the cohorts
to advance gradually

(Sallust *Cat.* 60.1)

Exercise 1

Indicate the conjugation of the following, then translate.

1	properāmus	18	aperīs	35	pugnat
2	veniunt	19	patet	36	dēbet
3	aedificō	20	ārdēmus	37	nūntiās
4	stant	21	fulgētis	38	respondeō
5	manēs	22	dormit	39	rogātis
6	habitat	23	excitant	40	monent
7	movētis	24	parō	41	stat
8	portātis	25	mūnītis	42	imperāmus
9	habent	26	servāmus	43	negō
10	teneō	27	dant	44	vocat
11	tacet	28	videō	45	audiunt
12	sentit	29	sciunt	46	nescīs
13	cōgitō	30	putās	47	docēmus
14	amāmus	31	rīdēmus	48	iubētis
15	optat	32	studet	49	cavent
16	valent	33	terrēs	50	flētis
17	timent	34	nocētis		

Exercise 2

Change the numbers of the words in Exercise 1, keeping the person constant. That is, if a word is singular then make it plural. If a word is plural then make it singular.

Exercise 3

Translate the following into Latin.

1	we desire	11	he warns	21	she does find
2	they are sleeping	12	we do know	22	I am afraid
3	you (sg.) laugh	13	you (pl.) ask	23	they hear
4	it is burning	14	I deny	24	we are hastening
5	we do carry	15	they teach	25	she is standing
6	we are coming	16	he is eager	26	he announces
7	it does harm	17	you (sg.) love	27	you (pl.) open
8	it is open	18	we are fighting	28	they weep
9	I frighten	19	it is shining	29	he does command
10	they are strong	20	I think	30	we do not know

Exercise 4

Each of the following unedited Latin passages contains a 1ˢᵗ, 2ⁿᵈ, or 4ᵗʰ conjugation verb. Match each passage with the English translation which follows. To assist you, try to think of English derivatives which stem from some of the Latin words.

1	asȳlum aperit	(Livy)
2	Eō praesente coniūrātiōnem aperit	(Sallust *Cat.*)
3	quae frontīs aperit hominum	(Cicero *Planc.*)
4	et haec tibi portō dōna prius	(Vergil *Aeneid*)
5	nam omnia mēcum portō mea	(Cicero *Parad.*)
6	quī iussa per aurās verba patris portō	(Ovid *Met.*)
7	"rīdēs" inquiēs "in talibus rēbus?"	(Cicero *Att.*)
8	rīdēs? nōn sunt haec rīdicula	(Cicero *Att.*)
9	"Quid rīdēs" inquit "vervēx?"	(Petronius)
10	et nūdō corpore pugnāre	(Caesar *Gal.*)
11	ac fortius pugnāre coepērunt	(Caesar *Gal.*)
12	nunc quoniam pugnāre contrā mē īnstituistī	(Cicero *Ver.*)

(a) You laugh? These things are not funny

(b) he opens a sanctuary

(c) and to fight with a naked body

(d) indeed I carry all my things with me

(e) and they began to fight more bravely

(f) you will say "you laugh on such matters?"

(g) He says, "why do you laugh, you wether?"

(i) which uncovers the appearances of men

(j) since now you have resolved to fight against me

(k) in his presence he uncovers the conspiracy

(l) and before I carry these gifts to you

(m) I, who carry the commands – the words – of my father through air

UNIT 3
Present tense: conjugation III

Background

The third conjugation is unique for two reasons:

- Its *thematic vowel* is short: **dūcere**
- It is divided into two sub-conjugations which differ with respect to the presence or absence of **-i-** in certain forms:

    - 3rd regular conjugation
    - 3rd *iō* conjugation

- The following two verbs will be used to illustrate the two sub-conjugations in this unit:

3rd-regular	**dūcō**	**dūcere**	**dūxī**	**ductus**	*to lead*
3rd-*iō*	**capiō**	**capere**	**cēpī**	**captus**	*to seize*

Latin structure

To form the present tense:

- Drop the **-ō** from the first principal part:

    dūcō → **duc-**
    capiō → **capi-**

- To these, add the endings:

	Singular	*Plural*
1	-ō	-(i)mus
2	-(i)s	-(i)tis
3	-(i)t	-unt

- The -(i)- is added in 3rd-regular verbs since these are the verbs whose stem does not end in the vowel -i- already:

1sg.	**dūcō** I lead	**capiō** I seize
2	**dūcis** you lead	**capis** you seize
3	**dūcit** s/he leads	**capit** s/he seizes
1pl.	**dūcimus** we lead	**capimus** we seize
2	**dūcitis** you lead	**capitis** you seize
3	**dūcunt** they lead	**capiunt** they seize

Notes

- The two sub-conjugations are identical except for the extra -i- in the 1st sg. and 3rd pl. in 3rd-*iō* verbs.
- 3rd-*iō* verbs differ from the 4th conjugation (cf. Unit 2) in that the -i- is always short in the former but long -ī- in the latter.

capis, capimus, capitis vs. **sentīs, sentīmus, sentītis**

	Synopsis of present tense thematic vowels + endings				
	1st	*2nd*	*3rd*	*3rd-iō*	*4th*
1sg.	**-ō**	**-eō**	**-ō**	**-iō**	**-iō**
2	**-ās**	**-ēs**	**-is**	**-is**	**-īs**
3	**-at**	**-et**	**-it**	**-it**	**-it**
1pl.	**-āmus**	**-ēmus**	**-imus**	**-imus**	**-īmus**
2	**-ātis**	**-ētis**	**-itis**	**-itis**	**-ītis**
3	**-ant**	**-ent**	**-unt**	**-iunt**	**-iunt**

Exercise 1

Indicate whether each of the following is a regular 3rd conjugation verb or a
3rd-*iō* (use the dictionary to help you). Then translate.

1 petis	16 currō	31 crēdunt
2 fugit	17 caditis	32 dēscendō
3 tangimus	18 geris	33 trahit
4 dūcitis	19 mittunt	34 discēdis
5 pellō	20 agit	35 cōgunt
6 iaciunt	21 pōnō	36 iungitis
7 bibit	22 capimus	37 incipiunt
8 emis	23 relinquis	38 vertō
9 clauditis	24 vīvunt	39 crēscimus
10 premimus	25 rēgit	40 dīvidit
11 tegō	26 faciō	41 interficiō
12 frangit	27 dīcō	42 quaeritis
13 canunt	28 cernitis	43 intellegitis
14 nōscis	29 crēdis	44 discunt
15 legitis	30 scrībimus	45 cupiunt

Exercise 2

Change the numbers of all of the words in Exercise 1, keeping the person constant. That is, if a word is singular then make it plural. If a word is plural, then
make it singular.

Exercise 3

Translate the following into Latin.

1 you (sg.) divide	8 he desires	15 it begins
2 I say	9 we buy	16 she rules
3 you (pl.) send	10 they break	17 it closes
4 we ask	11 he kills	18 we do
5 they place	12 we write	19 I sing
6 she drinks	13 you (pl.) believe	20 they grow
7 he reads	14 they depart	21 you (sg.) lead

Exercise 4

Each of the following unedited Latin passages contains either a 3rd or 3rd-*iō*
conjugation verb. Match each passage with the English translation which follows. To assist you, try to think of English derivatives which stem from some
of the Latin words.

 1 vērum esse īnscītī crēdimus   (Plautus *Truc.*)
 2 parvum hoc tandem esse crēdimus   (Livy)
 3 deum esse nōn tamquam iussī crēdimus   (Seneca *Cl.*)
 4 implentur fossae et cava flūmina crēscunt (Vergil *G.*)
 5 nam concordiā parvae rēs crēscunt   (Sallust *Jug.*)
 6 omnia quandō paulātim crēscunt   (Lucretius)
 7 sed scīre cupiō quid habeat   (Cicero *Cael.*)
 8 cupiō audīre, ut videam   (Cicero *Phil.*)
 9 audīre cupiō, quī in pāce et ōtiō   (Cicero *Caec.*)
10 iacit volturiōs quattuor   (Plautus *Cur.*)
11 ante ōs ipsum portūs ancorās iacit   (Livy)
12 lustrāmina pontō pōne iacit   (Valerius Flaccus)

(a) but I wish to know what it has
(b) the ditches fill and hollow rivers grow
(c) small states indeed grow by harmony
(d) we, ignorant, believe it to be true
(e) he throws the four vultures
(f) he throws the anchors before the mouth itself of the harbor
(g) not just, as if ordered, do we believe him to be a god
(h) I wish to hear, that I may see
(i) since all things grow little by little
(j) we just believe this to be small
(k) he throws the purifying offerings behind to the sea
(l) I wish to hear, who in peace and leisure

Exercise 5

Using the sentences in Exercise 4, try to determine the meanings of the following words.

vērum	deum	pāce
ante	ancorās	quattuor

UNIT 4
1st declension

Fundamentals

How do we know who's doing the loving in the sentence *John loves the girl next door* or who's being bitten in the sentence *The dog bit the mailman*? Simple enough, the word order tells us. In English, the subject almost always precedes the verb. Equally consistently, the object follows the verb. Not all languages work this way, however. Languages such as Russian and Latin do not rely on word order to indicate the subject or object. Rather, they rely on special endings placed on the end of a word, called *inflectional endings*. Therefore, in the Latin sentence **Puer puellam amat** *the boy loves the girl* we know that **puellam** is the person being loved (**amat**) by the boy (**puer**) not because it occurs in a specific position in the sentence, but because it ends in **-am**.

Why do languages have inflectional endings? Well, it grants the language much freer word order which can be utilized in different contexts (something which is largely done by *intonation* in English or by adverbs). For instance, our Latin sentence could also be written among other possibilities – as:

> **Puellam puer amat.** [stressing the *girl*] The boy loves **THE GIRL**.
> **Amat puellam puer.** [stressing the act of *loving*] The boy **LOVES** the girl.

Latin cases

Inflectional endings added to nouns or pronouns are called *case endings*. There are five cases in Latin (and two minor cases, the *locative* and the *vocative*, discussed in Unit 29):

1 **nominative** – used when the noun is the subject

> '*The son* of the man bought with money a ring for the woman.'

2 **genitive** – used when the noun *possesses* something, usually translated by *of* + the noun or noun + *'s*

'The son *of the man* bought with money a ring for the woman.'
'The *man's* son bought with money a ring for the woman.'

3 **dative** – used to express the *indirect object* translated by *to/for* + the noun

'The son of the man bought with money a ring *for the woman*.'

4 **accusative** – used to express the *direct object* of the verb

'The son of the man bought with money *a ring* for the woman.'

5 **ablative** – used to express the *means* by which some action is done

'The son of the man bought *with money* a ring for the woman.'

or to highlight the means aspect of the ablative, one may translate:

'The son of the man bought a ring for the woman *by means of money*.'

As an aid to learning the cases, only the single most frequent use of each case is listed above. As will be seen in later units every case aside from the nominative possesses other functions.

As can be seen by the example sentence, what will be expressed in Latin via inflectional endings is expressed in English by prepositions, for example:

of the man   *for* the woman   *with* the money

In Latin each of the above is expressed by a SINGLE word, whose ending indicates what the word is doing in the sentence (note that Latin has no word for *the* or *a*):

virī of the man   -ī indicates the genitive
fēminae to the woman   -ae indicates the dative
pecūniā with money   -ā indicates the ablative

The translation of the English sentence into Latin is given below with the case endings underlined:

Fīlius virī fēminae pecūniā ānulum ēmit.

Latin declensions

Every noun in Latin belongs to one *and only one* of five declensions, for example: **pecūnia** (*money*) is 1st declension while **equus** (*horse*) is 2nd declension. Why a word is one declension as opposed to another is just a historical artifact which must be memorized, much like the plural of English *goose* is *geese* and not **gooses*.

Declensions differ by what endings are used to express the cases. The dictionary forms of a noun are the nominative singular and the genitive singular. When the stem of the genitive is the same as the stem of the nominative, only the genitive ending is listed and not the whole genitive form itself:

> **pecūnia**, **-ae** money   vs.   **grex**, **gregis** herd

1st declension

In order to decline any 1st declension noun, simply remove the final **-ae** from the genitive singular and add the following endings:

	Singular	*Plural*
Nominative	**-a**	**-ae**
Genitive	**-ae**	**-ārum**
Dative	**-ae**	**-īs**
Accusative	**-am**	**-ās**
Ablative	**-ā**	**-īs**

As an example: **pecūniae** → **pecūni-**

	Singular	*Plural*
Nominative	**pecūnia**	**pecūniae**
Genitive	**pecūniae**	**pecūniārum**
Dative	**pecūniae**	**pecūniīs**
Accusative	**pecūniam**	**pecūniās**
Ablative	**pecūniā**	**pecūniīs**

- Note that some forms are identical. Context will allow you to determine how such an ambiguous word is being used in a given sentence.
- Some words only occur in the plural. In lieu of listing the nominative and genitive singular forms of such words in the glossary, the nominative and genitive plurals are listed:

> **tenebrae**, **-ārum** *darkness*

- Most 1ˢᵗ declension nouns are feminine. The exceptions are a handful of words most of which refer to a profession, such as **nauta** *sailor*, **agricola** *farmer*, **poēta** *poet*, **incola** *inhabitant*

Advanced topics

The words **dea**, -ae *goddess* and **filia**, -ae *daughter* usually take the special ending -**ābus** in place of -**īs** in the dative and ablative plural.

This is to avoid ambiguity with the words **deus**, -ī *god* and **filius**, -ī *son* (see Unit 5).

Exercise 1

Convert each form to the opposite number, then translate. Some words may have more than one possibility.

1	laetitia	4	amīcitiā	7	deās	10	cōpiārum
2	noxae	5	lacrimārum	8	vītā	11	coma
3	fēminīs	6	agricolam	9	īnsidiīs	12	turbae

Exercise 2

Determine the case of the underlined words in each sentence. Then translate the underlined words into Latin. Note that English *in* and *on* are translated by Latin ablatives.

1 The woman saw the eagle.
2 The women told the story to the girls.
3 A queen of an island has servants.
4 The sailor hit an eagle with an arrow.
5 The mob was filled with joy.
6 The farmers of the province entered the land of darkness.
7 The mob heard the story of the daughter of the queen.
8 The goddess gave a crown of victory to the inhabitant of the country.
9 The riverbank borders the road.
10 By means of the language the poet wrote a story.
11 The farmers and their daughters entered battle.
12 Do not do harm to the island.
13 By means of luck the daughter of the goddess found the forest.
14 The goddess destroyed the island by means of waves.
15 The farmer saw the shadow of the gate.
16 The anger of the goddess did not leave her memory.
17 It is your punishment to bring water to the nymphs.

18 Because of the stars and moon he found the loot in the country house.
19 He lost his soul on the flames of the altar.
20 She told the story of injustice by means of a letter.

Exercise 3

Translate the following. Note the following words which occur in some of the sentences:

- the prepositions:
  - **ad** [+ accusative] *to*
  - **in** [+ accusative] *into, onto*
  - **in** [+ ablative] *in, on*
  - **dē** [+ ablative] *about, concerning*
- the conjunction **sed** *but*
- the conjunction **-que** *and* is added to the second word of a pair
- the question word **quandō** *when?*

1   Fēmina corōnam rēgīnae in vīllam portat.
2   Incolae īnsulārum laetitiā canant.
3   Fīliae nautae poētaeque nōn in tenebrīs manent sed in silvam currunt.
4   Umbrā lūnae praedam nōn inveniō.
5   Aquila in aquā cēnam videt.
6   Fāmae incolārum dē deā crēdimus.
7   Quandō ad īnsulam venītis?
8   Sagittae nymphārum in rīpam cadunt.
9   Fābulās patriae īnsulaeque amāmus.
10 Incolae īram deae timent.

Exercise 4

Change the number of all of the nouns in Exercise 3 (unless the noun only has plural forms), keeping case the same. If a noun is singular, make it plural and vice versa. Do not forget that any changes in the number of the subject will affect the form of the verb too!

Exercise 5

Each of the following unedited Latin passages contains a 1st declension noun. Match each passage with the English translation which follows. To assist you, try to think of English derivatives which stem from some of the Latin words.

1 ēripis lacrimās nōn cōnsōlandō sed minandō (Cicero *Pis.*)
2 lacrimās gaudium, questūs adūlātiōnem miscēbant (Tacitus *Ann.*)
3 inter vectōrum lacrimās et mortis mētum (Phaedrus)
4 vīdī contermina rīpae cum gregibus stabula alta trahī (Ovid *Met.*)
5 tendēbantque manūs rīpae ulteriōris amōre (Vergil *Aeneid*)
6 continentemque rīpae collem imprōvīsō occupat (Caesar *Civ.*)
7 multitūdine sagittārum atque omnis generis tēlōrum (Caesar *Gal.*)
8 armōrum nūllō, sagittārum vel praecipuō
   studiō tenēbātur (Suetonius *Dom.*)
9 sīc illae mētū sagittārum (Apuleius *Met.*)
10 tū liquidī dūcēbās fontis ad undam (Ovid *Met.*)
11 quī deae vestīgiō discurrēns in lenem vibrātur undam (Apuleius *Met.*)
12 īte, ratēs, frangite virginis undam (Valerius Flaccus)

(a) you snatch away tears not by consoling but by threatening
(b) by a great number of arrows and of weapons of every type
(c) go, ships, crush the wave of a maiden
(d) I saw high stables near the riverbank being dragged away
    together with the herds
(e) he was held by no enthusiasm of arms, rather by
    a particular zeal of arrows
(f) which running by the footstep of the goddess sparkles
    in a gentle wave
(g) he occupies unexpectedly a hill adjacent to the riverbank
(h) they stretched out their hands because of a yearning
    for the farther shore
(i) in this way, they, out of fear of arrows
(j) you were leading to the water of the clear spring
(k) between the tears of the passengers and the fear of death
(l) joy was mixing with tears, laments were mixing with flattery

Exercise 6

Return to Exercise 4 in Unit 2, and try to locate the lone 1st declension form.
It is an:

accusative plural

Now do the same for Exercise 4 in Unit 3. The grammatical descriptions of the
three 1st declension forms are listed in the order in which they occur:

• a nominative plural
• an ablative singular
• an accusative plural

Review of units 1–4

A. Indicate where the stress falls on each of the following words and why.

1	intexunt	6	dēlēcta	11	amor
2	īnfandum	7	reditū	12	refūgit
3	lacrimīs	8	nōtissima	13	comitante
4	procul	9	suspecta	14	obtulerat
5	vīribus	10	ecce	15	īnsonuēre

B. Use the following verbs to translate.

amō, amāre to love
doceō, docēre to teach
veniō, venīre to come

1	**amāmus**	5	they come
2	**amant**	6	I teach
3	**docēs**	7	she loves
4	**venit**	8	you (pl.) teach

C. Use the following verbs to translate.

capiō, capere *to seize*
dūcō, dūcere *to lead*

1	**capis**	4	they lead
2	**dūcitis**	5	you (sg.) seize
3	**dūcunt**	6	we seize

D. Determine the case and number of each of the following nouns. Some may have multiple possibilities.

1	**fēminārum**	4	**deābus**
2	**turbam**	5	**aquilās**
3	**lūnae**	6	**portā**

UNIT 5
2nd declension

Background

As opposed to 1st declension nouns (Unit 4) which are primarily feminine, 2nd declension nouns are either *masculine* or *neuter*.

The endings are:

		Masculine endings	*Neuter endings*
sg.	Nom.	**-us**	**-um**
	Gen.	**-ī**	**-ī**
	Dat.	**-ō**	**-ō**
	Acc.	**-um**	**-um**
	Abl.	**-ō**	**-ō**
pl.	Nom.	**-ī**	**-a**
	Gen.	**-ōrum**	**-ōrum**
	Dat.	**-īs**	**-īs**
	Acc.	**-ōs**	**-a**
	Abl.	**-īs**	**-īs**

Notes

Neuter nouns take the same endings as those of the masculine except in three contexts:

- nominative singular: **-um**
- nominative plural: **-a**
- accusative plural: **-a**

Fortunately, the nominative plural and accusative plural of a neuter noun are always identical. This is true regardless of which declension the neuter noun belongs to.

The same is true of the nominative singular and accusative singular of neuter nouns.

Some masculine nouns do not end in **-us** in the nominative singular, but rather in **-r** or **-er**. These nouns simply add the other endings to the nominative form in **-r**, in some cases losing the **-e-** which precedes the **-r** (see **puer** and **ager** below).

This is one of the reasons why the genitive singular is always glossed with a word in a dictionary. Besides indicating which declension the noun belongs to, the genitive provides the stem to which the endings outside of the nominative singular are added. In this instance, the genitive singular shows whether or not the **-e-** which occurs before the **-r** in the nominative singular exists in the other forms of the noun.

Examples

equus, -ī horse **vir**, -ī man
puer, -ī boy   **ager**, **agrī** field
frūmentum, -ī grain

		Masculine				*Neuter*
sg.	Nom.	**equus**	**vir**	**puer**	**ager**	**frūmentum**
	Gen.	**equī**	**virī**	**puerī**	**agrī**	**frūmentī**
	Dat.	**equō**	**virō**	**puerō**	**agrō**	**frūmentō**
	Acc.	**equum**	**virum**	**puerum**	**agrum**	**frūmentum**
	Abl.	**equō**	**virō**	**puerō**	**agrō**	**frūmentō**
pl.	Nom.	**equī**	**virī**	**puerī**	**agrī**	**frūmenta**
	Gen.	**equōrum**	**virōrum**	**puerōrum**	**agrōrum**	**frūmentōrum**
	Dat.	**equīs**	**virīs**	**puerīs**	**agrīs**	**frūmentīs**
	Acc.	**equōs**	**virōs**	**puerōs**	**agrōs**	**frūmenta**
	Abl.	**equīs**	**virīs**	**puerīs**	**agrīs**	**frūmentīs**

Notes

- The 2ⁿᵈ declension has an **-ō-** in many instances where the 1ˢᵗ declension has an **-ā-**:

	1ˢᵗ decl.	*2ⁿᵈ decl.*
ablative singular	**-ā**	**-ō**
genitive plural	**-ārum**	**-ōrum**
accusative plural	**-ās**	**-ōs**

- For 2ⁿᵈ decl. masculine nouns, the genitive singular is the same as the nominative plural. The same situation holds in the 1ˢᵗ declension:

1ˢᵗ declension: genitive sg. = nominative pl. **-ae**
2ⁿᵈ declension masculine: genitive sg. = nominative pl. **-ī**

- Two endings are identical with the endings of the 1st declension:

	1st decl.	*2nd decl.*
dative plural	-īs	-īs
ablative plural	-īs	-īs

- The ending -a plays a different role in the 1st and 2nd declensions:

  1st declension   -a = nominative singular
  2nd declension neuter   -a = nominative and accusative plural

- In order to know the function of -a, one must know what declension the word belongs to.

  - If the word belongs to the 1st declension then the -a can *only* be a nominative singular.
  - If it belongs to the 2nd declension then the -a can be either the *nominative plural* or the *accusative plural* but not the nominative singular.

Word	*Declension*	*Dictionary entry*
fēmina *woman*	1st declension	**(fēmina, -ae)**
frūmenta *grains*	2nd declension	**(frūmentum, -ī)**

Exercise 1

Convert each form to the opposite number, then translate. Some words may have more than one possibility.

1	deī	5	templum	9	somnō
2	somnia	6	mundīs	10	caelōrum
3	aurō	7	ventī	11	pontus
4	vēlī	8	campus	12	antrīs

Exercise 2

Translate the following. Note the following words which occur in some of the sentences:

- the prepositions:
  - **ad** [+ accusative] *to*
  - **circum** [+ accusative] *around*
  - **contrā** [+ accusative] *against*
  - **dē** [+ ablative] *about, concerning*

- ē [+ ablative] *away from*
- in [+ ablative] *in, on*
- in [+ accusative] *into, onto*

- the conjunction **-que** *and* is added onto the second word of a pair

1 Saxa contrā mūrōs ferrī iaciunt.
2 Rāmī in viīs manent.
3 Fīlius nautae fābulam dē hortō deōrum deārumque nūntiat.
4 Semper equīs cibum nauta portat.
5 Hodiē bibimus vīnum!
6 Taurī in agrum agricolae movent et ibi stant.
7 Taurum equumque lupus silvae interficit.
8 Vulgīs rēgīna cibum dat et virī cibum fīliīs fīliābusque dīvidunt.
9 Populus īnsulae in antrīs vīvit et ibi dormit.
10 Puerī sociōrum īnsulae verba deae audiunt et nōn timent.
11 Servus ē vīllā dominī fugit et ad terram fīnitimōrum properat.
12 Quandō incolae īnsulae barbarōs vident, fēminae virīque arma et gladiōs ferrī capiunt.
13 Oculī et coma deī fulgent, bracchia deī valent, et animus deī ārdet.
14 In memoriā odium barbarōrum tenet.
15 Rēgīna negōtia vulgō dat.
16 Servīs mūrōs circum castra populus aedificat.
17 Barbarus contrā incolās oppidī bellum gerit.
18 Perīculō bellī auxilium deōrum vulgus petit.
19 Auxiliō populus puerō praemium dat.
20 Rēgīnae in locō numerus līberōrum canit.

Exercise 3

Translate into Latin.

1 The neighbours close the gates of the wall.
2 The children are weeping because of their hatred of barbarians.
3 The wind is strong and deep sea carries the sailors to the island.
4 The son of the goddess finds an eagle in the sky and kills a bull with a sword.
5 The queen commands the crowd to run to the caves.
6 We believe the words of the nymph.
7 Sleep seizes the mind when a man drinks.
8 The people depart by means of a sail and the help of the queen.
9 The poet writes stories for children of the town.
10 Around the field the inhabitants build a wall of iron and gold.

Exercise 4

Each of the following unedited Latin passages contains a 2nd declension noun. Match each passage with the English translation which follows. To assist you, try to think of English derivatives which stem from some of the Latin words.

1 intrā oppida ac mūrōs compelluntur   (Caesar *Gal.*)
2 vōbīs mūrōs atque urbis tēcta commendat   (Cicero *Catil.*)
3 hostis habet mūrōs   (Vergil *Aeneid*)
4 nēquīquam vānīs iactantem cornua ventīs   (Catullus)
5 tū, nisī ventīs dēbēs lūdibrium, cavē   (Horace *Od.*)
6 disiēcitque ratēs ēvertitque aequora ventīs   (Vergil *Aeneid*)
7 nōn sine candidā puellā et vīnō et sale et omnibus
   cachinnīs   (Catullus)
8 audīs in cibō et vīnō   (Cicero *Pis.*)
9 nunc vīnō pellite cūrās   (Horace *Od.*)
10 quī propter gravem morbum oculōrum tum nōn
   nāvigārit   (Cicero *Ver.*)
11 quamvīs sopor est oculōrum parte receptus   (Ovid *Met.*)
12 poena omnis oculōrum ad caecitātem mentis est
   conversa   (Cicero *Dom.*)

(a) flinging in vain its horns to the empty winds
(b) the enemy has the walls
(c) they are driven together within the towns and walls
(d) who then did not sail on account of a serious
    illness of the eyes
(e) although slumber was seized by some (of the) eyes
(f) not without a radiant girl and wine and humour
    and all laughs
(g) she scattered the ships and overturned the seas
    by means of the winds
(h) you listen (to them) in food and in wine
(i) beware you, lest you ought to be a laughing
    stock by means of the winds
(j) all the punishment of his eyes changed to
    blindness of his mind
(k) now drive away your cares by means of wine
(l) he entrusts to you the walls and houses of the city

Exercise 5

Return to Exercise 4 in Unit 2, and try to locate the following 2nd declension forms, which are listed in the sequence in which they occur:

- an accusative singular neuter
- an accusative plural neuter
- two accusative plural neuters in the same sentence

Now do the same for Exercise 4 in Unit 3, and try to locate the following 2nd declension forms:

- an accusative singular masculine
- an ablative singular neuter
- an accusative plural masculine
- dative singular

Now do the same for Exercise 5 in Unit 4, and try to locate the following 2nd declension forms:

- two ablative singular neuters in the same sentence (both forms are gerunds; see *Intensive Intermediate Latin*)
- an accusative singular neuter
- an accusative plural neuter
- genitive plural neuter
- a genitive plural neuter and an ablative singular neuter in the same sentence

Reading: Hercules and the Serpents I

Herculēs, fīlius Alcmēnae, in Graeciā habitat. **Est** puer **fortis**. Iūnō, rēgīna deōrum, Alcmēnam **ōdit**. Fīlium Alcmēnae interficere **vult**. Dea igitur duās **serpentēs** in domum Alcmēnae mittit.

Mediā nocte in cubiculum veniunt, ubi Herculēs dormit. Alcmēna fīlium nōn in lectō, sed in scūtō magnō ponit.

est *s/he is* **fortis** *strong*	**ōdit** *s/he hates* **vult** *s/he wants*
serpentēs *serpents* [acc. pl.]	**mediā nocte** *in the middle of the night*

UNIT 6
1st and 2nd declension adjectives

Background

Adjectives describe a noun.

When the adjective immediately precedes the noun it is describing, the adjective is being used *attributively*.

the **black** car	the **singing** birds
the **blue**, **cloudless** sky	a **happy-go-lucky** person

When the adjective is separated from the noun it is describing by a verb, the adjective is being used *predicatively*.

The verbs which have the ability to separate an adjective from its noun are *be, seem, smell, sound* and other verbs of sensation.

The dog is **hungry**.	The weather seems **terrible**.
The song sounds **fantastic**.	The pie smells **divine**.

Latin structure

Unlike some languages such as German, Latin exhibits no difference between *attributive* and *predicative* adjectives. They take the same form in both constructions.

Since adjectives work so closely with nouns it should be unsurprising that they decline like nouns, taking specific endings for *case* and *number*.

Additionally, however, since adjectives lack an inherent gender of their own, they acquire the *gender* of the noun they are modifying. They therefore select their *case, number*, and *gender* from the noun they modify.

For example, if a noun is accusative singular feminine, then the adjective – whether attributive or predicative – will likewise need to be accusative singular feminine.

29

Adjectives belong either to the *1st/2nd*-declension (Units 4 and 5) or to the *3rd* declension (Unit 15). The former simply take 1st declension endings when a feminine form is needed, and 2nd declension endings when a masculine or neuter form is needed.

Example

bonus, -a, -um good

		Masc.	*Fem.*	*Neut.*
sg.	Nom.	**bonus**	**bona**	**bonum**
	Gen.	**bonī**	**bonae**	**bonī**
	Dat.	**bonō**	**bonae**	**bonō**
	Acc.	**bonum**	**bonam**	**bonum**
	Abl.	**bonō**	**bonā**	**bonō**
pl.	Nom.	**bonī**	**bonae**	**bona**
	Gen.	**bonōrum**	**bonārum**	**bonōrum**
	Dat.	**bonīs**	**bonīs**	**bonīs**
	Acc.	**bonōs**	**bonās**	**bona**
	Abl.	**bonīs**	**bonīs**	**bonīs**

It is important to realize that the endings on the adjective and on the noun it modifies will not always agree. This will become apparent as other declensions are learned, but for the time being observe the following examples:

agricola bonus the good farmer (nom. sg.)
incolae bonō   to the good farmer (dat. sg.)

- Since **agricola** is masculine, 2nd declension endings are used on the adjective.
- The fact that **agricola** is 1st declension makes no difference whatsoever in the form of the adjective.

  - Adjectives agree for *person, number,* and *gender*, but ***not*** for declension!

As was the case with some 2nd declension nouns, the masculine nominative singular of some adjectives ends in **-r**:

līber, lībera, līberum free

Some of these adjectives that end in **-er** drop their **-e-** when endings are added:

noster, nostra, nostrum our

Latin word order

Attributive adjectives predominantly follow the noun they modify.

vir bonus	**fēmina pulchra**	**canis laetus**
a good man	a beautiful woman	a glad dog

When placed before the noun, the adjective expresses a crucial, stressed aspect of meaning. The difference is not often clear in English.

fugitīvus servus vs. **servus fugitīvus**
a runaway slave   a slave who's a runaway

Adjectives modifying a noun in a prepositional phrase (Unit 7) very often occur outside of the prepositional phrase.

cum taurō	**ferō cum taurō**
with a bull	with a wild bull

When unaccompanied by a noun, an adjective can serve as a noun, termed a *substantive adjective*. Based on the gender of the adjective, an appropriate English noun (*man, woman, people, thing, things, one*) may be inserted.

Magna videō.	I see great (things).
Iūcundus venit.	The joyful (man) is coming.

Advanced topics

In some set phrases the position of the adjective does not change the emphasis but the actual meaning:

rēs bonae	**bonae rēs**
good things	articles of value

mēnsa secunda	**secunda mēnsa**
a second table	dessert

When two nouns of different genders are being modified by a single predicative adjective, there is variation in what gender the adjective assumes.
General tendencies are:

* When both nouns refer to humans, the adjective is masculine

    Rēgīna et nauta sunt bonī.
    The queen and sailor are good.

- When both nouns refer to things, the adjective is sometimes neuter, even if neither noun is neuter, yet other times it agrees with the closer noun:

> **Librī et epistulae poētae sunt bona.**
> **Librī et epistulae poētae sunt bonae.**
> The books and letters of the poet are good.

Exercise 1

Write the form of **magnus, -a, -um** which agrees with each of the following. Be aware that some will have more than one answer.

1	verba	5	nautae	9	poētārum
2	agrō	6	praemiī	10	patriā
3	lūnam	7	ager	11	oppidō
4	corōnīs	8	aquilās	12	incolam

Exercise 2

Translate the following.

1 In pontō invenimus vēla alta.
2 Amīcī mūrōs lātōs altōsque populō oppidī aedificant.
3 Cūr ad parvam vīllam venīs?
4 Bracchiīs longīs vir aquilās vulgō capit.
5 Multī barbarī in īnsulam currunt et contrā incolās prosperōs pugnant.
6 Puer sōlus in āram deae pulchrae rāmum longum pōnit.
7 Terram firmam nautae dēfessī petunt.
8 Ventō lentō caelī coma nigra fīliae rēgīnae nōn movet.
9 Dē taurō albō et nymphā candidā scrībit poēta.
10 Stēllae in antrō obscūrō nōn fulgent.
11 Populus hortum pūblicum crēscit.
12 Magister dē antīquō populō docet.
13 Fīnitimī equōs novōs firmōsque emunt.
14 Oppidum magnum in agrum bonum patet.
15 Inimīcus rēgīnam interficit malō vīnō.
16 Īnsidiīs puellās līberās capit et barbarīs vēndit.
17 Poētam ignōtum caecumque epistulārum multārum puerī puellaeque nōn sciunt.
18 Rēgīnae clārae equōs nigrōs, aurum, et ferrum candidum mittit.
19 Dominō dīgnō laetitiā populus iūcundus in locō sacrō et pūrō canit.
20 Ventōs ferōs, pontum asperum, undās altās, et tenebrās nigrās dea saeva nautīs miserīs facit.

Exercise 3

Translate the following.

1 The good queen rules with joy the people of the great island.
2 The prosperous allies give aid to the wretched son of the bad sailor.
3 A shadow of darkness fills the place because of the anger of the gods.
4 Wild, shining white wolves depart the deep forest.
5 In a wide plain in darkness they find gold by means of a flame.
6 We, tired and alone, seek food and weapons from our neighbours.
7 Why do you (sg.) write a long letter to the beautiful daughter of the queen?
8 The men kill and drag the evil bull into the temple.
9 When does a new life for the inhabitants of the wretched town begin?
10 She does not say a worthy story to the joyful crowd.

Exercise 4

Each of the following unedited Latin passages contains a 1ˢᵗ–2ⁿᵈ declension adjective. Match each passage with the English translation which follows. To assist you, try to think of English derivatives which stem from some of the Latin words.

1 veterem atque antīquam rem novam ad vōs prōferam   (Plautus *Am.*)
2 redde cantiōnem veterī prō vīnō novam   (Plautus *St.*)
3 audēs persōnam fōrmāre novam   (Horace *Ars*)
4 et rabiē fera corda tument   (Vergil *Aeneid*)
5 atque aliquis positā mōnstrat fera proelia mēnsā   (Ovid *Ep.*)
6 postquam ēsurīre coepit societās fera   (Phaedrus)
7 multī erant praetereā clārī in philosophiā   (Cicero *de Orat.*)
8 quī quidem semper erunt clārī   (Cicero *Att.*)
9 cōnsul nihil offēnsus līberā admonitiōne tam clārī
   adulēscentis   (Livy)
10 fortūna saevō laeta negōtiō   (Horace *Od.*)
11 et tyrannō tam saevō, quam quī umquam fuit
    saevissimus   (Livy)
12 tum silva gemit murmure saevō   (Seneca *Phaed.*)

  (a) who will indeed always be famous
  (b) and some, with a table set, show the wild battles
  (c) then the forest groans with a wrathful roaring
  (d) moreover many were famous in philosophy
  (e) repay [with] a new song for the old wine
  (f) I will mention to you an old and ancient thing, [made] new

33

(g) after the wild alliance began to be hungry
(h) and her wild feelings swell with fury
(i) you dare form a new character
(j) fortune, happy with her cruel business
(k) the consul, not offended by the free reprimand of
    so famous a young man
(l) and with so cruel a tyrant, who was as cruel
    [a tyrant] as there ever was

Exercise 5

Return to Exercise 4 in Unit 2, and try to locate the following 1st–2nd declension adjectives, which are listed in the sequence in which they occur:

• neuter accusative plural
• neuter nominative plural
• neuter ablative singular

Now do the same for Exercise 4 in Unit 3.

• neuter accusative singular
• neuter accusative singular
• neuter nominative plural
• feminine nominative plural

Now do the same for Exercise 5 in Unit 4.

• two neuter accusative plurals in the same sentence
• neuter ablative singular

Now do the same for Exercise 4 in Unit 5.

• masculine dative plural
• feminine ablative singular

Reading: Hercules and the Serpents II

Serpentēs scūtō clam appropinquant. Tum Herculēs movet scūtum, quod ē somnō venit. Hercules nōn timet. **Manibus** parvīs **serpentēs** tenet et colla comprimit. Puer **fortius est** quam animālia. **Eās** interficit.

serpentēs serpents [nom. and acc. pl.]	**ē** out of
fortius stronger	**manibus** with (his) hands
est s/he is	**eās** them [acc. pl.]

UNIT 7
Prepositions

Background

A *preposition* indicates the *temporal* or *spatial* relationship of one noun or pronoun to the sentence.

> *She came home **after the symphony**.* (temporal relationship)
> *He is going **to the store**.* (spatial relationship)

A *preposition* may also establish a *logical* relationship between a noun or pronoun and some other word in the sentence in order to complete the meaning of this other word.

> *I am happy **for the newlyweds**.* (completing the meaning of the adjective *happy*)
> *He always talks **about politics**.* (completing the meaning of the verb *talks*)
> *He is the king **of England**.* (completing the meaning of the noun *king*)

Latin structure

Latin prepositions predominantly establish *temporal* or *spatial* relationships.

Where English uses prepositions to establish *logical* relationships, Latin often simply uses inflectional endings on the noun, such as the *genitive*, *dative*, and *ablative* (see Units 8, 12, 18, 40).

Latin prepositions are grouped by the case they demand on the noun or pronoun they control.

The following take the accusative:

ad to	**ante** before	**apud** at the house of, among
circum around	**contrā** against, opposite	**inter** between
intrā within	**ob** on account of	**per** through
post after	**praeter** beyond, except	**prope** near
propter on account of	**super** above	**trāns** through

The following take the ablative:

ā, ab away from	**cum** with	**dē** down from; concerning
ē, ex out of	**prō** in front of, for	**sine** without

- ā generally occurs before consonants, **ab** before vowels and **h-**

  ā terrā   **ab īnsulā**
  away from the land   away from the island

- ē generally occurs before consonants, **ex** before vowels and **h-**

  ē domō   **ex aquā**
  out of the house   out of the water

- **cum** follows and is attached to the *personal pronouns* (Unit 27), *reflexive pronouns* (Unit 27), and *interrogative pronouns* (Unit 26)

  Pāx tēcum.
  Peace (be) with you.

  Pāx vōbīscum.
  Peace (be) with you (plural).

  Quōcum vēnistī?
  With whom did you come?

Two prepositions take the accusative and the ablative with differences in meaning. The accusative implies *movement* while the ablative indicates *lack of movement*.

	Accusative	*Ablative*
in	into, onto	in, on
sub	under	under (neath)

In īnsulam īmus.	**Sub tēctum cucurrit.**
We are going onto the island.	He ran under the roof.
In īnsulā sumus.	**Sub tēctō sunt.**
We are on the island.	They are under the roof.

* **causā** *for the sake of* and **grātiā** *for the sake of* are unusual in that they take the *genitive* and are *postpositions*; that is, they follow the noun or pronoun they control.

> **Mīlitēs in oppidum bellī causā veniunt.**
> The soldiers come into the town for the sake of war.

Word order

It is very frequent for an adjective which modifies a noun in a prepositional phrase to precede the preposition:

ex antrō obscūrō
obscūrō ex antrō
out of the dark cave

Advanced topic

Super may occasionally take the ablative as in the following example from Vergil. Note that in addition to referring to physical location, with the ablative it may also bear the meaning *about*:

multa super Priamō rogitāns
asking many things about Priam

Exercise 1

Translate the following short phrases and sentences into Latin.

1 down from the dark sky
2 into the deep sea
3 away from broad camp
4 at the house of our daughter
5 near the high wall of the country house
6 without the aid of the tired inhabitants
7 through the road into the town
8 concerning the story of the famous poet
9 within the beautiful garden
10 before the unfriendly war
11 on account of the price of gold
12 for the sake of the joy of my family
13 against the wild barbarians
14 out of the water and away from the riverbank

15 The stars shine around the peaceful province.
16 We are afraid on account of the dream of the sacred boy.
17 The ancients believe in the great bear in the golden sky.
18 You (sg.) find food in a dark cave near our town.
19 For the sake of the good people the joyful children sing.
20 With the weapons we rule the wide land.

Exercise 2

Match the following unedited Latin texts from Caesar's *Dē Bellō Gallicō* with the correct translation. To assist you, try to think of English derivatives which stem from some of the Latin words.

1 ab extrēmīs Galliae fīnibus
2 ā flūmine Rhodanō
3 dīvīsa in partēs trēs
4 in eōrum fīnibus bellum gerunt
5 ad Hispāniam
6 prō glōriā bellī
7 eīque fīliam suam in mātrimōnium dat
8 per trēs potentissimōs ac firmissimōs populōs tōtīus Galliae
9 ex agrīs magistrātūs
10 eius exercitum sub iugum mīserat
11 ante hoc tempus
12 propter linguae Gallicae scientiam
13 sēsē cum hīs coniūnxisse
14 paulisper apud oppidum morātī
15 sine ūllō perīculō
16 intrā eās silvās
17 ob eāsque rēs ex litterīs
18 propter inīquitātem locī
19 ob eam causam
20 inter carrōs impedīmentaque proelium commīsērunt
21 quae sunt contrā Galliās
22 erat ob hās causās summa difficultās
23 hīberna praeter eam
24 sub ipsō vallō
25 ā suīs castrīs

(a) from the river Rhone
(b) they joined with those ones
(c) on account of the difficulty of the place
(d) he had sent his army under the yoke

(e) for the glory of war
(f) before this time
(g) divided into three parts
(h) and he gives to him his own daughter into marriage
(i) delayed for a short time at the town
(j) they wage war in their borders
(k) on account of these things from the letters
(l) through the three most powerful and most stable peoples
     of all of Gaul
(m) out of the fields of the magistrate
(n) from the farthest borders of Gaul
(o) they engaged in battle between carts and baggage
(p) there was the greatest difficulty on account of these reasons
(q) from their own camps
(r) the winter quarters except for that
(s) on account of knowledge of the Gallic tongue
(t) to Spain
(u) for that reason
(v) without any danger
(w) which are opposite the Gauls
(x) under this very rampart
(y) within those woods

Exercise 3

Using the sentences in Exercise 2, try to determine the meanings of the following words.

eōrum	eius	eī	fīnibus
erat	potentissimōs	firmissimōs	trēs

Reading: Hercules and the Serpents III

Alcmēna, **māter** puerī, **clāmōrem** audit et marītum ē somnō excitat. **Ille** gladium rapit et in cubiculum properat. Ubi intrat, **Herculem** vidit. Puer rīdet et **serpentēs** mortuās iūcundīs cum oculīs mōnstrat. **Haec est** fābula prīma poētārum Graecōrum dē vītā **Herculis**.

māter mother [nom. sg.]	**serpentēs** *serpents* [acc. pl.]
Herculem [acc. sg.]	**Herculis** [gen. sg.]
est s/he is	**ille** he [nom. sg.]
clāmōrem noise [acc. sg.]	**haec** this [nom. sg.]

UNIT 8
Uses of the ablative I

Background

One key to mastering Latin is to conquer the uses of the independent ablative. The independent ablative is an ablative which is often not accompanied by a preposition.

- The ablative is a multifaceted case with an array of uses.
- This unit and Unit 40 provide an overview of some of its more important and frequent uses.

The various uses differ in terms of:

- whether they complete the meaning of a verb, an adjective, or a noun
- whether or not a preposition is optional
- the sense that the ablative contributes.

These three properties will be highlighted in each of the following sections.

Ablatives which modify nouns

I. Ablative of description (also known as ablative of quality)

Basics:

- Preposition: ---
- Meaning: describing a characteristic of another *noun*
- Translation: *with*
    Observe that the noun in the ablative must be accompanied by an adjective in the ablative.

> **Rēgīna *magnā animā* īnsulam regit.**   modifies the noun **rēgīna**
> The queen with a great soul rules the island.

> **Agrōs *lātīs hortīs* vidēmus.**   modifies the noun **agrōs**
> We see the fields with wide gardens.

Ablatives which modify verbs

II. Ablative of means

Basics:

- Preposition: ---
- Meaning: instrument or means by which the action of the *verb* is completed
- Translation: *by means of, by*

> **Praedam *equīs* portant.**   modifies the verb **portant**
> They carry the loot by means of horses.

> **Incolās īnsulae *sagittīs* oppugnant.**   modifies the verb **oppugnant**
> They attack the inhabitants of the island
> by means of arrows.

This is frequent with passive verbs (Units 19 and 20)

> **Templum *flammīs* dēlētum est.**   modifies the verb **dēlētum est**
> The temple was destroyed by flames.

III. Ablative of manner

Basics:

- Preposition: **cum**

    - **cum** is mandatory when the noun is not modified by an adjective
    - **cum** is optional when the noun is modified by an adjective

- Meaning: manner by which the action of the *verb* is completed
- Translation: *with* or as an adverb

    - compare the two translations

	with + *noun*		*adverb*
cum spē	with hope	~	hopefully
cum noxā	with harm	~	harmfully
cum odiō	with hatred	~	hatefully

> **Poēta librōs *cum studiō* scrībit.**   modifies the verb **scrībit**
> The poet writes books with zeal.
> The poet writes books zealously.

> **Poēta *ferō (cum) studiō* legit.**   modifies the verb **legit**
> The poet reads with wild zeal.

IV. Ablative of price

Basics:

- Preposition: ---
- Meaning: what something costs, was sold for, was exchanged for.

    It is usual with the following verbs:

    emō, -ere, ēmī, emptus to buy
    mūtō (1) to change, exchange
    vendō, -ere, vendidī, venditus to sell

- Translation: *for*

    Equōs *aurō* vendunt.   modifies the verb **vendunt**
    They sell the horses for gold.

    Agrum *equīs fortibus* mūtat.   modifies the verb **mūtat**
    He exchanges the field for strong horses.

    Vīllam *bonō cibō* emis.   modifies the verb **emis**
    For good food, you buy the villa.

V. Ablative of cause

Basics:

- Preposition: ---
- Meaning: cause of a *verbal* action
- Translation: *because of*

    Incolae *īrā* pugnant.   modifies the verb **pugnant**
    The inhabitants fight because of anger.

    Poēta *praemiō magnō* scrībit.   modifies the verb **scrībit**
    The poet writes because of the great reward.

Ablatives which modify verbs *or* adjectives

VI. Ablative of respect (also known as ablative of specification)

Basics:

- Preposition: ---
- Meaning: the way in which the meaning of an *adjective* or *verb* is true
- Translation: *in, with respect to, of*

Fīlia dīgna *amōre* est.	modifies the adjective **dīgna**	**8** Uses of the ablative I
The daughter is worthy of love.		
Vir pulcher *comā* est.	modifies the adjective **pulcher**	
The man is beautiful with respect to hair.		
Nautae agricolās *praedā* praestant.	modifies the verb **praestant**	
The sailors surpass the farmers in loot.		

Exercise 1

Determine which type of ablative the underlined portions would be if translated into Latin.

1 We are walking <u>with great care</u>.
2 He sells the goats <u>for ten dollars</u>.
3 <u>Out of fear</u> they flee into the countryside.
4 She is beautiful <u>in appearance</u>.
5 They laugh <u>noisily</u>.
6 Blonde <u>in hair</u>, she is admired by everyone.
7 He was injured <u>by the fallen glass</u>.
8 It was exchanged <u>for the necklace</u>.
9 They see the boat <u>with a fresh white coating</u>.
10 Hercules was great <u>in strength</u>.
11 The name <u>with many letters</u> is difficult to spell.
12 <u>Because of love</u> they are kissing each other.
13 The door was shut <u>by wind</u>.
14 The dog runs <u>with speed</u>.
15 He far exceeds his friends <u>in health</u>.
16 The king is worthy <u>of praise</u>.
17 He wants a head <u>with much hair</u>.
18 They sing the song <u>out of joy</u>.
19 They sing the song <u>with their voices</u>.
20 I bought a new car <u>for nothing</u>.

Exercise 2

Each of the following unedited Latin passages contains an ablative from the 1st, 2nd or 3rd declensions. Match each passage with the English translation which follows. To assist you, try to think of English derivatives which stem from some of the Latin words.

1	animō īgnāvus, procāx ōre	(Tacitus *Hist.*)
2	nōmen erat magnā apud omnēs glōriā	(Cicero *de Orat.*)
3	ista turpiculō puella nāsō	(Catullus)
4	neque tangitur īrā	(Lucretius)
5	ēmit morte immortālitātem	(Quintilian *Inst.*)
6	flagrem dēsīderiō urbis	(Cicero *Att.*)
7	hominēs inimīcō animō	(Caesar *Gal.*)
8	summā virtūte adulēscēns	(Caesar *Gal.*)
9	dōte imperium vendidī	(Plautus *As.*)
10	populus Rōmānus animī magnitūdine excellit	(Cicero *Off.*)
11	clāvī ferreī digitī pollicis crassitūdine	(Caesar *Gal.*)
12	nēmō nisī victor pāce bellum mūtāvit	(Sallust *Cat.*)

(a) men with hostile mind

(b) youth with the greatest courage

(c) I sold command for a dowry

(d) no one, if not victorious, exchanged war for peace

(e) that damn girl with the somewhat ugly nose

(f) iron nails with the thickness of a thumb-finger

(g) lazy in mind, bold in mouth

(h) the name among everyone was of great glory

(i) he bought immortality by death

(j) I may burn from a longing of the city

(k) the Roman people excel in the greatness of mind

(l) and he is not touched by anger

Exercise 3

Looking at Exercise 2 again, what is the 3rd declension ablative singular ending?

Reading: Hercules Kills His Family I

Herculēs **iuvenis** Thēbās ab inimīcīs dēfendit. **Rēx** oppidī decorat Herculem magnīs praemiīs. Fīliam suam **eī** in mātrimōnium dat. Herculēs cum fēminā vītam beātam agit, sed post paucōs annōs subitō in īram cadit. **Manibus** propriīs trēs fīliōs occīdit.

> **iuvenis** young [nom. sg.]   **rēx** king [nom. sg.]   **eī** to him
> **manibus** with (his) hands

UNIT 9
Imperfect tense

Background

In English the *imperfect tense* emphasizes the continuity of an action in the past tense.

*He **was walking** to the store, when he saw his friend.*
*She **was singing** in the shower.*

The English imperfect consists of *was/were + present participle*. The *present participle* is the form of the verb which ends in *-ing* (see Unit 33).
Contrast the imperfect sentences above with:

He <u>walked</u> to the store.

This sentence does *not* emphasize the fact that the 'walking' occurred over a given point of time; rather, it treats it as a single event.
Therefore, the English past tense in *-ed* is similar in use to the Latin *perfect tense* (Unit 13).

Latin structure

The endings of the Latin imperfect are:

	Singular	Plural
1	-bam	-bāmus
2	-bās	-bātis
3	-bat	-bant

These endings are very similar to the present tense endings (Units 2 and 3) with two differences:

(a) The 1st singular ends in **-m** and not **-ō**
(b) An element **-bā-** occurs in every form. This is shortened to **-ba-** before word-final **-t**, **-nt** (as seen in the present tense) as well as before word-final **-m**. This is part of a larger Latin rule which prohibits a long vowel from occurring before a word-final **-t**, **-nt**, **-m**, or **-r**.

Unsurprisingly, the conjugations differ as to which vowel(s) precedes the imperfect endings. Specifically:

1st	**-ā-**
2nd	**-ē-**
3rd	**-ē-**
3rd-io	**-iē-**
4th	**-iē-**

		1st	2nd	3rd	3rd-io	4th
sg.	1	amābam	vidēbam	dūcēbam	capiēbam	sentiēbam
	2	amābās	vidēbās	dūcēbās	capiēbās	sentiēbās
	3	amābat	vidēbat	dūcēbat	capiēbat	sentiēbat
pl.	1	amābāmus	vidēbāmus	dūcēbāmus	capiēbāmus	sentiēbāmus
	2	amābātis	vidēbātis	dūcēbātis	capiēbātis	sentiēbātis
	3	amābant	vidēbant	dūcēbant	capiēbant	sentiēbant

Uses

Like English, Latin's imperfect tense is used to emphasize the continuity of a past activity.

Equōs pāscēbam.
I was feeding the horses.

Herculēs stābulum sordidum pūrgābat.
Hercules was cleaning the dirty stable.

Along these lines, the Latin imperfect is used to express a repeated or habitual action in the past:

Rēgīna lēgātōs interrogābat.
The queen kept asking the envoys.

Advanced topics

The verb **dare** *to give* maintains a short vowel before the **-bā-** of the imperfect, while **stare** does not:

dabam, dabās, dabat, dabāmus, dabātis, dabant
stābam, stābās, stābat, stābāmus, stābātis, stābant

Exercise 1

Convert the following present tense forms to their imperfect counterparts.

1	nūntiās	11	bibimus	21	canitis
2	cavet	12	vidēs	22	fugimus
3	nocent	13	veniunt	23	terreō
4	dīcō	14	properās	24	scrībit
5	audīmus	15	flētis	25	dās
6	crēscunt	16	pugnat	26	tacent
7	cupiō	17	currunt	27	amō
8	tenēs	18	geritis	28	claudō
9	habitat	19	interficitis	29	crēditis
10	tegitis	20	vīvō	30	scītis

Exercise 2

Translate the following.

1 Mūrōs altōs castrōrum mūniēbant.
2 Līberī parvī virōrum et fēminārum īrā rēgīnae timēbant.
3 In campō aurum incola prosperus inveniēbat.
4 Propter pugnam malam et feram fīnitimōrum nostra oppida relinquēbāmus.
5 In āram sacram serva dīgna ramum silvae pōnēbat.
6 Quandō fābulās iūcundās poētae ignōtī legēbātis?
7 Inter equum dēfessum et lupum parvum stābat taurus magnus.
8 Inimīcī ad nostram patriam nāvigābant. Timēbāmus.
9 Ex hortō pulchrō dominum lentum vocābāmus.
10 Properābās in antrum. Quid ibi faciēbās?

Exercise 3

Translate the following into Latin.

1 The god was ruling the world.
2 After the battle the teacher of the children was weeping.
3 She was seeking the aid of the master.
4 The unknown poet was writing friendly, new letters to the worthy people.
5 We were buying the broad, harsh field of the farmer.

Exercise 4

Each of the following unedited Latin passages contains an imperfect tense verbal form. Match each passage with the English translation which follows. To assist you, try to think of English derivatives which stem from some of the Latin words.

1	in altum vēla dabant laetī	(Vergil *Aeneid*)
2	vīna dabant animōs	(Ovid *Met.*)
3	recessumque prīmīs ultimī nōn dabant	(Caesar *Gal.*)
4	sīc ego currēbam, sīc mē ferus ille premēbat	(Ovid *Met.*)
5	quae necessitās eum tanta premēbat	(Cicero *S. Rosc.*)
6	premēbat illa resolūta marmoreīs cervīcibus aureum torum	(Petronius)
7	fugam quaerēbāmus omnēs	(Cicero *Phil.*)
8	nōs igitur dē orīgine et ratiōne verbī quaerēbāmus	(Gellius)
9	ecce pater tuus et ego dolentēs quaerēbāmus tē	(St Jerome)
10	igitur frātrem exhērēdāns tē faciēbat hērēdem	(Cicero *Phil.*)
11	itaque īnfrāctus furor tuus inānis faciēbat impetūs	(Cicero *Dom.*)
12	atque ultrō in nostrōs impetum faciēbat	(Caesar *Civ.*)

(a) and so your broken, empty rage was making attacks
(b) she, relaxed, was pressing a golden couch with her marble-like neck
(c) they, happy, were setting sail [literally: *gave sail*] into the deep
(d) what so great compulsion was pressing him
(e) lo, your father and I, weeping, were seeking you
(f) therefore disinheriting his brother he made you heir
(g) and voluntarily he made an attack on our [men]
(h) therefore we were seeking about the source and an account of the word
(i) we were all seeking flight
(j) in this way I was running, and in this way that one, wild, was pressing me
(k) the last were not giving a retreat to the first
(l) wines were giving courage

Exercise 5

Return to Exercise 5 in Unit 4, and try to locate the following active imperfect verbal forms, which are listed in the sequence in which they occur:

- 3rd pl. of the 2nd conjugation
- 3rd pl. of the 3rd conjugation
- 2nd sg. of the 3rd conjugation

Reading: Hercules Kills His Family II

Propter factum **crūdēlissimum** magnā tristitiā Herculēs vīvēbat. Volēbat **hanc** culpam maximam expiāre. Cōnstituēbat igitur ad clārum ōrāculum Delphicum **īre**. Ibi in templō **Apollinis** fēmina, **nōmine** Pȳthia, cōnsilium virīs dabat. **Apollō** autem fēminam docēbat. Pȳthia **voluntātēs Apollinis** sciēbat et virīs **eās** nūntiābat.

crūdēlissimum most cruel	**hanc** this [acc. sg.]	**īre** to go
Apollinis [gen. sg.]	**nōmine** *by name*	**Apollō** [nom. sg.]
voluntātēs wishes [acc. pl.]	**eās** them [acc. pl.]	

UNIT 10
Future tense

Background

The English future is rather straightforwardly formed by *will* + the base form of a verb:

> *It **will rain** for sure tonight.*
> *We **will see** each other next week.*

Latin structure

The Latin future, like the present (Units 2 and 3) and imperfect (Unit 9), is formed by the addition of endings. This clearly differs from the situation in English.

Recall that the four conjugations differ only with respect to the vowel or vowels which occur before the endings (in the present tense) and stem extension -bā- (in the imperfect tense).

This is not the situation in the future tense. Rather,

- the 1ˢᵗ and 2ⁿᵈ conjugations take a stem extension.
- the 3ʳᵈ and 4ᵗʰ conjugations do not take a stem extension but only change their thematic vowel.

1ˢᵗ and 2ⁿᵈ conjugations

To form the future tense:

- drop the -ō or -eō of the 1ˢᵗ principal part
- add the stem vowel -ā- and -ē- to 1ˢᵗ and 2ⁿᵈ conjugation verbs respectively
- add the stem extension -b-
- finally, add the following endings: **-ō, -is, -it, -imus, -itis, -unt**

    - Observe that these vowel + endings are identical to the present tense vowel + endings of a regular 3ʳᵈ conjugation verb.

A synopsis of the conglomeration of stem vowel, extension, and ending is the following:

	1ˢᵗ conjugation	*2ⁿᵈ conjugation*
1sg.	-ābō	-ēbō
2	-ābis	-ēbis
3	-ābit	-ēbit
1pl.	-ābimus	-ēbimus
2	-ābitis	-ēbitis
3	-ābunt	-ēbunt

Example:

amō, amāre, amāvī, amātus to love   **video, vidēre, vīdī, vīsus** to see

1sg.	**amābō** I will love	**vidēbō** I will see
2	**amābis** you will love	**vidēbis** you will see
3	**amābit** s/he will love	**vidēbit** s/he will see
1pl.	**amābimus** we will love	**vidēbimus** we will see
2	**amābitis** you will love	**vidēbitis** you will see
3	**amābunt** they will love	**vidēbunt** they will see

3ʳᵈ and 4ᵗʰ conjugations

As stated above there is no stem extension -b- in the future of the 3ʳᵈ and 4ᵗʰ conjugations. They are only characterized by the interchange of the vowels -a- and -ē-.

To form the future:

- Drop the final -ō of the first principal part
  - if the verb ends in -iō, only drop the -ō
- Add the stem vowel -a- in the 1ˢᵗ person sg. form and -ē- in every other form
- Add the endings: -m, -s, -t, -mus, -tis, -nt
  - shorten -ē- to -e- before -t and -nt

A synopsis of the stem vowel and endings is:

	3rd conjugation	*3rd-iō conjugation/4th conjugation*
1sg.	-am	-i-am
2	-ēs	-i-ēs
3	-et	-i-et
1pl.	-ēmus	-i-ēmus
2	-ētis	-i-ētis
3	-ent	-i-ent

Note that the 3rd *-iō* and 4th conjugations are identical.
Recall that their **-i-** is from the 1st principal part.

Example

dūcō, dūcere, dūxī, ductus to lead
capiō, capere, cēpī, captus to seize
sentiō, sentīre, sēnsī, sēnsus to feel, perceive

	3rd conjugation	*3rd-iō conjugation*	*4th conjugation*
1sg.	**dūcam** *I will lead*	**capiam** *I will seize*	**sentiam** *I will feel*
2	**dūcēs**	**capiēs**	**sentiēs**
3	**dūcet**	**capiet**	**sentiet**
1pl.	**dūcēmus**	**capiēmus**	**sentiēmus**
2	**dūcētis**	**capiētis**	**sentiētis**
3	**dūcent**	**capient**	**sentient**

Note Knowing the conjugation of a verb is essential in differentiating a 2nd conjugation present tense from a 3rd conjugation future:

docent *they teach*   present of **docēre**;   its future is **docēbunt**
dūcent *they will lead*   future of **dūcere**;   its present is **dūcunt**

Exercise 1

Translate the following. Be aware of the conjugation, since some of these may be presents!

1	docēbis	11	canet	21	vidēbimus
2	valēbō	12	crēdent	22	capit
3	ārdēbit	13	nocētis	23	franget
4	parant	14	bibēmus	24	relinquēs
5	discēdētis	15	vertet	25	monet
6	putābit	16	discēdunt	26	curret
7	cupiēmus	17	servābit	27	aperiam
8	cernam	18	rīdēbimus	28	claudēmus
9	cadit	19	pugnābit	29	emēs
10	fugiet	20	sentiētis	30	cōgitābō

Exercise 2

Convert the present tense forms in Exercise 1 into the future, keeping the person and number the same.

Exercise 3

Translate the following.

1 Inveniēmus aurum rēgīnae.
2 Hodiē sciō. Crās nōn sciam.
3 Post bellum mūrum novum ferrō aedificābimus.
4 Quandō per silvās in undās aquae currēs?
5 Poenam saevam īrā incolīs inimīcīs deī dābunt.
6 Rāmī magnī contrā vīllam prement.
7 Iniūriā oculōrum poēta inimīcus numquam vidēbit.
8 Cum inimīcīs pugnābō, et īnsulam sōlus magnā cum laetitiā regam.
9 Tenebrīs pontī nautae timēbunt.
10 Ante cēnam fīliae virī in rīpā equōs pāscent.

Exercise 4

Translate the following into Latin.

1 You (sg.) will press the wild enemies into the small cave by means of arrows.
2 I will build a road to the town.
3 The goddess will save our wretched neighbours.
4 They will prepare dinner for the crowd.
5 The star will shine tomorrow.

Exercise 5

Each of the following unedited Latin passages contains a future tense verbal form. Match each passage with the English translation which follows. To assist you, try to think of English derivatives which stem from some of the Latin words.

1	līberō tē metū; nēmo crēdet umquam	(Cicero *Phil.*)
2	quid faciam; crēdō, nōn crēdet pater	(Plautus *Mer.*)
3	in diēbus vestrīs quod nēmo crēdet cum nārrābitur	(St Jerome)
4	et ventīs dare vēla iubēbō	(Vergil *Aeneid*)
5	mortālem ēripiam fōrmam magnīque iubēbō aequoris esse deās	(Vergil *Aeneid*)
6	iubēbō nōbīs cēnam continuō coquī	(Plautus *Rud.*)
7	quae mihi venient in mentem	(Cicero *Fam.*)
8	venient super eum horribilēs	(St Jerome)
9	cum canibus timidī venient ad pōcula dammae	(Vergil *Ecl.*)
10	sīc igitur faciēs mēque amābis et scrīptō aliquō lacessēs	(Cicero *Fam.*)
11	quem nunc amābis, cuius esse dīcēris, quem bāsiābis	(Catullus)
12	valēbis igitur mēque, ut ā puerō fēcistī, amābis	(Cicero *Fam.*)

(a) therefore you will do like this and you will love me and will exasperate me with some writing

(b) whom will you now love? Whose will you be said to be? Whom will you kiss?

(c) I free you from fear; no one will ever believe

(d) I will order dinner be cooked for us immediately

(e) and I will order to set sail by the winds

(f) whatever will come into my mind

(g) which in your days no one will believe although it will be told

(h) therefore you will be strong and, as you have done since boyhood, you will love me

(i) what will I do? I believe, that (my) father will not believe

(j) terrifying things will come upon him

(k) I will snatch away their mortal form and will order them to be goddesses of the great sea

(l) with dogs shy deer will come to drink

Reading: Hercules Kills His Family III

Pӯthia verba **Herculis** audiēbat. Ubi vir **tristis** fābulam faciēbat, Pӯthia dīcēbat: "Adveniēs ad **urbem Tīryntha**. Ibi manēbis et petēs Eurystheum, **rēgem** oppidī. Ubi **eum** inveniēs, **ille tibi** imperābit. Expiābis culpam tuam."

Ubi Herculēs verba Pȳthiae audiēbat, ad **urbem** contendēbat. Ibi Eurystheō sē servum faciēbat. Duodecim annōs Eurystheō serviēbat et duodecim negōtia cōnficiēbat. Negōtiīs tantum expiābat culpam maximam **crūdēlissimam**que.

Herculis of Hercules	**tristis** sad [nom. sg.]	**urbem** city [acc. sg.]
Tīryntha Tiryns [acc. sg.]	**rēgem** king [acc. sg.]	**eum** him
ille he	**tibi** to you	**sē** himself [acc. sg.]
crūdēlissimam most cruel		

Review of units 5–10

A. Determine the case and number of each of the following nouns. Some may have multiple possibilities. Be sure to determine whether they are masculine or neuter.

1	**antrum**	4	**virīs**
2	**ventī**	5	**puer**
3	**campōrum**	6	**auxilia**

B. Make the adjective **meus, -a, -um** *my* agree with each of the following nouns.

1	**templum**	4	**somniōrum**
2	**nautam**	5	**fīliīs**
3	**fīliās**	6	**vīllae**

C. Fill in the blanks with the following prepositions: **ante, causā, cum, prō, sine, trāns.** Use each preposition only once.

Currimus _____ silvam _____ cēnam. Stāmus _____ templō _____ equīs. Laetitiae _____ canimus. _____ morā currimus domum (*to home*).

D. Which types of ablative would the following be rendered into Latin as?

1 They drink the wine *by means of glasses.*
2 We could not arrive *by car* on time *because of the traffic.*
3 *With joy* she exchanged her old car *for a new bicycle.*

E. Use the following verbs to translate.

Review of
units 5–10

amō, **amāre** *to love*
capiō, **capere** *to seize*
doceō, **docēre** *to teach*
dūcō, **dūcere** *to lead*
veniō, **venīre** *to come*

1 **docēbās**
2 **capiet**
3 **amābis**
4 **veniēbāmus**
5 **dūcent**

6 she was loving
7 they were seizing
8 you (pl.) will teach
9 I was leading
10 we will come

UNIT 11
Irregular verbs I: *esse* and *posse*

Background

Most languages possess verbs which do not fit the predicted patterns. Such *irregular verbs* consist of forms which simply need to be individually memorized.

As compared to other Indo-European languages, Latin has a relatively small set of such irregular verbs:

sum	**esse**	**fuī**	**futūrus**	to be
possum	**posse**	**potuī**	---	to be able, can
volō	**velle**	**voluī**	---	to want
nōlō	**nōlle**	**nōluī**	---	to not wish, be unwilling
mālō	**mālle**	**māluī**	---	to prefer
eō	**īre**	**īvī, iī**	**itus**	to go
ferō	**ferre**	**tulī**	**lātus**	to bring, carry

Latin has the advantage that *all verbs are regular in the perfect system* (Units 13, 14, 20). The peculiarities of the verbs listed above are all confined to the *present system: present, imperfect*, and *future tenses*.

This unit focuses on the first pair of verbs above while the remaining five are discussed in Unit 23.

Latin structure

Esse to be

- **esse** does not follow any of the patterns of the four conjugations because:
  - it lacks a clear vowel between the stem and the endings – at least in the present tense
  - it lacks a clear stem
    - the stem in the imperfect and future is **er-** while the stem in the present flips between **es-** and **s-**

- Its forms are:

		Present	*Imperfect*	*Future*
sg.	1	sum	eram	erō
	2	es	erās	eris
	3	est	erat	erit
pl.	1	sumus	erāmus	erimus
	2	estis	erātis	eritis
	3	sunt	erant	erunt

INFINITIVE: **esse**

Notes

- The endings in the imperfect are the same as for the four conjugations: **-m, -s, -t, -mus, -tis, -nt**.

  - The imperfect simply has an **-ā-** in every form and not **-bā-** as do the four conjugations.

- The future tense shows a change in vowels:

  - **-ō** (1st sg.)
  - **-i-** (2nd sg., 3rd sg., 1st pl., 2nd pl.)
  - **-u-** (3rd pl.)

  - This change of vowels is *identical* to what we saw in:

    - the present tense of regular 3rd conjugation verbs (**ducō, ducis, ducit, ducimus, ducitis, ducunt**)
    - the future tense of 1st and 2nd conjugation verbs after the stem extension **-b-** (**amābō, amābis, amābit, amābimus, amābitis, amābunt**)

- Third person forms of **sum** can be translated with *there* as subject when the context allows it.

  Vulgus hīc est.
  The crowd is here.
  There is a crowd here.

Posse *to be able, can*

- Knowing the verb **esse**, one gets the verb **posse** for nothing.

  - It is formed using the verb **esse**:

    - Add **pos-** before those forms of **esse** which start in a consonant.
    - Add **pot-** before those forms of **esse** which start in a vowel

		Present	*Imperfect*	*Future*
sg.	1	*possum*	poteram	poterō
	2	potes	poterās	poteris
	3	potest	poterat	poterit
pl.	1	*possumus*	poterāmus	poterimus
	2	potestis	poterātis	poteritis
	3	*possunt*	poterant	poterunt

INFINITIVE: **posse**

Syntactic structure

The verb **esse** is like an equals sign. Every noun that depends on it takes the *nominative*.

Vir servus est.   **Virī agricolae sunt.**
The man is a slave.   The men are farmers.

As in English, **posse** usually requires an infinitive to accompany it in order to complete its meaning:

Fīlia hominem *vidēre* poterat.
The daughter was able to see the man.

Advanced topics

Besides **posse** a few other verbs are also built using **esse**:

absum, abesse, āfuī to be absent
adsum, adesse, adfuī to be present
prōsum, prōdesse, prōfuī to benefit, be useful to [+ dat.]

- for the first two verbs **ab-** and **ad-** are added directly to the forms of **sum**

   abest s/he, it is absent   **adsunt** they are present

- for the third verb, **prō-** is added to forms of **esse** starting in a consonant and **prod-** to forms starting in a vowel

   prōdest s/he, it is useful to   **prōsunt** they are useful to

Exercise 1

Fill in the blanks with either a present tense form of **esse** or a present tense form of **posse**. Sentences which do not have a pronoun listed in parentheses have an expressed noun subject in the sentence.

1 Virī gladiīs inimīcōs interficere _____.
2 Laetae fīliae _____, quod lūnam _____ vidēre.
3 Quandō *(you, sg.)*_____ hūc venīre?
4 *(I)*_____ verbīs sacrīs poētae caecus.
5 Nāvigāmus illinc, quod pecūnia hīc _____.
6 Cibum miserum equus ad vīllam meam in oppidō magnō portāre
    _____.
7 Postquam in antrō *(you, pl.)*_____, relinquimus.
8 Rāmīs barbarī castra alta _____ aedificāre.
9 Līberī nōn bibere _____ vīnum!
10 Deae _____ in templīs.

Exercise 2

Go back to Exercise 1, and first convert the present tense forms to imperfect forms and then to future tense forms.

Exercise 3

Each of the following unedited Latin passages contains a verbal form built from the verb **esse**. Match each passage with the English translation which follows. To assist you, try to think of English derivatives which stem from some of the Latin words.

1 sī quidem tibi vīvus nōn prōsum   (Cicero *Planc.*)
2 quae prōsum sōla nocendō   (Ovid *Met.*)
3 quibus et rē salvā et perditā prōfueram,
    et prōsum saepe   (Terence *Eu.*)
4 sī nūllī prōsum, nisī ut in vicem ille mihi prōsit   (Seneca *Ben.*)
5 neque abest suspīciō   (Caesar *Gal.*)
6 fīlius tuus ā mē abest   (Cicero *ad Brut.*)
7 quia ille hinc abest quem ego amō praeter omnēs   (Plautus *Am.*)
8 dum timor abest, ā tē nōn discēdit   (Cicero *Phil.*)
9 quī aderant magnō flētū   (Caesar *Gal.*)
10 quisquis adest, aderant comitēs, terrētur   (Ovid *Met.*)
11 propinquīs necessāriīsque eius, quī tum aderant,
     verbum nūllum facit   (Cicero *Ver.*)
12 datō iūre iūrandō ab omnibus quī aderant   (Caesar *Gal.*)

(a) an oath was given by all who were present
(b) and suspicion is not lacking
(c) if I benefit no one, unless that he may benefit me in turn
(d) your son is absent from me
(e) whoever is present – companions were present – is frightened
(f) he does not make a word to his relatives and kinsmen is, who were
then present
(g) because he whom I love beyond all is away from here
(h) if indeed I alive am no benefit to you
(i) I, who alone benefit by harming
(j) it does not depart from you, while fear is absent
(k) whom I had benefited in both good times and in destitute times,
and whom I often [still] benefit
(l) who were present with great weeping

Reading: The Nemean Lion (Labor I), part 1

Leō formīdolōsus agrum oppidō Nemeae propinquum reddēbat perīculōsum.
Eurystheus **Herculī** imperābat **hanc** bēstiam occīdere. Vir intrepidus in silvās
intrābat. In **hīs** silvīs **leō** habitābat. Hōrās frūstrā Herculēs bēstiam quaerēbat.
Tandem post hōrās mōnstrum appārēbat. In viā angustā ambulābat. Herculēs
volēbat bēstiam ē silvā dēnsā vulnerāre, sed **id** nōn capiēbat. Sagittae **Herculis**
in terram cadēbant, quod mōnstrum enim **pellem** dūram habēbat.

> **leō** lion [nom. sg.] **Herculī** [dat. sg.] **hanc** this [acc. sg.]
> **hīs** these [abl. pl.] **id** it [acc. sg.] **Herculis** [gen. sg.]
> **pellem** skin, hide [acc. sg.]

UNIT 12
Uses of the genitive

Background

Up till now the only use of the genitive we have seen is to indicate *possession*.

fīlius nautae   the son of the sailor

Since Latin is a heavily inflectional language, the genitive is unsurprisingly used in other situations where English uses a preposition.

While some of these other uses of the genitive do translate as *of* in English, others do not.

Latin structure

I. Subjective genitive

- A noun which is the <u>agent</u> behind an *act* or *feeling* expressed in another noun is placed in the genitive

  somnus *fīliī*   the sleep of the boy, the boy's sleep
  odium *rēgīnae*   the hatred of the queen, the queen's hatred

- The noun requiring a genitive-subject (**somnus** and **odium** above) represents either an action or feeling and not a physical object.

  - A genitive with a physical object expresses possession and not agency.

II. Objective genitive

- A noun which is the <u>result</u> of an *act* or of a *feeling* expressed in another noun or adjective is placed in the genitive

memoria *rēgīnae*	memory of the queen
	[*i.e. one remembers the queen*]
odium *rēgīnae*	hatred of the queen
	[*i.e. one loathes the queen*]
cupidus *glōriae*	desirous of glory

- In cases of ambiguity context will determine whether a genitive is the agent or the result of another noun.

III. Partitive genitive

- In order to indicate the whole from which a subset comes, the genitive is used

pars *aquae*	part of the water
nihil *librōrum*	none of the books
satis *saxōrum*	enough rocks

IV. Genitive of description

- A noun in the genitive modified by the following adjectives is used to express the inherent quality of someone or something.

  magnus, -a, -um great
  maximus, -a, -um greatest
  summus, -a, -um greatest, most
  tantus, -a, -um so great

- These are most naturally translated into English by means of the preposition *with*.

  fēmina *maximī animī*
  a woman with the greatest spirit

  Nautās *tantī timōris* vincimus.
  We conquer sailors with so great fear.
  We conquer sailors who have so great fear.

  ○ Note that this use is very similar to the *ablative of description* (Unit 8) and there is in fact no difference in meaning.

- The genitive of the demonstrative (Unit 21) eius *this* can also be used in this construction.

  puer *eius fāmae*   a boy of/with this reputation

- The genitive of description may be used with the verb **esse** *to be* (Unit 11) instead of depending on a noun. Such a use is termed the *genitive of characteristic* or a *predicate genitive*:

    tantae mōlis **erat Rōmānam condere gentem** (Vergil *Aeneid*)
    founding the Roman race was <u>of such great effort</u>

V. Genitive of material

- Related to the genitive of description is the use of a genitive to describe the material of which something is made.

    gladius *eius aurī*   a sword of/with this gold

VI. Genitive of value

- A *substantive adjective* in the genitive can indicate the value of something.

    ○ Recall that a *substantive adjective* is unaccompanied by a noun.

    - In translating the nouns *value* or *worth* can be added.
    - Note that since the value does not contain a noun (e.g. *dollars*, *gold*), it is indefinite.

Līberōs *magnī* **habēmus.**	We have children of great worth.
Parvī **dūcitur.**	S/he is considered of little value.

VII. Genitive with certain verbs

- Certain verbs take their objects in the genitive, particularly verbs of *remembering* and *forgetting*

    meminī, meminisse to remember
    oblīvīscor, -ī, oblītus sum to forget

    - **meminī** takes perfect forms (Unit 13) but has present meanings
    - **oblīvīscor** is a *deponent verb* (see *Intensive Intermediate Latin*)

        ○ it takes passive endings (Units 19, 20) yet has active meaning

Tuae patriae **meministī.**	You (sg.) remember your fatherland.
Librōrum **oblīvīscitur.**	S/he forgets the books.

• Other verbs take a genitive in addition to an accusative in order to complete their meaning, such as verbs of *accusing* and *condemning*:

accūsō (1) to accuse
culpō (1) to blame
damnō (1) to condemn

Barbarōs *iniūriae meae* accūsō.
I accuse the barbarians for my injury.

Tenebrās *perīculī* culpāmus.
We blame the darkness for the danger.

Fīnitimōs nostrōs *īnsidiārum* damnant.
They condemn our neighbours for treachery.

Advanced topic

With numerals and **quīdam** *certain* (Unit 31), the preposition **ē/ex** is used instead of the partitive genitive.

quīnque ē virīs   five of the men
quīdam ē agrōrum   certain of the fields

Exercise 1

Determine which type of genitive the underlined portions would be if translated into Latin.

 1 We remember <u>our parents</u>.
 2 A woman <u>of great stature</u> rules this country.
 3 They consider the table worth <u>nothing</u>.
 4 The sword <u>of iron</u> is too heavy to lift.
 5 Love <u>of his family</u> is what drives him.
 6 They blame some <u>of the men</u> for the fire.
 7 When did you forget <u>my name</u>?
 8 Walking through the forest is not <u>a great task</u>.
 9 The walls <u>of clay</u> did not survive the storms.
10 Why do you blame him <u>for the crime</u>?
11 The love <u>of a parent</u> for a child is unmatched.
12 Enough <u>of the money</u> was stolen unfortunately.

13 The man <u>with so great a beard</u> is looking right at you!

14 <u>How much</u> is this table worth?

15 Listening to her sing is <u>a great pleasure</u>.

16 The attack <u>of the city</u> was unexpected.

17 We will never forget <u>you</u>.

18 The judge condemned him <u>for arson</u>.

19 I saw a tail <u>of a mouse</u> and screamed.

20 The idea <u>of my sister</u> worked.

Exercise 2

Each of the following unedited Latin passages contains a genitive from the 1st, 2nd, 3rd, or 5th declensions. Match each passage with the English translation which follows. To assist you, try to think of English derivatives which stem from some of the Latin words.

1 vīr magnae auctōritātis	(Caesar *Gal.*)
2 maximus vīnī numerus fuit	(Cicero *Phil.*)
3 satis ēloquentiae, sapientiae parum	(Sallust *Cat.*)
4 ipse iubet mortis tē meminisse deus	(Martial)
5 sed illōs damnātōs esse caedis	(Cicero *Ver.*)
6 nōn multī cibī hospitem accipiēs	(Cicero *Fam.*)
7 damnātiō est iūdicum, quae manēbat, poena lēgis	(Cicero *Sul.*)
8 virī fīunt dōtis nōmine	(Cicero *Top.*)
9 vērnī temporis suāvitāte	(Cicero *Sen.*)
10 cōnsiliī ambiguus	(Tacitus *Hist.*)
11 omnium rērum īnscium	(Cicero *Brut.*)
12 cupidus pecūniae	(Cicero *Ver.*)

(a) a god himself orders you to remember death

(b) by the sweetness of the spring time

(c) a man of great power

(d) desirous of money

(e) but those ones are condemned of murder

(f) you will receive a guest who doesn't (eat) much food

(g) ignorant of all things

(h) enough eloquence, too little wisdom

(i) they are made the man's under the name of a dowry

(j) there was the greatest amount of wine

(k) doubtful of plan

(l) condemnation is of judges, which was remaining, punishment of the law

Exercise 3

Using Exercise 2 try to answer the following.

1 What is the genitive singular ending of the 3rd declension?
2 What is the 5th declension genitive plural ending?

Reading: The Nemean Lion (Labor I), part 2

Leō cum īrā nunc virum post **arborēs** cōnspiciēbat. Celeriter ad **eum** currēbat. Bēstia virum lacerāre volēbat. Herculēs sagittās in terram iaciēbat. Līgnō magnō, **quod** semper portābat, **caput** bestiae discutere volēbat. Sed frūstrā! Tum vir **fortissimus** collum corripiēbat et comprimēbat. Leō **ōs** magnum aperiēbat, quod Herculem dēvorāre volēbat. Sed **manūs** Herculis **fortēs** erant, et bēstia mortua in terram cadēbat.

leō lion [nom. sg.]	**arborēs** trees [acc. pl.]	**eum** him [acc. sg.]
quod which [acc. sg.]	**caput** head [acc. sg.]	**fortissimus** strongest
ōs mouth [acc. sg. nt.]	**manūs** hands [nom. pl.]	**fortēs** strong [nom. pl.]

UNIT 13
Perfect active

Background

As seen in Unit 9 the *imperfect tense* is used to highlight the continuity of an action in the past tense and is effectively equivalent to the English imperfect.

> *I was walking.*

The *perfect tense* is used to state a one-time action or an action whose duration is not being emphasized. The English equivalent of the Latin perfect is twofold: the *simple past* and the *present perfect*:

Simple Past	*I walked.*
Present Perfect	*I have walked.*

- The simple past is formed by adding *-ed* to the base form of the verb (or by vowel change for *strong verbs*: *sing ~ sang*).
- The present perfect is formed by using *has/have* + the past participle.
- The use of these two English past tenses varies from dialect to dialect, but two general rules of thumb for those dialects that maintain a more rigid distinction are that the present perfect is used to:

  - give recent information

    > *It has rained again in Wales.*   (present perfect)

  - express an action in a time period which is not finished yet

    > *She has read three books this week.*   (present perfect) vs.
    > *She read three books last week.*   (simple past)

    > *She has lived in France since May.*   (present perfect) vs.
    > *She lived in France from May to July.*   (simple past)

    - In the second pair, *she* still lives in France in the first example while *she* reasonably no longer lives in France in the second.

Latin structure

Surprisingly Latin simplifies things by expunging the differences between the two English past tenses and simply possessing one tense: the *perfect tense*.

The *perfect tense* is one of three tenses which make up the Latin *perfect system*. The other two will be presented in the following unit.

- The perfect system is formed from the third principal part of the verb.
- All conjugations form the tenses of the perfect system identically. **There are no conjugational differences in the endings or in the stems.**

To form the *perfect active*:

- go to the third principal part of the verb (remember a verb has four principal parts):

  amō, amāre, *amāvī*, amātus to love
  videō, vidēre, *vīdī*, vīsus to see
  dūcō, dūcere, *dūxī*, ductus to lead
  capiō, capere, *cēpī*, captus to seize
  sentiō, sentīre, *sēnsī*, sēnsus to feel

  - The third principal part is the *1ˢᵗ sg. perfect active* so:

    amāvī I loved, have loved   **cēpī** I seized, I have seized
    vīdī I saw, I have seen   **sēnsī** I felt, I have felt
    dūxī I led, I have led

  - The shape of the third principal part is unpredictable outside of the 1ˢᵗ conjugation.

    - 1ˢᵗ conjugation verbs (with a few exceptions) always have an **-āv-** added to the root.
    - For every other verb it is pretty much unpredictable though some regular tendencies do apply which you will come to see as you acquire more verbs.

- drop the **-ī** from the 3ʳᵈ principal part and add the following endings:

	Singular	Plural
1	-ī	-imus
2	-istī	-istis
3	-it	-ērunt

Example:

1sg.	**dūxī**	I led, I have led
2	**dūxistī**	you led, you have led
3	**dūxit**	s/he led, s/he has led
1pl.	**dūximus**	we led, we have led
2	**dūxistis**	you led, you have led
3	**dūxērunt**	they led, they have led

Advanced topics

Preterite-Present

There are several verbs (*preterite-presents*) which have perfect forms but present meanings. These verbs can be broken into two groups:

- those that are defective and lack a present system altogether, their principal parts simply being the 1st sg. perfect active and the perfect active infinitive (see *Intensive Intermediate Latin*)

meminī, meminisse [+ gen.]	to remember
ōdī, ōdisse	to hate

- those that have four principal parts but the perfect system forms have a present meaning which is different from the present system's meaning

nōscō, -ere, nōvī, nōtus	present system: *to get to know, learn*
	perfect system: *to know*
cōnsuēscō, -ere, cōnsuēvī, cōnsuētus	present system: *to get accustomed*
	perfect system: *to be accustomed*

The perfect forms of these verbs are translated as presents:

meminī, meministī, meminit . . .	I remember, you remember, s/he remembers
ōdī, ōdistī, ōdit . . .	I hate, you hate, s/he hates
nōvī, nōvistī, nōvit . . .	I know, you know, s/he knows
cōnsuēvī, cōnsuēvistī, cōnsuēvit . . .	I am accustomed, you are accustomed, s/he is accustomed . . .

The past and future tenses of these verbs are filled by the pluperfect and future perfects respectively (see next unit).

Alternative ending

A less frequent 3rd pl. ending **-ēre** exists alongside the ending **-ērunt** with no difference in meaning.

Rēgīnam vīdērunt.
Rēgīnam vīdēre.
They saw the queen.

- Note that the present infinitive *to see* has a short **-i-** in the root: **vidēre**

Exercise 1

Translate the following.

1 you (pl.) ruled	6 they taught	11 he saw
2 we believed	7 she seized	12 I carried
3 she loved	8 you (sg.) remember	13 you (sg.) heard
4 I know	9 we hate	14 they said no
5 you (pl.) are accustomed	10 you (pl.) prepared	15 we sang

Exercise 2

Translate the following.

1 Cūr bellōrum antīquōrum nōn meministis? Nōscētis.
2 Socius novus equum prētiō bonō ēmit.
3 Nautae ad terram novam vēla dedērunt.
4 Caecum virum ignōtum gladiō ferrī interfēcērunt.
5 Deō pontī cecinimus.
6 Relīquī, quod timuī.
7 In somniō meō perīculum saevum sēnsī.
8 Cūr in antrō magnīs tenebrīs cum incolīs mānsistis?
9 Corōnam auream deae pulchrae incolae in āram posuērunt.
10 Inter hortōs agrōsque mūrum altum aedificāre cōnsuēvērunt.

Exercise 3

Translate the following.

1 When did you (sg.) see the god of the winds?
2 Why do you (pl.) not remember the story of the blind poet?
3 The crowd did not read the letter of the male slave.
4 Out of joy we ran to the riverbank.
5 The horses descended from the town through the gates of the high walls.

Exercise 4

Each of the following unedited Latin passages contains a perfect. Match each
passage with the English translation which follows. To assist you, try to think
of English derivatives that stem from some of the Latin words.

1 aliās terrās petiērunt; iūra, lēgēs, agrōs, lībertātem
   nōbīs reliquērunt   (Caesar *Gal.*)
2 vēnērunt, quae fortūnās suās reliquērunt   (Cicero *Att.*)
3 quī illōrum temporum historiam reliquērunt   (Nepos *Them.*)
4 ego vērō neque vēnī et domō mē tenuī   (Cicero *Dom.*)
5 vēnī nec puppe per undās, nec pede per terrās   (Ovid *Met.*)
6 inter pompae fercula trium verbōrum praetulit titulum,
   vēnī, vīdī, vīcī   (Suetonius *Jul.*)
7 quī illīus culpā cecidit velut prātī ultimī flōs   (Catullus)
8 cecidit arma contrā patriam ferēns   (Cicero *Att.*)
9 sīc cūnctus pelagī cecidit fragor   (Vergil *Aeneid*)
10 dedimus summam certāminis ūnī   (Ovid *Met.*)
11 hunc vestītum atque arma dedimus   (Cicero *Phil.*)
12 at tibi nōs dedimus dābimusque etiam   (Plautus *Per.*)

(a) who left a history of those times
(b) I came neither by ship through waves nor by foot through lands
(c) we gave the chief part of the contest to a sole one
(d) we gave this clothing and arms
(e) and in truth I did not come and kept myself in my house
(f) in this way the entire uproar of the sea fell
(g) they sought other lands, they left to us our rights, laws, fields, and freedom
(h) who fell by his own fault just as a flower at the edge of the meadow
(i) they came, who left their own fortunes
(j) between the litters of the procession he carried before him an inscription
     of three words: I came, I saw, I conquered
(k) he fell, carrying arms against his fatherland
(l) but we have given you it and will give it to you again

Exercise 5

Return to the listed exercises in previous units and try to locate the following
perfect tense forms, which are listed in the sequence in which they occur:

- Unit 2, Exercise 4:   3rd pl., 2nd sg.
- Unit 4, Exercise 5:   1st sg.
- Unit 5, Exercise 4:   3rd sg., 3rd sg.
- Unit 6, Exercise 4:   3rd sg., 3rd sg.
- Unit 7, Exercise 2:   3rd pl.
- Unit 8, Exercise 2:   3rd sg., 1st sg., 3rd sg.
- Unit 10, Exercise 5:   2nd sg.
- Unit 12, Exercise 2:   3rd sg.

Reading: The Nemean Lion (Labor I), part 3

Herculēs nunc bēstiam in umerīs in oppidum **rettulit**. Multī virī et fēminae
oppidum incolēbant.

Magnopere gaudēbant, **cum** Herculem cum mōnstrō vīdērunt. Nunc erant
līberī perīculōsō ā mōnstrō. Herculī magna praemia dedērunt. Herculēs autem
pellem bēstiae prō amīculō gerēbat.

rettulit *look under* **referō**   **cum** when   **pellem** skin, hide [acc. sg.]

UNIT 14
Pluperfect and future perfect active

Background

The *pluperfect* and *future perfect* are used to express an activity that occurs before another action.

- The *pluperfect* expresses an activity which occurred further in the past than another activity.

  - In English it is formed by *had* + past participle

    *I remembered that I **had read** about that.*
    *You **had left** it on the table.*

  - The second example would be used in the course of a narrative which is in the past tense. For instance:

    *I came early and found the book. You **had left** it on the table.*

- The *future perfect* expresses a future activity which will occur *before* another future action.

  - It is formed by *will have* + past participle

    *I **will have seen** the letter by the time I get home.*
    *When the case ends, the jurors **will have spent** three weeks in court.*

Latin structure

To form the *pluperfect* and *future perfect*:

- Go to the third principal part and drop the final -ī:

amāvī	→	amāv-
vīdī	→	vīd-
dūxī	→	dūx-
cēpī	→	cēp-
sēnsī	→	sēns-

• Add the following endings:

	Pluperfect	*Future perfect*
1sg.	**-eram**	**-erō**
2	**-erās**	**-eris**
3	**-erat**	**-erit**
1pl.	**-erāmus**	**-erimus**
2	**-erātis**	**-eritis**
3	**-erant**	**-erint**

Example:

Pluperfect		*Future perfect*	
dūxeram	I had led	**dūxerō**	I will have led
dūxerās	you had led	**dūxeris**	you will have led
dūxerat	s/he had led	**dūxerit**	s/he will have led
dūxerāmus	we had led	**dūxerimus**	we will have led
dūxerātis	you had led	**dūxeritis**	you will have led
dūxerant	they had led	**dūxerint**	they will have led

Note Aside from the third pl. future perfect **-erint**, the endings are identical to the forms of the imperfect and future of **esse** (Unit 11).

Exercise 1

Translate the following.

1 you (sg.) had been strong
2 he will have placed
3 I will have hastened
4 you (pl.) had begun
5 they will hate
6 she will have had
7 they had opened
8 we will have fortified
9 we had said
10 they had shone
11 you (pl.) will have responded
12 we knew
13 he had abandoned
14 it will have extended
15 she had sung
16 they will have forced

Exercise 2

Translate the following.

1 Postquam puerī vēnerant, laetae erāmus.
2 Quandō vīllam novam aedificāveris?
3 Cibus bonus fuerat in ārā lātā antrī.
4 Agrōrum intrā patriam meminerant incolae īnsulae.
5 Nōn nāvigābunt quandō ventus malus trāns undās pontī incēperit.
6 Cūr rēgīnae litterās iūcundās scrīpserātis? Nōn respondēbit.
7 Noxam fīnitimīs nostrīs lupī lentī et dēfessī nōn dederant.
8 Comam longam puellae pulchrae et līberae vīderit fīlius servae servīque.
9 Vulgus contrā barbarōs pugnāverat, quandō equōs rēgīnae gladiīs ferrī
   interfēcērunt.
10 In mundō antīquō multī poētae caecī et ignōtī fuerant.

Exercise 3

Each of the following unedited Latin passages contains either a pluperfect or a
future perfect. Match each passage with the English translation which follows.
To assist you, try to think of English derivatives which stem from some of the
Latin words.

1	praeclārē enim vīxerō, sī quid mihi acciderit	(Cicero *Mil.*)
2	seu maestus omnī tempore vīxeris	(Horace *Od.*)
3	ego crās hīc erō, crās habuerō, uxor, ego tamen convīvium	(Plautus *Cas.*)
4	quae vitia quī fūgerit	(Cicero *Orat.*)
5	sī potuerō, faciam vōbīs satis	(Cicero *Brut.*)
6	mulier virum et fīlium eōdem tempore venēnīs clam datīs vītā interfēcerat	(Gellius)
7	dein catēnīs onerātum, postrēmō interfēcerat	(Tacitus *Ann.*)
8	impotēns amōris interfēcerat	(Tacitus *Hist.*)
9	cōnsulem interfēcerat et eius exercitum sub iugum mīserat	(Caesar *Gal.*)
10	mē, quī līber fueram, servom fēcit	(Plautus *Capt.*)
11	cōnsēderam, ubi hesternō diē fueram	(Petronius)
12	ille quī vester comes ubique fueram	(Seneca *Her. O.*)

(a) indeed I shall have lived excellently, if something will have happened to me
(b) violent of love he had killed her
(c) I will be here tomorrow, tomorrow, wife, I will have had a banquet all the same
(d) then loaded with chains, finally he had killed him
(e) poison having been given, that woman had killed from life her husband and her son at the same time
(f) whether you will have lived always as gloomy
(g) he who will have escaped these faults
(h) he had killed the consul and had sent his army under the yoke
(i) he made me, who had been free, a slave
(j) I, who had been your companion everywhere
(k) if I will have been able, I will be enough for you
(l) I had sat down, where I had been yesterday

Exercise 4

In the previous exercise there is an example of an archaic 2nd declension accusative singular masculine ending. Can you find it?

Reading: The Lernean Hydra (Labor II), part 1

Paulō posteā Eurystheus iussit Herculī Hydram necāre. Erat mōnstrum alterum, **nōmine** Hydra.

Campōs circum Lernam dēvastābat. Mōnstrum novem **capita mortālia** habēbat. **Caput** autem decimum **immortāle** erat. Herculēs quadrīgā ad locum vēnit, ubi Hydra habitābat. Vir intrepidus sagittīs mōnstrum excitāvit. Cum sonīs formīdolōsīs Herculem appropinquāvit. Minimē timuit. **Manū** sinistrā collum corripuit et novem capita ūnum post alterum abscidit. Sed frūstrā labōrābat. Locō **cuiusque capitis** duo nova crēvērunt.

nōmine by name	**immortāle** immortal [nom. sg.]
caput head [nom. sg. nt.]	**capitis** of head [gen. sg.]
cuiusque of each [gen. sg.]	**mortalia** mortal [acc. pl.]
capita heads [acc. pl.]	**manū** with (his) hand [abl. sg. f.]

UNIT 15
3rd declension

Background

We have already dealt with the 1st declension (Unit 4) and 2nd declension (Unit 5). They are both characterized by a specific *nominative singular* ending:

- 1st declension: **-a**
- 2nd declension:

  - masculine: **-us**   (some in **-r**)
  - neuter: **-um**

Additionally, they are both lopsided towards one or two genders:

- 1st declension: feminine
- 2nd declension: masculine and neuter

Both of these hallmarks, which occur again in the 4th and 5th declensions (Unit 36), are strikingly absent from the *3rd declension*.

The nominative singular does not have a generic ending. Additionally, since the *nominative* stem can differ somewhat drastically from the *genitive* stem – the stem used in every other form – both the *nominative* and the *genitive singulars* will need to be memorized.

The gender of a 3rd declension noun will also need to be memorized since it is not predictable. Some general tendencies do occur, as you will see as you progress and encounter more vocabulary.

For example nouns in **-tūs** (**virtūs** *courage*) and **-tās** (**aetās** *age*) are feminine while nouns in **-men** (**nōmen** *name*) are neuter.

To illustrate, the dictionary form of *soldier* is **mīles, mīlitis** (m.).

- The nominative singular of this masculine noun has no discernible ending, so the nominative stem is the entire form **mīles**.

• The genitive singular form consists of the stem **mīlit-** and the genitive singular
ending **-is**. From this stem **mīlit-**, the remaining forms are derived.

Latin structure

The endings of the 3rd declension are:

		Masc./Fem.	Neuter
sg.	Nom.	-----	-----
	Gen.	**-is**	**-is**
	Dat.	**-ī**	**-ī**
	Acc.	**-em**	-----
	Abl.	**-e**	**-e**
pl.	Nom.	**-ēs**	**-a**
	Gen.	**-um**	**-um**
	Dat.	**-ibus**	**-ibus**
	Acc.	**-ēs**	**-a**
	Abl.	**-ibus**	**-ibus**

Notes

1 *Masculine* and *feminine* words take the same endings.
2 *Neuter nouns* take special endings in 3 forms:

   • accusative singular
   • nominative plural
   • accusative plural

3 The slots filled with ----- indicate that there is no set, predictable ending and
  that the nominative singular form must simply be memorized.

   • For neuters the nominative singular = accusative singular

In order to decline a 3rd declension noun, drop the **-is** from the genitive singular and add the appropriate endings:

mīles, mīlitis (m.) soldier
lēx, lēgis (f.) law
flūmen, flūminis (nt.) river

		mīles, mīlitis (m.)	*lēx, lēgis* (f.)	*flūmen, flūminis* (nt.)
sg.	Nom.	mīles	lēx	flūmen
	Gen.	mīlitis	lēgis	flūminis
	Dat.	mīlitī	lēgī	flūminī
	Acc.	mīlitem	lēgem	flūmen
	Abl.	mīlite	lēge	flūmine
pl.	Nom.	mīlitēs	lēgēs	flūmina
	Gen.	mīlitum	lēgum	flūminum
	Dat.	mīlitibus	lēgibus	flūminibus
	Acc.	mīlitēs	lēgēs	flūmina
	Abl.	mīlitibus	lēgibus	flūminibus

Overview of first three declensions

You can tell which declension a noun belongs to by seeing how it's listed in the dictionary. The *genitive singular ending* indicates which declension it belongs to.

1st declension: **aqua, -ae** water
2nd declension (masculine):   **vir, -ī** man
2nd declension (neuter):   **frūmentum, -ī** grain
3rd declension (masculine):   **mīles, mīlitis** soldier
3rd declension (feminine):   **lēx, lēgis** law
3rd declension (neuter):   **flūmen, flūminis** river

Exercise 1

Translate the following. Some words may have more than one possibility.

1	hospitēs	11	itinera	21	pectus
2	pāce	12	pēdum	22	vulnerī
3	flōribus	13	opus	23	patrum
4	aequor	14	gregī	24	ōra
5	nōmina	15	aetāte	25	tempestās
6	mulierēs	16	frātribus	26	equitēs
7	capitī	17	virtūs	27	sōlis
8	sīderis	18	temporis	28	legiō
9	laudum	19	āerem	29	leōnem
10	lēgibus	20	āēr	30	sēmine

Exercise 2

Convert the nouns in Exercise 1 to the opposite number while keeping case constant. If singular, make then plural; if plural, make them singular. Some words may have more than one possibility.

Exercise 3

Translate the following.

1 Nēmō sorōrem meam et frātrēs altōs vīderat.
2 Prīnceps mīlitēs dēfessōs in legiōnem mōribus Rōmānīs posuit.
3 Agricolae ab rūre fugiunt odōre pecoris.
4 Inimīcī cum mīlitibus nostrīs pugnāvērunt. Post bellum virī nostrī auxilium petēbant ā sorōribus rēgis et rēgīnā.
5 Poētam caecum sceleribus contrā honōrem cīvitātis in carcerem obscurum iaciēmus.
6 Auctor epistulārum librōrumque opus magnum cīvitātī plēbīque fēcit.
7 Puer laetus sēmina flōrum sub arbore altā invēnit.
8 Cūr labor hominum corpus frangit?
9 Canēs vātis sanguinem taurī bibunt.
10 Rūmōrem mātrī meae dīcam, quod nōn intellegō.
11 Fīlius fīnitimōrum scelera inimīcī ōdit.
12 Custōdēs ārae stant ante vātem.
13 Odor flōrum in vīllam parvam patēbit.
14 Agricola novum gregem taurō ēmit.
15 Mōre īnsulae sacrae virī in itineribus in vīllā rēgis rēgīnaeque dormiunt.
16 Sōl mundī fulget et tenebrās ā terrīs remōvet.
17 Laetī sunt hominēs canēsque, quod pater deōrum nōn tempestātēs facet.
18 Leōnēs taurōs invēnērunt et interfēcērunt.
19 Laudem rēgīnae damus, quod pulchra est.
20 Nēmō mīlitum prīncipem legiōnis vidēre poterat.

Exercise 4

Translate the following.

1 The sister of my mother is coming today.
2 The horsemen are able to carry swords of iron on horses.
3 According to the law the king will kill a man on account of a crime of blood.

4 Why do you (pl.) not see the famous legion of the good king?
5 When will you (sg.) make food for the many dogs?
6 My father and mother love my brothers, because they are not in prison.
7 With courage we will be able to conquer!
8 The guardians of the prison give food to the men.
9 The storm will come to the towns of the island tomorrow.
10 The heads of the enemies are in a cave.

Exercise 5

Each of the following unedited Latin passages contains a 3rd declension noun. Match each passage with the English translation which follows. To assist you, try to think of English derivatives which stem from some of the Latin words.

1	canem istam ā foribus aliquis abdūcat face	(Plautus *Mos.*)
2	satis habuit canem appellāre	(Suetonius *Ves.*)
3	canem illum, invīsum agricolīs sidus, vēnisse	(Horace *S.*)
4	magnam partem aestātis faciēbant, quod nostrae nāvēs tempestātibus dētinēbantur	(Caesar *Gal.*)
5	tum quod hīs tempestātibus es prope sōlus in portū	(Cicero *Fam.*)
6	sed tempestātibus et ingravēscente vī morbī retentus	(Suetonius *Tib.*)
7	o tempora, o mōrēs, senātus haec intellegit	(Cicero *Catil.*)
8	ad mea perpetuum dēdūcite tempora carmen	(Ovid *Met.*)
9	hīs ego nec mētās rērum nec tempora pōnō	(Vergil *Aeneid*)
10	magnō cum perīculō nostrōrum equitum cum eīs cōnfligēbat	(Caesar *Gal.*)
11	magister equitum, bellī prīnceps, crūdēlitātis auctor	(Cicero *Phil.*)
12	equitum levia improbus arma praemīsit	(Vergil *Aeneid*)

(a) with great danger to our cavalry he would engage with them
(b) they did [this] a great part of the summer, because our ships were kept back by storms
(c) make it so that someone may lead that damn dog away from the doors
(d) lead this continuous song to my times
(e) then because you are alone in the harbour despite these storms
(f) o times, o customs, the senate understands these things
(g) master of the cavalry, leader of war, author of cruelty
(h) but held back by storms and the increasing strength of his illness
(i) I place on them neither bounds of things nor time
(j) he, wicked, sent forth light arms of the cavalry
(k) [like] that dog, hated constellation for farmers, had come
(l) he had enough to [only] call him a dog

Exercise 6

Return to the listed exercises in previous units and try to locate the following
3rd declension forms, which are listed in the sequence in which they occur.
Gender is indicated for the nominative and accusative forms, the two cases in
which non-neuters and neuter take different endings.

- Unit 2, Exercise 4:   fem. accusative singular, genitive plural, genitive singular, ablative singular
- Unit 3, Exercise 4:   neuter accusative plural, ablative singular, neuter accusative singular, neuter accusative plural
- Unit 4, Exercise 5:   fem. accusative singular, genitive singular, ablative
plural, ablative singular, masc. accusative singular,
ablative singular, genitive singular, genitive singular,
fem. accusative plural, genitive singular
- Unit 5, Exercise 4:   genitive singular, fem. accusative plural, neuter accusative plural, ablative singular, ablative singular, fem.
accusative singular, genitive singular
- Unit 6, Exercise 4:   fem. accusative singular, ablative singular, genitive
singular, ablative singular
- Unit 7, Exercise 2:   ablative plural, ablative singular, fem. accusative plural,
ablative plural, neuter accusative singular, fem. accusa-
tive singular
- Unit 8, Exercise 2:   ablative singular, ablative singular, fem. accusative
singular, genitive singular, masc. nominative plural,
ablative singular, ablative singular, ablative singular,
genitive singular, ablative singular, ablative singular
- Unit 9, Exercise 4:   ablative plural, ablative singular, ablative singular,
masc. accusative singular, masc. accusative singular
- Unit 10, Exercise 5: genitive singular, fem. accusative singular, ablative
plural
- Unit 11, Exercise 3: fem. accusative singular, masc. nominative plural
- Unit 12, Exercise 2: genitive singular, genitive singular, genitive singular,
masc. accusative singular, genitive plural, genitive
singular, genitive singular, ablative singular, genitive
singular, ablative singular
- Unit 13, Exercise 4: neut. accusative plural, fem. accusative plural, fem.
accusative singular, genitive plural, ablative singular,
ablative singular, genitive singular
- Unit 14, Exercise 3: ablative singular, genitive singular, masc. accusative
singular

Reading: The Lernean Hydra (Labor II), part 2

Herculēs interrogāvit, "Quid facere dēbeō? Sīc bēstiam numquam interficere poterō." **Manū** ergō līberā ignem accendit atque līgnō **ārdentī** novem capita adūssit. **Hoc** facere poterat quod **mortālia** erant. Sed vir intrepidus caput decimum occīdere nōn poterat. **Id** igitur vīvum in terrā sepelīvit et lapidem magnum **eī** imposuit. Herculēs nunc etiam corpus mōnstrī necāre dēbuit. Gladiō bēstiam in duās partēs dīvīsit. Sanguis tamquam flūmen ex corpore mōnstrī flūxit. Herculēs sagittās immersit. Venēnum, **quod** in sanguine erat, vulnera reddidit mortifera. **Hic** erat labor secundus, **quem** Herculēs cōnfēcit.

manū with (his) hand [abl. sg. f.]
mortālia mortal [nom. pl. nt.]
quod which [nom. sg.]
ārdentī burning [abl. sg.]
id it [acc. sg. nt.]

hic this [nom. sg.]
hoc this [acc. sg.]
eī to it [dat. sg.]
quem which [acc. sg.]

UNIT 16
3rd declension *i*-stems

Background

The last unit introduced *3rd declension nouns*. Among 3rd declension nouns there is a predictable subset which takes certain endings with **-i-** or **-ī-** in them. These nouns are creatively termed *3rd declension i-stems.*

Latin structure

The endings of the 3rd declension *i*-stem are as follows:

	Singular			*Plural*	
	Masc./Fem.	*Neut.*		*Masc./Fem.*	*Neut.*
Nom.	-----	-----	Nom.	**-ēs**	**-ia**
Gen.	**-is**	**-is**	Gen.	**-ium**	**-ium**
Dat.	**-ī**	**-ī**	Dat.	**-ibus**	**-ibus**
Acc.	**-em**	-----	Acc.	**-ēs**	**-ia**
Abl.	**-e**	**-ī**	Abl.	**-ibus**	**-ibus**

The unique endings are:

Masc./Fem.:	genitive plural	**-ium**
Neuter:	genitive plural	**-ium**
	nominative plural	**-ia**
	accusative plural	**-ia**
	ablative singular	**-ī**

Three rules dictate whether a noun is a regular 3rd declension noun or an *i*-stem one. If a noun satisfies *just one* of the following three rules, then it is an *i*-stem:

1 If the nominative sg. and genitive sg. have the same number of syllables:

ignis, **ignis** (m.) fire
cīvis, **cīvis** (m./f.) citizen
caedēs, **caedis** (f.) slaughter
mare, **maris** (nt.) sea

- Note that **canis**, **canis** (m./f.) *dog* is not an *i*-stem despite satisfying this rule.

2 The stem of the word ends in *two consonants*, the second one NOT being *-l-* or *-r-*.

nox, **noctis** (f.) *night*   stem: **noct-**
mēns, **mentis** (f.) *mind*   stem: **ment-**

- **pater**, **patris** (m.) *father* and **māter**, **mātris** (f.) *mother* do not satisfy this rule since the second consonant of the stems **patr-** and **mātr-** is *-r*. They are also exceptions to rule 1.
- **parēns**, **parentis** (m./f.) *parent* unexpectedly is not an *i*-stem even though it fits this rule

3 The nominative sg. of a *neuter* noun ends in **-e**, **-al**, or **-ar**:

animal, **animālis** (nt.) animal
sedīle, **sedīlis** (nt.) seat

	fire (m.)	*night* (f.)	*sea* (nt.)
Nom.	**ignis**	**nox**	**mare**
Gen.	**ignis**	**noctis**	**maris**
Dat.	**ignī**	**noctī**	**marī**
Acc.	**ignem**	**noctem**	**mare**
Abl.	**igne**	**nocte**	**marī**
Nom.	**ignēs**	**noctēs**	**maria**
Gen.	**ignium**	**noctium**	**marium**
Dat.	**ignibus**	**noctibus**	**maribus**
Acc.	**ignēs**	**noctēs**	**maria**
Abl.	**ignibus**	**noctibus**	**maribus**

Advanced topics

Certain other masculine/feminine *i*-stem endings occur, some more frequently
with specific words.

Masc./Fem.: accusative singular   **-im**
               ablative singular: **-ī**
               accusative plural: **-īs**

Sē ex *nāvī* prōiēcit (Caesar *Gal.*)   **nāvis, nāvis** (f.) ship
He threw himself forth from the ship.

Illa metū *puppim* dīmīsit (Ovid *Met.*)   **puppis, puppis** (f.) ship
She let go of the ship out of fear

Hīc fessās nōn vincula *nāvīs* ūlla tenent
(Vergil *Aeneid*)   **nāvis, nāvis** (f.) ship
Here no chains hold the tired ships

Exercise 1

Convert each form to the opposite number, then translate. Some words may
have more than one possibility.

1 dentī	6 cordia	11 famēs
2 cīvibus	7 serpentium	12 urbēs
3 vātium	8 marī	13 avium
4 adulēscēns	9 amnis	14 animālia
5 vestibus	10 nocte	15 sortī

Exercise 2

Translate the following.

1 In amnem flūmenque piscēs iacimus.
2 Prōlēs rēgis deōrum pācem faciet et urbēs magnās aedificābit.
3 Inter partēs oppidī est pons longa et alta.
4 Postquam auxilium dē fīnitimīs quaesīverant, fīliōs et fīliam invēnērunt.
5 Hostēs barbarī dē montibus dēscendent et nāvēs nostrās ad aequor trahere
   incipient.

6 Moenia alta nūbēs tangent.
7 Fame agricolae ovibus mel novum dant.
8 Sociōs vir igne rubrō monēbat.
9 Incolās īnsulae inimīcī igne terrent.
10 Mortis mātris poēta caecus meminit.
11 Nōn nōvimus fīnēs orbis terrārum.
12 Mēns mea in capite meō est.
13 Corpora, aurēs, dentēs, ōra, comam, cordia, oculōs habēmus.
14 Animālia in amne stant, quod piscēs quaerunt.
15 Custōdēs ārae sacrae ignem rāmīs crēscunt.
16 Pontem trāns flūmen aedificābimus.
17 Aqua dē nūbibus tegit orbem terrārum, et populī laetī sunt.
18 Quod serpēns malus puerum interfēcerat, auxilium dē rēge quaesīvimus.
19 Dē ponte novō in amnem parvum cecidit.
20 Sīdera nūbibus multīs vidēre nōn possumus.

Exercise 3

Translate the following.

1 The young men always find sacred animals because of luck.
2 The enemies broke our new bridge.
3 When will you (sg.) give wine to the offspring of the queen?
4 The small, radiant ships were sailing on the deep sea.
5 Because of hunger we went into the forest and found fish in streams.
6 Because of the ramparts the barbarians could not attack the country house of my parents.
7 We do not sell clothing for honey.
8 The soothsayers say words to the citizens in front of a wild fire.
9 They heard the rumours about the high mountains under the seas.
10 Why will you have (pl.) run around the world?

Exercise 4

Each of the following unedited Latin passages contains a 3rd declension *i*-stem noun. Match each passage with the English translation which follows. To assist you, try to think of English derivatives which stem from some of the Latin words.

1 at certē longinquā obsidiōne famēs esset timenda   (Caesar *Gal.*)
2 crēscentem sequitur cūra pecūniam māiōrumque
   famēs   (Horace *Od.*)
3 famēs hominī vetitōrum tanta cibōrum   (Ovid *Met.*)
4 spatia omnis temporis nōn numerō diērum sed
   noctium fīniunt   (Caesar *Gal.*)
5 inde est quod magnam partem in imāgine tuā
   vigil exigō   (Pliny the Younger)
6 quōnam modo noctium suārum ingentia nōtēscerent   (Tacitus *Ann.*)
7 cum dēvolūtum ex igne prōsequēns pānem   (Catullus)
8 videt igne micantēs sīderibus similēs oculōs   (Ovid *Met.*)
9 glomeratque sub antrō fūmiferam noctem
   commīxtīs igne tenebrīs   (Vergil *Aeneid*)
10 lūstrāvit aethera album, sola dūra, mare ferum   (Catullus)
11 quod mare nōn trānsierim   (Cicero *Att.*)
12 reliquum corpus trāctum atque laniātum abiēcit
   in mare   (Cicero *Phil.*)

(a) care follows growing money as does a hunger of more
(b) for man such a hunger of forbidden foods
(c) he threw the remaining body, dragged and mangled into the sea
(d) the periods of all time are not bound by the number of days but of nights
(e) he sees her eyes sparkling like stars with fire
(f) when she, chasing the bread which rolled out of the fire
(g) from there it is such that I, awake, spend a great part of the night on your image
(h) just how the huge deeds of his nights became known
(i) but certainly by an extended siege, hunger was to be feared
(j) he rolled up from under the cave a smoky night mixed with darkness and fire
(k) that I did not cross over the sea
(l) it illuminated the white sky, the hard land, the wild sea

Reading: The Fight with the Centaurs (Labor III), part 1

Dum Herculēs iter in Arcadiam fēcit, in regiōnem Centaurōrum vēnit. Ūnus ex
Centaurōrum, nōmine Pholus, Herculem benīgnē excēpit et cēnam **eī** parāvit.
Post cēnam vīnum ā Pholō postulāvit, quod vīnum amābat. Centaurī amphoram
vīnō optimō in antrum dēposuerant.

  "**Cuius** vīnum est hoc?" interrogāvit Herculēs.
  Pholus dīxit, "vīnum Centaurōrum est."
  "Possum**ne** id bibere?" postulāvit.
  "Nōn potes. Centaurī **mē** interficient, sī amphoram aperuerō."

eī to him [dat. sg.]	**cuius** whose	**hoc** this [nom. sg. nt.]
-ne [indicates a question]	**id** it [acc. sg.]	**mē** me [acc. sg.]

UNIT 17
3rd declension adjectives

Background

Not all adjectives are *1st–2nd declension adjectives* (Unit 6). Those that are not are *3rd declension adjectives*. As the name suggests, they take *3rd declension endings.*

They have two noteworthy peculiarities:

1 They are all *i*-stems (Unit 16)
2 They are broken into three groups depending upon how many gender distinctions are made in the nominative singular:

- *3 terminations*: 3-way gender contrast in the nominative sg.
- *2 terminations*: 2-way gender contrast in the nominative sg.
- *1 termination*: no gender contrast in the nominative sg.

Each adjective follows only one of the patterns. That is, each adjective is either a *1st–2nd declension adjective* or a *3rd declension adjective*, and within the latter a *3*, *2*, or *1* termination adjective.

- Note that every *1st–2nd declension adjective* is *3 terminations* since there is a 3-way gender contrast in the nominative sg.

Latin structure

Three terminations (**ācer, ācris, ācre** *sharp*)

		M	*F*	*Nt*
singular	Nom.	**ācer**	**ācris**	**ācre**
	Gen.	**ācris**	**ācris**	**ācris**
	Dat.	**ācrī**	**ācrī**	**ācrī**
	Acc.	**ācrem**	**ācrem**	**ācre**
	Abl.	**ācrī**	**ācrī**	**ācrī**
		M	*F*	*Nt*
plural	Nom.	**ācrēs**	**ācrēs**	**ācria**
	Gen.	**ācrium**	**ācrium**	**ācrium**
	Dat.	**ācribus**	**ācribus**	**ācribus**
	Acc.	**ācrēs**	**ācrēs**	**ācria**
	Abl.	**ācribus**	**ācribus**	**ācribus**

Two terminations (**fortis, forte** *strong*)

	Singular			*Plural*	
	M/F	*Nt*		*M/F*	*Nt*
Nom.	**fortis**	**forte**	Nom.	**fortēs**	**fortia**
Gen.	**fortis**	**fortis**	Gen.	**fortium**	**fortium**
Dat.	**fortī**	**fortī**	Dat.	**fortibus**	**fortibus**
Acc.	**fortem**	**forte**	Acc.	**fortēs**	**fortia**
Abl.	**fortī**	**fortī**	Abl.	**fortibus**	**fortibus**

One termination (**ingēns, ingentis** *huge*)

	Singular			*Plural*	
	M/F	*Nt*		*M/F*	*Nt*
Nom.	**ingēns**	**ingēns**	Nom.	**ingentēs**	**ingentia**
Gen.	**ingentis**	**ingentis**	Gen.	**ingentium**	**ingentium**
Dat.	**ingentī**	**ingentī**	Dat.	**ingentibus**	**ingentibus**
Acc.	**ingentem**	**ingēns**	Acc.	**ingentēs**	**ingentia**
Abl.	**ingentī**	**ingentī**	Abl.	**ingentibus**	**ingentibus**

- The ablative singular is -ī for all three genders, not just neuters as was the case with *3rd declension i*-stem nouns (Unit 16)
- -īs occurs in lieu of **-ēs** as the masculine/feminine accusative plural sometimes in poetry
- An adjective has:

  - *3-terminations* if the dictionary presents three forms
  - *2-terminations* if the dictionary presents *two* forms, the second of which ends in **-e**
  - *1-termination* if the dictionary presents *two* forms, the second of which ends in **-is**

- As with 1st–2nd declension adjectives, 3rd declension adjectives may also be used substantively:

  Nunc *fortēs* **pugnant.**   Now they fight the strong (men).

Exercise 1

Make the following three adjectives agree with each of the nouns below. Since some of the nouns may be in more than one case, there may be more than one answer for a few.

ācer, ācris, ācre
fortis, forte
recēns, recentis

1 gladiōs	8 ovēs	15 auctōrem
2 sanguinis	9 vulnera	16 igne
3 sociī	10 rēgīnae	17 aequorī
4 puerō	11 fīliārum	18 vīnum
5 ager	12 mīlitum	19 famēs
6 canibus	13 ārīs	20 pugnās
7 silvā	14 cīvibus	21 cordī

Exercise 2

Translate the following.

1 Fēlīcēs virī vident sōlem et antrum triste relinquunt.
2 Avis sapiēns inveniet mel dulce in arbore parvā.
3 Postquam mātrem nōbilis virī interfēcerat, turpis ex oppidō cucurrit.
4 Ob bellum ācre crūdēleque parentēs multōrum mīlitum fortium flent.
5 Nōn potestis in frequentī vīllā stāre.
6 Equus celer fuit animal deī immortālis, rēgis omnium hominum animāliumque.
7 Cūr nōn dat pauperibus populīs dīves dominus?
8 Poterant ingentēs vīllās laetīs urbis aedificāre.
9 Honōrem senibus nostrīs līberī oppidōrum īnsulae semper dant.
10 Gravēs librōs dē īnfēlicibus rēgīnae rēgisque scrīpsit.
11 Post brevem annum, nōn regam et discēdam.
12 Nāvēs nautārum īnfēlīcium nōn mōvit ventus levis.
13 Multus numerus nostrōrum sociōrum auxilium portābit et recentī bellō mūrōs novōs aedificābit.
14 Nōn bibō vīnum mītem, sed canēs meī bibunt.
15 Servus humilis labōrem facit, sed pecūniam nōn optat. Optat novam līberam vītam.
16 Omnēs urbis ibi aderunt.
17 Poēta caecus, sapiēns, et senex docet līberōs oppidī.
18 Timēmus ventum celerem fortemque in tempestāte crūdēlī.
19 Quis nōn immortālis vītae meminit?
20 Odor mītis flōris implēbat vīllam.

Exercise 3

Translate the following.

1 The cruel masters close the borders of the camp.
2 The immortal god made all men of the world.
3 Disgraceful men and women had run through the crowded streets.
4 The soothsayer will have divided the fat sheep and sweet wine for the crowd.
5 The author will write about all the sweet smells of the flowers of the small garden.
6 The animals fought with keen eyes.
7 The sad and old servants will seek aid of the wise soothsayer.
8 The life of the soldier is short. An arrow through the heart can kill him.
9 Happy children always sing with the beautiful birds on the riverbank.
10 You (pl.) will fight for your noble fatherland and you (pl.) will save our humble king.

Exercise 4

Each of the following unedited Latin passages contains a 3rd declension adjective. Match each passage with the English translation which follows. To assist you, try to think of English derivatives which stem from some of the Latin words.

1 quae pōmīs intersita dulcibus ornant   (Lucretius)
2 dulcibus indulget lacrimīs aperitque dolōrem   (Valerius Flaccus)
3 sed in dulcibus aquīs lūnae alimentum esse, sīcut
   in marīnīs sōlis   (Pliny the Elder)
4 quam septem ingentia victor corpora fundat humī   (Vergil *Aeneid*)
5 tantōrum ingentia septem terga boum plumbō īnsūtō
   ferrōque rigēbant   (Vergil *Aeneid*)
6 intrāque quartum mēnsem periit, ingentia
   facinora ausus   (Suetonius *Cal.*)
7 quod supplicium satis ācre reperiētur   (Cicero *S. Rosc.*)
8 et genus ācre lupōrum atque canum   (Vergil *G.*)
9 et missae cohortēs ācre proelium fēcēre   (Tacitus *Ann.*)
10 fortem et līberum animum, quō et cōnsul et nunc
   cōnsulāris rem pūblicam vindicastī   (Cicero *ad Brut.*)
11 inventum tamen esse fortem amīcum ex eādem
   familiā   (Cicero *Ver.*)
12 eum sorōrem dēspondisse suam in tam fortem
   familiam   (Plautus *Trin.*)

(a) what sufficiently severe punishment will be found
(b) till he, victorious, laid low seven huge bodies on the ground
(c) that he had pledged his own sister into so strong a family
(d) seven huge hides of such great oxen were rigid, with lead
     and iron having been sewn in
(e) which they adorn placed amongst sweet fruit trees
(f) and the sent cohorts made a fierce battle
(g) both the fierce kind of wolves and dogs
(h) he indulges sweet tears and opens his sorrow
(i) nevertheless a strong friend was found from the same family
(j) within the fourth month he died, having dared enormous crimes
(k) but as the nourishment of the moon is in sweet waters, likewise
     that of the sun is in sea waters
(l) that strong and free spirit, by which you both as consul and
     now as ex-consul have protected the republic

Reading: The Fight with the Centaurs (Labor III), part 2

Herculēs Centaurōs nōn timēbat. Amphoram aperuit et plūrimum bibit. Centaurī
odōrem sēnsērunt. Undique ad antrum convēnērunt. Ibi vīdērunt Herculem ōre
lātō bibere. Īrātī ergō impetum in virum fortem fēcērunt. Nescīvērunt Herculem
sagittās mortiferās habēre. Omnēs igitur, **quōs** Herculēs sagittīs vulnerāvit, miserē
vītam fīnīvērunt. Reliquī Centaurī, ubi mortem amīcōrum vīdērant, terga vertērunt
et fugā salūtem petīvērunt. Pholus ex antrō vēnit. Sīve forte sīve cōnsiliō deōrum
pedem sagittā leviter vulnerāvit. Statim dolōrem gravem sēnsit et mortuus in
terram cecidit. Herculēs, **quī** cēterōs Centaurōs longē fugāverat, magnā cum
tristitiā Pholum mortuum invēnit. Corpus Pholi multīs cum lacrimīs sepelīvit.

quōs whom [acc. pl.]   **quī** who [nom. sg.]

Review of units 11–17

A. Translate the following.

1 they can	3 we are	5 there is	7 I will be
2 you (sg.) could	4 you (pl.) will be	6 I will be able to	8 they were

B. Which types of genitive would the following be rendered into Latin as?

1 Out of love *for my mother* I called her on mother's day.
2 Some *of the men* do not have houses *of wood*.
3 He forgot *his fear* which was *so great*.

C. Use the following verbs to translate.

amō, amāre, amāvī to love
capiō, capere, cēpī to seize
doceō, docēre, docuī to teach
dūcō, dūcere, dūxī to lead
veniō, venīre, vēnī to come

1 they had come	6 we will have seized
2 I taught	7 they had loved
3 she seized	8 you (pl.) have taught
4 you (sg.) will have loved	9 he had come
5 you (pl.) led	10 I will have led

D. Convert the following words to the desired forms.

animal, animālis (nt.) animal
flūmen, flūminis (nt.) river
mīles, mīlitis (m.) soldier
nox, noctis (f.) night

1 nominative plural	3 genitive plural
2 ablative singular	4 accusative singular

E. Make the adjective **fortis, forte** *strong* agree with each of the following nouns.

1 **templum**   4 **somniōrum**
2 **nautam**   5 **fīliīs**
3 **fīliās**   6 **vīllae**

UNIT 18
Uses of the dative

Background

Up till now the dative has been confined to expressing the indirect object. As with the ablative (Unit 8) and genitive (Unit 12), however, the independent dative possesses a range of other uses, not all of which are naturally translatable into English as *to/for + noun*.

Latin structure

I. Dative of possession

Many languages do not have a verb *to have* but rather indicate possession by means of the verb *to be*.
  Latin has both structures:

- **habeō, -ēre, habuī, habitus**
- dative of possession which uses the verb **esse**

The dative of possession has the following structure:

  thing possessed [nominative] + possessor [dative] + form of **esse**

Vīllae *incolīs* sunt.	The inhabitants have country houses. literally: Country houses are to the inhabitants.
Praeda *barbarō* est.	The barbarian has the loot. literally: The loot is to the barbarian.

II. Dative of reference

A noun in the dative may indicate the person for whom something occurs, whom something affects, or to whom something refers.

Tempestātēs *agricolīs* nocent.
The storms are harmful to the farmers

Est vīnum bonum hīc *parentibus*.
There is good wine here for the parents.

A subclass of the dative of reference is the *ethical dative*. It is the use of a personal pronoun (Unit 27) to indicate someone with a vested interest in the contents of a sentence. The pronoun is not closely linked to any one item in the sentence.

Hīc est nēmō clārus *mihi*.
There is no one famous here, in my opinion.
As for me, there is no one famous here.

***Vōbīs* nunc lūmen sōlis agrōs implet.**
Now the light of the sun fills the fields, in your opinion.
As for you, now the light of the sun fills the fields.

III. Dative of purpose

A noun in the dative may indicate the reason why something occurs.

Mīlitēs contrā hostēs *lībertātī* pugnant.
Soldiers fight enemies for freedom.

Pontem *viae* faciēmus.
We will build a bridge for a road.

IV. Double dative

A dative of reference and a dative of purpose often occur together in a single sentence. This structure is referred to as a *double dative*.

Pontem *viae populō* faciēmus.
We will build a bridge for a road for the people.

Aqua nōn *noxae* est *cīvibus*.
Water is not as a harm for the citizens.

Lībrum scrīpsit *rēgī honōrī*.
He wrote a book as an honour for the king.

V. Dative with adjectives

Several adjectives (Units 6 and 17) take a noun in the dative to complete their meanings. A handful are:

amīcus, -a, -um	friendly
inimīcus, -a, -um	unfriendly, hostile
dissimilis, dissimile	dissimilar
similis, simile	similar
idōneus, -a, -um	suitable
pār, paris	equal
proximus, -a, -um	nearest

Oppidum fīnitimōrum proximum *nostrō* est.
The town of the neighbours is nearest to our own.

Hostēs *līberīs nostrīs* inimīcī sunt.
The enemies are hostile to our children.

Cibus hic *rēgī rēgīnaeque* idōneus est.
This food is suitable for the king and queen.

Exercise 1

Determine which type of dative the underlined portions would be if translated into Latin.

1 I do not find that man suitable <u>for you</u>.
2 <u>As for me</u> that man is not friendly <u>to you</u>.
3 We want to attack the enemies <u>for our safety</u>.
4 The father's new job is a benefit <u>to the family</u>.
5 Why does he look similar <u>to him</u>?
6 What does <u>the lady</u> have?
7 The courts rejected the plea <u>with respect to us</u>.
8 They should not have done that <u>in our opinion</u>.
9 <u>For what</u> are they doing all that work?
10 <u>For whom</u> are they doing all that work?
11 <u>The men</u> have money.
12 He is equal in strength <u>to the gladiator</u>.
13 The attack serves <u>as a danger</u> <u>to the city</u>.
14 The iron will be good material <u>for the sword</u>.
15 He sits nearest <u>to her</u>.

Exercise 2

Each of the following unedited Latin passages contains a dative. Match each
passage with the English translation which follows. To assist you, try to think
of English derivatives which stem from some of the Latin words.

1	castrīs idōneus locus	(Caesar *Gal.*)
2	an nescīs longās rēgibus esse manūs	(Ovid *Ep.*)
3	sī quid peccat . . . mihi peccat	(Terence *Ad.*)
4	nēminī meus adventus labōrī aut sūmptuī fuit	(Cicero *Ver.*)
5	vērē aestimantī	(Livy)
6	ut mihi dēfōrmis, sīc tibi magnificus	(Tac. *Hist.*)
7	in cōnspectum vēnerat hostibus	(Caesar *Gal.*)
8	praedam mīlitibus dōnat	(Caesar *Gal.*)
9	tuō virō oculī dolent	(Terence *Ph.*)
10	habēre quaestuī rem pūblicam turpe est	(Cicero *Off.*)
11	dōnō neque accipitur	(Sallust *Jug.*)
12	lībertātī tempora sunt impedīmentō	(Cicero *S. Rosc.*)

(a) nor is it accepted as a present

(b) a place suitable for camp

(c) he gives the loot to the soldiers

(d) the eyes of your husband grieve

(e) truly to the one judging

(f) my arrival was neither work nor an expense for anyone

(g) the times are an obstacle to (my) freedom

(h) or you do not know that kings have long arms?

(i) as disfigured to me, thus grand to you

(j) it is disgraceful to have the republic as a profit

(k) if he makes some mistake, he makes it to me

(l) he had come into the view of the enemies

Reading: The Running Stag (Labor IV)

Eurystheus quartum labōrem nūntiāvit. Erat cervus, **cuius** caput aurea cornua
habēbat. Animālī fuit maxima celeritās, quod pedēs fortēs erant. Vestīgia cervī
Herculēs invēnerat. Quandō Herculem vīdit, saluit et cucurrit. Post animal
Herculēs frūstrā cucurrit. Mēnsēs et mēnsēs cucurrērunt, sed Herculēs cervum
capere nōn potuit. Tandem post annum cervus sēdit, quod dēfessus fuit. Herculēs
corpus cēpit et **id** rēgī dedit.

cuius whose   **id** it [acc. sg. nt.]

UNIT 19
Passive voice

Background

Up till now every verb has been in the *active* voice. In the active voice, the <u>subject does the action</u> *expressed in the verb.*

English has a second voice: ***passive voice***. It is used when the <u>subject has the action</u> ***done to it***.

English examples:

Active: The man loves the dog.
Passive: The dog is loved (by the man).

In expressing the passive, English always needs a form of the verb *to be* (underlined in the sentences below).

It also uses the past participle form of the verb (*loved* in the sentences below).

PASSIVE

Present   The dog <u>is</u> loved.
         The dog is <u>being</u> loved.
Imperfect   The dog was <u>being</u> loved.
Future   The dog will <u>be</u> loved.

The agent is expressed in an optional prepositional phrase introduced by *by*:

The dog is loved *by the man*.

Latin structure

The passive of the present system (present, imperfect, future tenses) is expressed via endings alone.

103

The passive endings which occur in the three tenses of the present system are:

	Singular	Plural
1	-r	-mur
2	-ris	-minī
3	-tur	-ntur

The tenses – and within each tense the conjugations – differ with respect to the stem extensions and thematic vowels used.

Present passive

The verbal root and thematic vowels are the same as those which were used in the present active (Units 2 and 3). The sole difference is -e- in the 2ⁿᵈ sg. of 3ʳᵈ conjugation verbs instead of the expected -i-.

	Thematic vowels + endings			
	1ˢᵗ	*2ⁿᵈ*	*3ʳᵈ*	*4ᵗʰ*
1sg.	-or	-eor	-(i)or	-ior
2	-āris	-ēris	-eris	-īris
3	-ātur	-ētur	-itur	-ītur
1pl.	-āmur	-ēmur	-imur	-īmur
2	-āminī	-ēminī	-iminī	-īminī
3	-antur	-entur	-(i)untur	-iuntur

The -(i)- in the 3ʳᵈ conjugation endings is used by 3ʳᵈ-*iō* verbs.

This will be the case in the imperfect and future passives as well.

Note that the endings -r and -ntur shorten the vowel which precedes. This is always true of these two endings.

Example

> **amō, amāre, amāvī, amātus** to love
> **doceō, docēre, docuī, doctus** to teach
> **dūcō, dūcere, dūxī, ductus** to lead
> **capiō, capere, cēpī, captus** to seize
> **audiō, audīre, audīvī, audītus** to listen

1sg.	amor	I am (being) loved	doceor	I am (being) taught
2	amāris	you are loved	docēris	you are being taught
3	amātur	s/he, it is loved	docētur	s/he, it is being taught
1pl.	amāmur	we are loved	docēmur	we are being taught
2	amāminī	you are loved	docēminī	you are being taught
3	amantur	they are loved	docentur	they are being taught

dūcor, dūceris, dūcitur, dūcimur, dūciminī, dūcuntur
capior, caperis, capitur, capimur, capiminī, capiuntur
audior, audīris, audītur, audīmur, audīminī, audiuntur

Imperfect passive

The verbal root, thematic vowels, and stem extension **-bā-** are the same as were used in the imperfect active (Unit 9).

| | *Thematic vowels, stem extension + endings* | | | |
	1ˢᵗ	*2ⁿᵈ*	*3ʳᵈ*	*4ᵗʰ*
1sg.	-ābar	-ēbar	-(i)ēbar	-iēbar
2	-ābāris	-ēbāris	-(i)ēbāris	-iēbāris
3	-ābātur	-ēbātur	-(i)ēbātur	-iēbātur
1pl.	-ābāmur	-ēbāmur	-(i)ēbāmur	-iēbāmur
2	-ābāminī	-ēbāminī	-(i)ēbāminī	-iēbāminī
3	-ābantur	-ēbantur	-(i)ēbantur	-iēbantur

1sg.	amābar	docēbar
	I was being loved	I was being taught
2	amābāris	docēbāris
	you were being loved	you were being taught
3	amābātur	docēbātur
	s/he, it was being loved	s/he, it was being taught
1pl.	amābāmur	docēbāmur
	we were being loved	we were being taught
2	amābāminī	docēbāminī
	you were being loved	you were being taught
3	amābantur	docēbantur
	they were being loved	they were being taught

dūcēbar, dūcēbāris, dūcēbātur, dūcēbāmur, dūcēbāminī, dūcēbantur
capiēbar, capiēbāris, capiēbātur, capiēbāmur, capiēbāminī, capiēbantur
audiēbar, audiēbāris, audiēbātur, audiēbāmur, audiēbāminī, audiēbantur

Future passive

The verbal root, thematic vowels, and presence or absence of the stem extension
-b- are the same as were used in the future active (Unit 10).

Recall that the 1st and 2nd conjugations are characterized by the stem extension -b- whereas the 3rd and 4th conjugations are characterized by the thematic
vowel interchange -a- ~ -ē-.

	Thematic vowels + endings			
	1st	*2nd*	*3rd*	*4th*
1sg.	-ābor	-ēbor	-(i)ar	-iar
2	-āberis	-ēberis	-(i)ēris	-iēris
3	-ābitur	-ēbitur	-(i)ētur	-iētur
1pl.	-ābimur	-ēbimur	-(i)ēmur	-iēmur
2	-ābiminī	-ēbiminī	-(i)ēminī	-iēminī
3	-ābuntur	-ēbuntur	-(i)entur	-ientur

Note the short -e- in the 2nd sg. of 1st and 2nd conjugation verbs instead of
expected -i-:

    active **amāb*i*s**   passive **amāb*e*ris**

This is the same change which occurs in the 2nd sg. of the present tense of 3rd
conjugation verbs (active **dūc*i*s** vs. passive **dūc*e*ris**).

1sg.	**amābor**	I will be loved	**capiar**	I will be seized
2	**amāberis**	you will be loved	**capiēris**	you will be seized
3	**amābitur**	s/he, it will be loved	**capiētur**	s/he, it will be seized
1pl.	**amābimur**	we will be loved	**capiēmur**	we will be seized
2	**amābiminī**	you will be loved	**capiēminī**	you will be seized
3	**amābuntur**	they will be loved	**capientur**	they will be seized

docēbor, docēberis, docēbitur, docēbimur, docēbiminī, docēbuntur
dūcar, dūcēris, dūcētur, dūcēmur, dūcēminī, dūcentur
audiar, audiēris, audiētur, audiēmur, audiēminī, audientur

Syntactic structure

As in English the agent of a passive is optional.

When the agent is a person, the preposition **ā/ab** is used. This is termed the *ablative of agent.*

Rēgīna *ā mīlitibus* interficiētur.
The queen will be killed by the soldiers.

Oppidum *ā populō* nōn servābātur.
The town was not being saved by the people.

When the cause is not a person, **ā/ab** is not used. Rather, a simple *ablative of means* is employed (Unit 8).

Rēgīna *gladiō* interficiētur.
The queen will be killed by the sword.

Oppidum *igne* nōn servābātur.
The town was not being saved by the fire.

Advanced topic

There is an alternative 2nd sg. ending **-re**. For example:

- **amāre** you are loved   (**amāris**)
- **amābāre** you were being loved   (**amābāris**)
- **amābere** you will be loved   (**amāberis**)

Note that this alternative is identical in form to the infinitive in the present tense.

Exercise 1

Translate the following.

1 interficitur	8 mūniēbātur	15 bibētur
2 iubeor	9 vidēminī	16 vocāberis
3 dūcentur	10 faciuntur	17 iungēbāris
4 audiēbar	11 excitantur	18 scrībitur
5 regētur	12 vertēbāmur	19 cupimur
6 pāscēminī	13 optor	20 claudēbantur
7 emar	14 datur	21 trahēmur

Exercise 2

Change the numbers of all of the words in Exercise 1, keeping tense and person constant. That is, if a word is singular then make it plural. If a word is plural then make it singular.

Exercise 3

Translate the following.

1 Verba fortia ā clārō sapientīque poētā scrībuntur.
2 Saxum magnum ā mīlitibus contrā moenia urbis saevōrum iaciēbātur.
3 Quandō hodiē cēna parābitur?
4 Vir in tenebrīs antrī nigrī inveniētur.
5 Odor flōrum hortī ventō per āerem portābātur.
6 Moenia nova ā senibus et iuvenibus aedificantur.
7 Nōn capiar ā hostibus meīs pācis dulcis causā.
8 Avis parvus in arbore altā nunc vidētur.
9 Cīvitātibus ā rēgibus prosperīs dīvitibusque dulce mel dabitur.
10 Bellum hodiē nōn incipiētur, quod prīncipēs pācem facere potērunt.
11 Bracchium laevum meī sociī sagittā frangitur.
12 Nāvis nova tempestātibus fortibus contrā undās iaciēbātur.
13 Mīlitēs ā prīncipibus iubēbuntur pugnāre.
14 Taurus ferus sagittīs incolae interficiētur.
15 Fugere cōgimur.
16 Ovēs in agrīs montis ab agricolīs dīvidēbantur.
17 Verba auctōris ā fīliābus fīliīsque canentur.
18 Vīlla movēbātur ventīs tempestātis.
19 Verbīs auctōris poētaeque tangēris.
20 Lupus ex agrīs nostrīs trahitur, quod ovēs interficiēbat.

Exercise 4

Translate the following.

1 The letters were being sent by the boys.
2 The kingdom of the nymphs was ruled by the god of the seas.
3 The white sheep will be killed by the farmer.
4 The land was covered by the shade of the clouds.
5 Help will be sought by the sad inhabitants.
6 The danger of the city is not seen by the children.
7 The good food will be seized by the cruel enemies.

8 The sweet wine will be drunk by the happy men and women.
9 The radiant gold on the land was seen by the birds in the air.
10 Why will you (pl.) be driven out of your own fields?

Exercise 5

Each of the following unedited Latin passages contains a passive verbal form. Match each passage with the English translation which follows. To assist you, try to think of English derivatives which stem from some of the Latin words.

1 scelus herbāriōrum aperiētur in hāc mentiōne (Pliny the Elder)
2 sed suō tempore tōtīus huius sceleris fōns aperiētur (Cicero *Phil.*)
3 quaerite et inveniētis pulsāte et aperiētur (St Jerome)
4 nōn ea quae finguntur aut optantur (Cicero *Amic.*)
5 et sī esse vīs fēlīx, deōs ōrā, nē quid tibi ex hīs,
  quae optantur, ēveniat (Seneca *Ep.*)
6 saepe etiam salsē, quae fierī nōn possunt, optantur (Cicero *de Orat.*)
7 ubi dīvidēbātur, eōque minus altō alveō trānsitum
  ostendere (Livy)
8 inter concordēs dīvidēbātur (Seneca *Ep.*)
9 quī annus ōlim in duās tantum partēs dīvidēbātur (Servius Honoratus)
10 tetigīque puellam, sīc etiam tunicā tangitur illā suā (Ovid *Am.*)
11 nec bene prōmeritīs capitur neque tangitur īrā (Lucretius)
12 ex eō cum tangitur ūmōre (Vitruvius)

(a) the crime of herbalist will be disclosed in this mention
(b) where it was divided, there the passage showed less with
   respect to a deep riverbed
(c) but the source of all this wickedness will be revealed in
   its own time
(d) neither is he well seized by merits nor touched by anger
(e) it was divided between harmonious men
(f) and if you wish to be happy, ask the gods that what is
   desired does not turn out for you
(g) the year was formerly divided into only two parts
(h) seek and you will find, knock and it will be opened
(i) not as those things are imagined or desired
(j) from this when it is touched by moisture
(k) often even humorously, those things which are not
   able to be done are desired
(l) I touched a girl, in the same way even that she is
   touched by her own undergarment

Exercise 6

Several passives (or at least passive-looking forms) have occurred in previous units. Locate the passive forms in the previous units. The number and order of their occurrence in each unit is listed below. One of these forms is a *deponent verb* (see *Intermediate Latin*) and is only passive in form but active in meaning. Can you determine which verb this is?

- Unit 3, Exercise 4:   3rd pl. present of the 2nd conjugation
- Unit 4, Exercise 5:   3rd sg. imperfect of the 2nd conjugation
                         3rd sg. present of the 1st conjugation
- Unit 5, Exercise 4:   3rd pl. present of the 3rd conjugation
- Unit 8, Exercise 2:   3rd sg. present of the 3rd conjugation
- Unit 10, Exercise 5:   3rd sg. future of the 1st conjugation
                         2nd sg. future of the 3rd conjugation
- Unit 11, Exercise 3:   3rd sg. present of the 2nd conjugation
- Unit 15, Exercise 5:   3rd pl. imperfect of the 2nd conjugation
- Unit 16, Exercise 4:   3rd sg. present of the 3rd conjugation
- Unit 17, Exercise 4:   3rd sg. future of the 4th conjugation
- Unit 18, Exercise 2:   3rd sg. present of the 3rd conjugation

Reading: The Augean Stables (Labor V), part 1

Eurystheus nunc labōrem difficilem quīntum iussit. Illō tempore rēx, nōmine Augēās, **tria** mīlia boum habēbat. Animālia in stabulō ingentis magnitūdinis inclūdēbantur. Stabulum squālōre terribilī erat quia nōn purgābātur. Eurystheus Herculem ad rēgem Augēam mīsit. Rēx nescīvit Herculem. Causa **adventūs** ā rēge nōn sciēbātur.

"Quid dabis, sī stabulum intrā vīgintī hōrās purgābitur?" interrogāvit Herculēs. Rēx nōn crēdidit. Opus tam celeriter nōn cōnficiētur.

"Bene," inquit, "dabō decimam partem omnium boum **quī** in stabulō sunt."

tria three [acc. pl. nt.]
adventūs of (his) arrival [gen. sg.]
quī which [nom. pl.]

UNIT 20
Passive of the perfect system

Background

The three tenses of the perfect system (i.e. *perfect, pluperfect, future perfect*) form their passives with the help of the verb **esse** *to be*.

These passives consist of two words:

4th principal part + form of the verb **esse**

Fourth principal part

The fourth principal part is the fourth and last part of a verb which must be memorized. It is used to form the *passive* of the *perfect system*.

It is translated as *-ed* or *-en* (see the examples below)

Aside from 1st conjugation verbs which predictably end in **-ātus** in the fourth principal part, all other verbs take unpredictable fourth principal parts, though you will notice sub-patterns as more verbs are learned:

1ˢᵗ conjugation

amō,	**amāre,**	**amāvī,**	*amātus*
(I love)	(to love)	(I loved)	(loved)
vulnerō,	**vulnerāre,**	**vulnerāvī,**	*vulnerātus*
(I wound)	(to wound)	(I wounded)	(wounded)

2ⁿᵈ conjugation

videō,	**vidēre**	**vīdī**	*vīsus*
(I see)	(to see)	(I saw)	(seen)
teneō	**tenēre**	**tenuī**	*tentus*
(I hold)	(to hold)	(I held)	(held)

3rd conjugation

capiō,	**capere**	**cēpī**	*captus*
(I seize)	(to seize)	(I seized)	(seized)

crēdō	**crēdere**	**crēdidī**	*crēditus*
(I believe)	(to believe)	(I believed)	(believed)

4th conjugation

audiō	**audīre**	**audīvī**	*audītus*
(I hear)	(to hear)	(I heard)	(heard)

sciō	**scīre**	**scīvī**	*scītus*
(I know)	(to know)	(I knew)	(known)

The fourth principal part is a verbal adjective. As such it will always take *gender*, *number*, and *case agreement* with the noun it is modifying.

In the passives of the perfect system, the fourth principal part will be agreeing with the subject of the sentence.

Perfect passive

Fourth principal part   +   present tense forms of **esse**

amātus sum	I was loved ~ I have been loved
amātus es	you were loved ~ you have been loved
amātus est	he was loved ~ he has been loved
amātī sumus	we were loved ~ we have been loved
amātī estis	you were loved ~ you have been loved
amātī sunt	they were loved ~ they have been loved

The forms above are used when the subject is masculine:

Rēx ā populō amātus est.
The king was loved by the people.

If the subject is feminine, **amāta** and **amātae** are used in place of **amātus** and **amātī** respectively.

Likewise if the subject is neuter, **amātum** and **amāta** are used in the singular and plural respectively.

	Feminine	*Neuter*
1sg.	amāta sum	amātum sum
2	amāta es	amātum es
3	amāta est	amātum est
1pl.	amātae sumus	amāta sumus
2	amātae estis	amāta estis
3	amātae sunt	amāta sunt

Examples:

Rēgīna ā populō amāta est.
The queen was loved by the people.

Oppidum ā populō amātum est.
The town was loved by the people.

Pluperfect passive

Fourth principal part   +   imperfect tense forms of **esse**

amātus, -a, -um eram	I had been loved
amātus, -a, -um erās	you had been loved
amātus, -a, -um erat	s/he, it had been loved
amātī, -ae, -a erāmus	we had been loved
amātī, -ae, -a erātis	you had been loved
amātī, -ae, -a erant	they had been loved

Future perfect passive

Fourth principal part   +   future tense forms of **esse**

amātus, -a, -um erō	I will have been loved
amātus, -a, -um eris	you will have been loved
amātus, -a, -um erit	s/he, it will have been loved
amātī, -ae, -a erimus	we will have been loved
amātī, -ae, -a eritis	you will have been loved
amātī, -ae, -a erunt	they will have been loved

Exercise 1

Translate the following.

1	she had been loved	6	the war was begun
2	the city will have been divided	7	our food has been prepared
3	the kings had been touched	8	the people had been driven
4	we will have been frightened	9	a wall will have been made
5	the crowns had been placed	10	the stories have been written

Exercise 2

Translate the following.

1 Nāvēs tempestātibus crūdēlibus āctae erant.
2 Fēlīx puer ā mātre patreque amātus est.
3 Ubi vīsa erās?
4 Vīnum per noctem ā mīlitibus bibitum erit.
5 Amor inter fīliam rēgis et fīlium agricolae sēnsus est.
6 Servus vocātus erat semper ā dominō.
7 Rūmor dē immortālibus urbī terrārum nūntiātus est.
8 Cupītus odor flōrum erat.
9 Saxa sagittaeque contrā moenia inimīcōrum nostrōrum iacta sunt.
10 Sōl nūbibus tēctus est.
11 Rāmīs arbōrum aedificātae sunt vīllae.
12 Litterae poētae rēgīnae scrīptae erant.
13 Lupus sagittīs puerōrum interfectus erit.
14 Ante bellum mūnīta sunt oppida īnsulae ab incolīs.
15 Numerus iūcundōrum agricolārum magnīs dē tempestātibus ā fīliō nautae monitus erat.
16 Ēmptus est canis senex ā dominō novō.
17 Rāmī aquā portātī sunt.
18 Coāctī sumus īre.
19 Verba auctōris clārī audīta erunt.
20 Aurum obscūrō in antrō ā mulieribus pulchrīs inventum erat.

Exercise 3

Translate the following.

1 The fields of beautiful flowers had been desired by the enemies.
2 The young will have been asked by the old.

3 The frightened boy was held by the mother.
4 The song was sung by all.
5 When had you (pl. m.) been seen?

Exercise 4

Each of the following unedited Latin passages contains a passive verbal form
in the perfect system. Match each passage with the English translation which
follows. To assist you, try to think of English derivatives which stem from some
of the Latin words.

1	nōn causa quae ācta timidē est	(Cicero *Att.*)
2	posteā rēs ācta est in senātū alia nūlla	(Cicero *Red. Pop.*)
3	spectātōrēs, fābula haec est ācta, vōs plausum date	(Plautus *Mos.*)
4	sed ita fēcistis quō modō paucī nōbilēs in hāc	
	cīvitāte cōnsulēs factī sunt	(Cicero *Agr.*)
5	lūdī sunt nōn rīte factī	(Cicero *Har.*)
6	sī patrēs auctōrēs nōn erant factī	(Cicero *Planc.*)
7	incitātō equō sē hostibus obtulit atque interfectus est	(Caesar *Gal.*)
8	ab cīvitāte erat interfectus	(Caesar *Gal.*)
9	interfectus est propter quāsdam sēditiōnum	
	suspīciōnēs	(Cicero *Catil.*)
10	parātae īnsidiae sunt: in statū stat senex	(Plautus *Mil.*)
11	sine meō sūmptū parātae iam sunt scapulīs	
	symbolae	(Plautus *Epid.*)
12	parātae sunt lactūcae singulae, cochleae ternae,	
	ōva bīna	(Pliny the Younger)

(a) his horse having been roused, he exposed himself to the
     enemies and he was killed
(b) but you have done so in such a way that few nobles have been
     made consuls in the state
(c) the games have not been made properly
(d) he has been killed on account of certain suspicions of insurrections
(e) this story has now been done, you, spectators, give applause
(f) one lettuce each, three snails each, two eggs each have been prepared
(g) without my own expense contributions have been prepared for my
     shoulder blades
(h) not the cause which has been done out of fear
(i) he had been killed by the state
(j) afterwards no other thing was done in the senate
(k) if the fathers had not been made authors
(l) treachery has been prepared, the old man stands in position

Reading: The Augean Stables (Labor V), part 2

Herculēs negōtium suscēpit, quamquam nōverat **id** difficile esse. Vīdit stabulum, quod numquam purgātum erat. Nam nōn longē ā domō rēgiā flūmen aquae cōpiōsae fluēbat. Herculēs prīmum magnō labōre fossam ad mūrum stabulī dūxit. Deinde mūrum perrūpit et aquam in stabulum immīsit. Clāmor horribilis erat. Aqua intrā mūrōs incrēdibilī cum celeritāte ruēbat et omnem squālōrem portābat. Herculēs tamquam dux victor post pugnam adstābat. Magnopere gaudēbat quod cōnsiliō opus difficile contrā opīniōnem omnium cōnfēcit. Sed nōn laetus erat, quod rēx nihil dedit, **quod** prōmissum erat.

id it [acc. sg.]   **quod** which [nom. sg. nt.]

UNIT 21
Demonstratives I

Background

There are a variety of pronouns in English and Latin. The following gives some illustration as to the different types and where they are dealt with in this book.

- <u>demonstrative pronouns</u>: *this one, that one, these ones, those ones*   (this unit)
- <u>intensive pronouns</u>: *the very one*   (Unit 22)
- <u>relative pronouns</u>: *who, whom, whose, that*   (Unit 25)
- <u>interrogative pronouns</u>: *who?, whom?, whose?, what?*   (Unit 26)
- <u>personal pronouns</u>: *I, you, he, she, it, we, they*   (Unit 27)
- <u>reflexive pronouns</u>: *myself, yourself, himself, herself, ourselves . . .*   (Unit 27)
- <u>indefinite pronouns</u>: *someone, anyone, something, anything*   (Unit 31)

This unit discusses *demonstrative pronouns*. A demonstrative is used to point out something definite, whether singular or plural. They differ as to *deixis*, or their reference points; namely, whether the person or thing which is being pointed out is *near* the speaker, *away* from the speaker but still *in view*, or *away* from the speaker but *not in view*.

	singular	**plural**
near	*this one*	*these ones*
distant	*that one*	*those ones*
distant out of sight	*that one (out of sight)*	*those ones (out of sight)*

- The pointing out function of demonstratives is encapsulated in the name *demonstrative*, which comes from Latin **dēmōnstrāre** (1) *to point out.*

When followed by a noun directly, an English *demonstrative pronoun* becomes a *demonstrative adjective*.

- Demonstrative Pronoun

  *I see **that**.*
  *Do you understand **this**?*

- Demonstrative Adjective

  *I see **that** dog.*
  *Do you understand **this** question?*

Latin structure

There are three sets of *demonstratives*. The first two contrast in deixis whereas the third is unemphatic and predominantly used as a 3rd person pronoun.

- **hic, haec, hoc** *this, these*
- **ille, illa, illud** *that, those*
- **is, ea, id** *this, that, these, those* – unemphatic

  - as a pronoun, **is, ea, id** is used to express the 3rd person personal pronouns *he, she, it, they, him, her, them*

Being pronouns and adjectives, the demonstratives are unsurprisingly declined. Fortunately, there is no difference between the pronominal and adjectival forms.

- Remember, all that differentiates the pronominal guise from the adjectival one is their use in a sentence. When no noun follows, a demonstrative is pronominal (i.e. substantive). When a noun follows, it is adjectival.

I. *hic, haec, hoc* this, these

	Singular			*Plural*		
	Masc.	*Fem.*	*Neut.*	*Masc.*	*Fem.*	*Neut.*
Nom.	hic	haec	hoc	hī	hae	haec
Gen.	huius	huius	huius	hōrum	hārum	hōrum
Dat.	huic	huic	huic	hīs	hīs	hīs
Acc.	hunc	hanc	hoc	hōs	hās	haec
Abl.	hōc	hāc	hōc	hīs	hīs	hīs

- The plural is pretty easy. Aside from **haec**, the endings are all from the *1ˢᵗ and 2ⁿᵈ declensions*.
- The singular is much more peculiar. A strange final **-c** appears in all the endings.
- There are at least two unsurprising facts:

  - Ablative singulars in **-ō-** and **-ā-**
  - The neuter nom. and acc. sg. are identical

Examples:

Hī mīlitēs hoc oppidum vīcērunt.   (demonstrative adjectives)
These soldiers conquered this town.

Hī haec vīcērunt.   (demonstrative pronouns)
These (men) conquered these (things).

II. *ille, illa, illud* that, those

	Singular			*Plural*		
	Masc.	*Fem.*	*Neut.*	*Masc.*	*Fem.*	*Neut.*
Nom.	**ille**	**illa**	**illud**	**illī**	**illae**	**illa**
Gen.	**illīus**	**illīus**	**illīus**	**illōrum**	**illārum**	**illōrum**
Dat.	**illī**	**illī**	**illī**	**illīs**	**illīs**	**illīs**
Acc.	**illum**	**illam**	**illud**	**illōs**	**illās**	**illa**
Abl.	**illō**	**illā**	**illō**	**illīs**	**illīs**	**illīs**

Notes:

- This time *all* the plural endings are *1ˢᵗ and 2ⁿᵈ declension* endings
- The singular is yet again more peculiar, though we see **-ō** and **-ā** in the ablative sg.
- We also see **-um** and **-am** in the accusative singular

Examples:

Illī mīlitēs illud oppidum vīcērunt.   (demonstrative adjectives)
Those soldiers conquered that town.

Illī illa vīcērunt.   (demonstrative pronouns)
Those (men) conquered those (things).

III. ***is***, ***ea***, ***id*** *he, she, it, they ~ [unemphatic] this, that, these, those*

	Singular			*Plural*		
	Masc.	*Fem.*	*Neut.*	*Masc.*	*Fem.*	*Neut.*
Nom.	**is** he	**ea** she	**id** it	**eī** they	**eae** they	**ea** they
Gen.	**eius** his	**eius** her	**eius** its	**eōrum** their	**eārum**	**eōrum**
Dat.	**eī** to him	**eī** to her	**eī** to it	**eīs** to them	**eīs**	**eīs**
Acc.	**eum** him	**eam** her	**id** it	**eōs** them	**eās**	**ea**
Abl.	**eō** by him	**eā** by her	**eō** by it	**eīs** by them	**eīs**	**eīs**

Notes:

- Aside from the masculine nom. sg., the endings are identical to those of **ille, illa, illud**
- All the plural forms with **eī**- have alternatives in **iī**- or just **ī**-

  - masc. nom. pl.: **eī, iī, ī**
  - dat. and abl. pl.: **eīs, iīs, īs**

- The genitive is used to show possession (see the second and third examples below). This is different from the situation with personal pronouns where special possessive adjectives are used (Unit 27).

Example

Eī eum vīcērunt.
They conquered it.

Canem eius videō.
I see his dog. ~ I see her dog.

Canēs eōrum videō.
I see their dogs.

- **Suus, -a, -um** *his own, her own, their own* is a reflexive adjective and can only refer back to the subject.
- **eius** *his, her* **eōrum** *their* (m.), **eārum** *their* (f.) are not reflexives and hence do <u>not</u> refer back to the subject.

  Canem eius audit.
  He hears his (someone else's) dog.

  Canem suum audit.
  S/he hears his/her own dog.

Exercise 1

Translate the following. Where there is gender ambiguity, provide all possibilities.

1 The daughter of that man loves him.
2 His daughter had come.
3 This daughter of those men is happy.
4 I know this daughter of these men
5 When did you (sg.) see their daughter?
6 By their own luck they will find gold.
7 By that luck we will wage war.
8 You (pl) remember all these things.
9 That king ruled this island.
10 These gods give swords to them.

Exercise 2

Translate the following.

1 Lūna fulget et lūx eius hanc terram tegit.
2 Illī nautae in pontō illō fuērunt.
3 Eius pater tacet quod dormit.
4 Vīnum illum hortī eārum bibēmus.
5 Praemium hoc ā deō illō huic vātī datum est.
6 Hic poēta caecus scrīpserat illās litterās eī.
7 Quandō invēnistis haec loca?
8 Saxīs illīs vīllae huius oppidī ab eīs aedificābuntur.
9 Līberī eōrum in silvā cucurrērunt et ibi animālibus illīs cecinērunt.
10 Hāc sagittā ille interfectus est.
11 Is fīliō suam fābulam dīcit.
12 Is fīliō eius fābulam dīcit.
13 Per hās portās altās venient illī mīlitēs urbis illīus.
14 In āere est hic odor illōrum flōrum.
15 Suīs vulneribus interfectus erit ille mīles.
16 Illīs tempestātibus gravibus nōn nāvigāre illī potuerant.
17 In hāc urbe frequentī nōn est cibus aquaque.
18 Hoc mel dulce uxōrī eius dedit rēgīna.
19 Soror eius legit librōs illōrum clārōrum auctōrum.
20 Verba sua nōn audiunt.

Exercise 3

Each of the following unedited Latin passages contains a demonstrative pronoun or adjective. Match each passage with the English translation which follows. To assist you, try to think of English derivatives which stem from some of the Latin words.

1	ad haec igitur prius equidem dīcō	(Josephus *Ap.*)
2	haec vidēbis et ferēs	(Catullus)
3	celeriter haec ad hostēs dēferuntur	(Caesar *Gal.*)
4	haec genera mūnītiōnis īnstituit	(Caesar *Gal.*)
5	quī fortūnae illīus perīculum fēcerat	(Caesar *Gal.*)
6	nec sēsē ā gremiō illīus movēbat	(Catullus)
7	aetās illīus hoc caecā nocte tegat studium	(Catullus)
8	in quibus ad mē epistulārum illīus exempla mīsistī	(Cicero *Att.*)
9	post eius mortem	(Caesar *Gal.*)
10	eius exercitum sub iugum mīserat	(Caesar *Gal.*)
11	fīliumque eius impūberem lēgātum ā patre missum in carcere necātum esse	(Cicero *Catil.*)
12	nam eum pater eius subēgit	(Plautus *Cist.*)
13	mīsērunt sēque eī dēdidērunt	(Caesar *Gal.*)
14	eī cāra patria est	(Cicero *Dom.*)
15	huic puerō quī est eī vītā suā multō cārior metuit	(Cicero *Sul.*)
16	grātiās agō eī	(St Jerome)
17	hāc pugnā nūntiātā	(Caesar *Gal.*)
18	hāc animās ille ēvocat	(Vergil *Aeneid*)
19	hāc super rē scrībam ad tē	(Cicero *Att.*)
20	sī nārrem tibi hāc nocte quod ego somniāvī dormiēns	(Plautus *Cur.*)

(a) if I tell you that I dreamt of this night while sleeping
(b) after his death
(c) on this thing I will write to you
(d) I thank him
(e) time may cover this zeal of that one with blind night
(f) these are conveyed quickly to the enemies
(g) in which you sent to me examples of his letters
(h) and his youthful son, sent as a delegate by his father, was killed in prison
(i) he had sent his army under the yoke
(j) he undertook these kinds of fortification
(k) after this battle had been announced
(l) who had experienced the danger of that fate
(m) by which he calls forth spirits
(n) he fears for this boy who is dearer to him than his own life by much
(o) and he was not moving himself from that one's bosom

(p)   the fatherland is dear to him
(q)   for his father compelled him
(r)   they sent and they gave themselves to him
(s)   you will see these things and bear them?
(t)   therefore before I indeed speak to these things

Reading: The Stymphalian Birds (Labor VI), part 1

Post paucōs **diēs** Herculēs ad oppidum Stymphālum iter fēcit. Avēs in **lacū** vīcīnō habitābant. Tōtam regiōnem perīculōsam reddēbant. Hae avēs horribilēs erant. Rostrīs ācribus omnia trānsfīgere poterant. Multī hominēs in illā regiōne vīvēbant. Multī ab eīs occīsī erant. Herculēs ad lacum vēnit. Magnam difficultātem superāre dēbēbat. Lacus enim nōn ex aquā, sed ē līmō cōnstābat. Avēs in arboribus altīs in mediō **lacū** sedēbant.

   diēs days [acc. pl.]   **lacū** lake [abl. sg. masc.]

UNIT 22
Demonstratives II

Background

Demonstrative pronouns/adjectives were introduced in the previous unit.

Recall that demonstratives point out a *definite* person or thing.

They are opposed to the *indefinite pronouns/adjectives* (Units 31 and 32), which do not point out a specific person or thing.

There are three additional *demonstratives* in Latin:

īdem, eadem, idem same
iste, istad, istud that/those (damn one(s)), that/those (of yours)
ipse, ipsa, ipsum self, very

Latin formation

Idem, eadem, idem is formed by adding the unchangeable suffix **-dem** to the forms of **is, ea, id** (Unit 21).

same

		Masc.	*Fem.*	*Nt.*
sg.	Nom.	**īdem**	eadem	idem
	Gen.	**eiusdem**	eiusdem	eiusdem
	Dat.	**eīdem**	eīdem	eīdem
	Acc.	**eundem**	eandem	idem
	Abl.	**eōdem**	eādem	eōdem
		Masc.	*Fem.*	*Nt.*
pl.	Nom.	**eīdem**	eaedem	eadem
	Gen.	**eōrundem**	eārundem	eōrundem
	Dat.	**eīsdem**	eīsdem	eīsdem
	Acc.	**eōsdem**	eāsdem	eadem
	Abl.	**eīsdem**	eīsdem	eīsdem

- The neuter **idem** has only one **-d-** and not two as expected *****id-dem**.
- The masculine **īdem** has an **ī-** in place of expected **is-**.
- An **-n-** occurs wherever an **-m-** is expected:

  - **eundem, eandem, eōrundem, eārundem.** A similar thing happens in the forms of **quīdam, quaedam, quiddam** *certain* (Unit 31)

- **īdem** is a variant of the masculine nominative pl. **eīdem** which is frequent in poetry.
- **īsdem** is a variant of the dative plural **eīsdem** of all genders.

that/those (damn one(s)); that/those (of yours)

Iste, ista, istud is declined identically to **ille, illa, illud** (Unit 21).

		Masc.	*Fem.*	*Nt.*
sg.	Nom.	iste	ista	istud
	Gen.	istīus	istīus	istīus
	Dat.	istī	istī	istī
	Acc.	istum	istam	istud
	Abl.	istō	istā	istō
		Masc.	*Fem.*	*Nt.*
pl.	Nom.	istī	istae	ista
	Gen.	istōrum	istārum	istōrum
	Dat.	istīs	istīs	istīs
	Acc.	istōs	istās	ista
	Abl.	istīs	istīs	istīs

This demonstrative often refers to something associated with the 2nd person (*you*) and also often has a pejorative connotation.

Iste canis semper lātrat.
That (damn) dog (of yours) always barks.

Virī oppidī istīus veniunt.
The men of that (damn) town (of yours) are coming.

self, very

Ipse, ipsa, ipsum is also declined identically to **ille, illa, illud** (Unit 21) except its neuter ends in **-um** instead of **-ud**.

		Masc.	Fem.	Nt.
sg.	Nom.	ipse	ipsa	ipsum
	Gen.	ipsīus	ipsīus	ipsīus
	Dat.	ipsī	ipsī	ipsī
	Acc.	ipsum	ipsam	ipsum
	Abl.	ipsō	ipsā	ipsō
		Masc.	Fem.	Nt.
pl.	Nom.	ipsī	ipsae	ipsa
	Gen.	ipsōrum	ipsārum	ipsōrum
	Dat.	ipsīs	ipsīs	ipsīs
	Acc.	ipsōs	ipsās	ipsa
	Abl.	ipsīs	ipsīs	ipsīs

This demonstrative intensifies the noun it modifies or is taking the place of. The translation *self* here is not the same *self* as used in the reflexive in English (Unit 27).

Ipse canis semper lātrat.
That very dog always barks.
That dog itself always barks.

Ipse ipsam fēminam vīdī.
I myself saw that very woman.
I myself saw that woman herself.

Exercise 1

Translate the following.

1 He himself had been killed by that damn lion of yours.
2 The same sailors saw the queen herself.
3 In the age of knights kings themselves fought the same enemies.
4 We will drink the wine of that island of yours.
5 She will have been seen by the same neighbours.
6 When did you (sg.) feel that wind itself?
7 I was throwing my eyes on the same gold.
8 That temple of yours is being built between our fields.
9 The same blind men had read the same books of the same poets.
10 The damn immortal gods give the poor farmers nothing.

Exercise 2

Translate the following.

1 Scelera istīus virī faciunt mātrem īnfēlīcem.
2 Ipse līberōs amō.
3 Tempestās nova hominēs animāliaque ab eīsdem oppidīs fūgere coēgerat.
4 Quid imperat rēx iste?
5 Interfēcērunt agricolae īdem gregem ovium, sed eīs nōn est.
6 Similis istī fēminae fuit ipsa puella huius nautae miserī.
7 Possumus nōn in urbem ipsam moeniīs īre.
8 Per noctem longam audīvīmus nihil altō dē ipsō monte.
9 Mīlitēs dederint vēla cum praedā prōvinciae istīus.
10 Omnī nocte somnium idem puerō est.
11 Dēfessī sumus, quod cucurrimus lātum circum hortum dominī.
12 Vulgus barbarōrum prope portam ipsam erat.
13 Litterae eaedem ab ipsō scrībuntur.
14 Lūna eadem fulsit in tempore antīquōrum, ipsa fulget hodiē, et ipsa fulgēbit
līberīs nostrīs.
15 Fēlīcēs puellae gladium eundem ferrī fortis mīlitis vīdērunt.
16 Ventō fortī ille rāmus arbōris istīus meum caput frēgit.
17 Dēbēs ipsa vulgō canere.
18 Meminerāmus nōn verbārum auctōris ipsīus.
19 Ipsa nympha pulchra movēbit illa saxa montis nautīs dēfessīs.
20 Taurōs sociī nostrī portāverant in eadem antra.

Exercise 3

Each of the following unedited Latin passages contains a demonstrative pronoun
or adjective. Match each passage with the English translation which follows.
To assist you, try to think of English derivatives which stem from some of the
Latin words.

1 reperiō apud scrīptōrēs senātōrēsque eōrundem
   temporum (Tacitus *Ann.*)
2 scrīpta ēgregiam eōrundem memoriam trādunt (Tacitus *Ann.*)
3 tertium eōrundem genus ērudītā operātiōne cōnspicuum (Pliny the Elder)
4 eōrundem lībertātī mē parcere certum est (Cicero *Off.*)
5 vīdistis ipsō rapere dē rogō cēnam (Catullus)
6 quī in ipsō negōtiō cōnsilium capere cōguntur (Caesar *Gal.*)
7 cum ipsō annī tempore ad gerendum bellum vocārētur (Caesar *Gal.*)
8 neque enim ab ipsō ūllae litterae (Cicero *Brut.*)
9 tālis iste meus stupor nīl videt (Catullus)
10 ut quō iste vester expolītior dēns est (Catullus)
11 unde iste amor tam imprōvīsus ac tam repentīnus (Cicero *Agr.*)
12 rogus iste cremet mea viscera (Ovid *Met.*)
13 aut ipsī in eōrum fīnibus bellum gerunt (Caesar *Gal.*)
14 ipsī inter sē prōvinciās partiuntur (Caesar *Gal.*)
15 unde mare et terrās ipsī mihi saepe vidēre fit timor (Ovid *Met.*)
16 arma dabunt ipsī (Vergil *Aeneid*)
17 cētera quae ad mē eīsdem litterīs scrībis (Cicero *Att.*)
18 quod ab eīsdem inlectī sumus (Cicero *Att.*)
19 ut putem esse commodius nōs eīsdem in locīs esse (Cicero *Att.*)
20 adēmit eīsdem agrōs (Cicero *Dom.*)

(a) the rest which you wrote to me by the same letter
(b) that we have been misled by the same people
(c) or they themselves wage war in their borders
(d) I find it stated among writers and senators of the same times
(e) so that by it your tooth is more polished
(f) from where is this love of yours which is so unexpected and so hasty
(g) the writings hand down a distinguished memory of the same men
(h) and indeed from him himself there has been no letter
(i) a third kind of the same is noticeable because of its accomplished
    working
(j) may this funeral pyre burn my entrails
(k) they themselves will give weapons
(l) from where seeing the sea and lands, fear often comes to me
(m) it is resolved that I spare the same men freedom
(n) and it took away the fields from the same people
(o) when he was called at the time of year itself to wage war
(p) they themselves distribute the provinces between themselves
(q) who are forced to take advice in the task itself
(r) that I think it to be more proper that we be in the same place
(s) such this my bewilderment sees nothing
(t) you have seen (her) snatching dinner from a funeral pyre itself

Reading: The Stymphalian Birds (Labor VI), part 2

Herculēs locum exāmināvit. "Quōmodo avēs pellere possum? Eae in illīs arboribus sedent. Quōmodo ad eās appropinquāre possum?" Dea eum ā tergō tetigit.
Ea adstābat et duo crepundia tenēbat. Crepundia ā Vulcānō ex aere fabricāta
erant. Herculī ea trādidit, deinde ēvānuit. Herculēs nunc collem propinquum
ascendit et crepundiīs ācrem crepitum fēcit. Avēs perterritae āvolāvērunt.
Herculēs magnam partem avium sagittīs trānsfīxit. Cīvēs illīus urbis ā perīculō
līberātī sunt. Herculī magnās grātiās ēgērunt.

Note

ā tergō   from behind (literally: *from the back*)

Review of units 18–22

A. Which types of dative would the following be rendered into Latin as?

1 He sent money *for help*.
2 The man, who is unfriendly *to us*, has five children.
3 *As for me*, this is a crazy idea.

B. Use the following verbs to translate.

> amō, amāre, amāvī, amātus   to love
> capiō, capere, cēpī, captus   to seize
> doceō, docēre, docuī, doctus   to teach
> dūcō, dūcere, dūxī, ductus   to lead
> audio, audīre, audīvī, audītus   to hear

1 **doctus erit**
2 **audiēbātur**
3 **capiēmur**
4 **amātae sunt**
5 **dūcuntur**

6 you (pl. m.) had been taught
7 I will be heard
8 they (pl. nt.) will have been seized
9 you (sg.) were being loved
10 we will be led

C. Rewrite the following Latin sentences replacing every noun with the correct form of the demonstrative pronoun **hic, haec, hoc**. Then rewrite the same sentences adding **ipse, ipsa, ipsum** to modify each noun.

1 Puer mātrem amat.
2 Poēta rēgīnae litterās mittit.

3 Sagittīs virum interficiam.
4 Rēgī līberī sunt.

UNIT 23
Irregular verbs II

Latin structure

This unit deals with the remaining five irregular verbs of Latin. For the other two see Unit 11.

I. eō, īre, īvī ~ iī, itus to go

Like **esse** (Unit 11) **īre** is irregular because of its changing stems:

- **e-** and **ī-** in the present
- **ī-** in the imperfect and future

Its forms are:

		Present	*Imperfect*	*Future*
sg.	1	eō	ībam	ībō
	2	īs	ībās	ībis
	3	it	ībat	ībit
pl.	1	īmus	ībāmus	ībimus
	2	ītis	ībātis	ībitis
	3	eunt	ībant	ībunt

INFINITIVE: **īre**
PRESENT PARTICIPLE: **iēns, euntis**   (cf. Unit 33)

Notes

- The stem **ī-** is predictably shortened before the final **-t** in **it** *s/he goes*
- The imperfect exhibits the same affix **-bā-** which occurs in the imperfect of the four conjugations (Unit 9).
- The future exhibits the form of a 1ˢᵗ or 2ⁿᵈ conjugation verb (Unit 10) because of the presence of the stem extension **-b-**.

131

- The nominative singular of the present participle **iēns** is what is expected of 4th conjugation verbs. The stem **eunt-** used for the other forms, however, is unexpected (see Unit 33 for discussion of participles).
- The perfect has two stems, **īv-** and **i-**. Either is acceptable.

Advanced topics

Passive forms of **īre** occur in transitive compounds formed from it. The expected passive endings are added to the same stems the active endings are added to.

praeter-eō, praeter-īre, praeter-iī, praeter-itus to overtake

Present Passive:

praetereor I am overtaken   **praeterīmur** we are overtaken

praeterīris you (sg.) are overtaken   **praeterīminī** you (pl.) are overtaken
praeterītur s/he, it is overtaken   **praetereuntur** they are overtaken

Imperfect Passive: **praeterībar, praeterībāris, praeterībātur . . .**
Future Passive: **praeterībor, praeterīberis, praeterībitur . . .**

II. *ferō, ferre, tulī, lātus to bring, carry*

The most striking feature about the principal parts of this verb is the *total suppletion*, or use of different roots, observed between the present system with **fer-**, the perfect active with **tul-** and the perfect passive with **lāt-**.

As with all irregular verbs in Latin, however, irregularities in form exist *only in the present system*. Therefore, even though the stems are different, all perfect system forms of this verb – both active and passive – are formed regularly with the expected endings (Units 13, 14, 20).

The present tense and imperative mood are alone irregular:

	Present Active		*Present Passive*	
	singular	*plural*	*singular*	*plural*
1	**ferō**	**ferimus**	**feror**	**ferimur**
2	**fers**	**fertis**	**ferris**	**feriminī**
3	**fert**	**ferunt**	**fertur**	**feruntur**

INFINITIVE: **ferre**
PRESENT PARTICIPLE: **ferēns, ferentis** (cf. Unit 33)
IMPERATIVE: **fer, ferte**   (cf. Unit 28)

- **Ferre** is effectively conjugated like a regular 3rd conjugation verb which simply loses its stem vowel in five forms:

  fers, **fert**, **fertis** in the active
  ferris, **fertur** in the passive.

  - The same occurs in the imperative where the expected stem vowel is missing from both the singular and plural forms (see Unit 28).

- The imperfect and future are formed regularly according to the 3rd conjugation (Units 9 and 10):

  - *Imperfect*: **ferēbam, ferēbās, ferēbat, ferēbāmus, ferēbātis, ferēbant**
  - *Future:* **feram, ferēs, feret, ferēmus, ferētis, ferent**

Compounds

Ferre forms many compounds by the affixation of prefixes, many of which occur independently as prepositions (Unit 7).

- The forms are conjugated exactly as **ferre** is.
- The one caveat to watch out for is the transformation of the prefixes before **ferre**'s different roots.

af-ferō	**af-ferre**	**at-tulī**	**al-lātus**	to bring to, present
au-ferō	**au-ferre**	**abs-tulī**	**ab-lātus**	to carry away
cōn-ferō	**cōn-ferre**	**con-tulī**	**col-lātus**	to collect
dif-ferō	**dif-ferre**	**dis-tulī**	**dī-lātus**	to differ
ef-ferō	**ef-ferre**	**ex-tulī**	**ē-lātus**	to carry out
of-ferō	**of-ferre**	**ob-tulī**	**ob-lātus**	to offer
re-ferō	**re-ferre**	**re-ttulī**	**re-lātus**	to bring back, report
suf-ferō	**suf-ferre**	**sus-tulī**	**sub-lātus**	to undergo, endure

Note

- The perfect **tulī** was historically reduplicated **tetulī** (cf. **canō** *I sing*, **cecinī** *I have sung*). While this reduplication has been lost, a trace of it survives in the **-tt-** of **rettulī** *I brought back*.

III. volō, nōlō, mālō

The last batch of irregular verbs is:

volō, velle, voluī, ---	to want, wish
nōlō, nōlle, nōluī, ---	to not want
mālō, mālle, māluī, ---	to prefer

Aside from their irregular present infinitives, these three verbs are only irregular in the *present tense* and *imperative mood*.

Their present forms are:

sg.	1	**volō** I want	**nōlō** I do not want	**mālō** I prefer
	2	**vīs**	**nōn vīs**	**māvīs**
	3	**vult**	**nōn vult**	**māvult**
pl.	1	**volumus**	**nōlumus**	**mālumus**
	2	**vultis**	**nōn vultis**	**māvultis**
	3	**volunt**	**nōlunt**	**mālunt**

- **nōlō** derives from **nōn** + the forms of **volō**

  - contraction has applied in those three forms which begin with **vo-**
  - **mālō** is derived from **magis** *more* + the forms of **volō**

The imperfect forms are regular:

volēbam, volēbās, volēbat, volēbāmus, volēbātis, volēbant
nōlēbam, nōlēbās, nōlēbat, nōlēbāmus, nōlēbātis, nōlēbant
mālēbam, mālēs, mālēbat, mālēbāmus, mālēbātis, mālēbant

The future follows the 3rd conjugation:

volam, volēs, volet, volēmus, volētis, volent
nōlam, nōlēs, nōlet, nōlēmus, nōlētis, nōlent
mālam, mālēs, mālet, mālēmus, mālētis, mālent

Only **nōlle** has an imperative. It unexpectedly takes 4th conjugation forms:

sg. **nōlī**   pl. **nōlīte**

As seen in Unit 28, these imperative forms are used to form negative commands of other verbs.

Exercise 1

Translate the following.

1 Vēla dare volēbant nautae, sed nāvēs erant parvae et tempestās fortis erat.
2 Quid māvīs? In īnsulam cum mātribus līberōrum īre aut in vīllā manēre?
3 Hostēs crūdēlēs ab oppidō nostrō abstulimus.
4 Ītis nunc ad agrum. Ibi animālia pascētis.
5 Verba rēgīnae incolīs laetīs poēta, socius rēgis, feret.
6 Pugnāre cum fīnitimīs dē fīnibus eōrum voluit, quod eī nihil fuit.
7 Hic gladius ferebātur ā mīlite in bellum istud.
8 Voluērunt ponere rāmum pācis in āram templī, quod in somniō eōs deī terruērunt.
9 Vīlla sapientis virī praeterītur armīs turbā saevā.
10 Cibus in silvā lātā ā fīliō dēfessō collātus est.
11 Quid eī est? Vult offerre rēgīnae ovem pinguem.
12 In urbem frequentem ībunt fortēs, quod ibi erunt eīs bona.
13 In aetāte hāc māluerant scrībere sapientēs, sed nōn verba omnibus dīxērunt.
14 Cūr fertur fīlia tua trāns pontem? Quod nōn illa currere potest.
15 Corōnam pulchram invēneram. Eam servae rēgīnae dare voluī.
16 Quō eunt et quid ferunt? Ad rīpam amnis currunt, quod piscēs rāmīs capere volunt.
17 In aquam lūx lūnae candidae stellārumque fulserat, sed nūbēs nigrae lūcem abstulērunt.
18 Oculī hominum lūcem etiam in antrīs vidēre volent, sed nōn poterunt.
19 Amīcī poētae mālunt dē antīquibus temporibus audīre.
20 Ferrum et arborēs ferunt in urbem templō deae.

Exercise 2

Translate the following.

1 When will you (sg.) want to sing the words of those famous poets?
2 My brother preferred to not frighten the joyful dogs by the smell of blood.
3 The wind carries the smell of the flowers across the wide fields.
4 The state had not wanted to wage war against its neighbours.
5 Why did you (pl.) not wish to remain here at my country house after you had drunk wine?
6 His fortunate son was not overtaken by the wild horses in the darkness.
7 Because of my tears I wish to ask the wise goddess for food and water.
8 On account of the dream of my sister, we went to the fatherland of our father.
9 Why does he carry a sword? He cannot find peace with it.
10 They will not want to build a new wall of the villa, because a strong storm will break it.

Exercise 3

Each of the following unedited Latin passages contains one of the irregular verbs discussed in this unit. Match each passage with the English translation which follows. To assist you, try to think of English derivatives which stem from some of the Latin words.

1 sī vītant, fūgiunt, audīre dē tē nōlunt   (Cicero *Vat.*)
2 populus nōn cūrat, prīncipēs nōlunt, ego quiēscō   (Cicero *Q. fr.*)
3 hunc hominem tam crūdēlem, tam scelerātum, tam
    nefārium nōlunt iūdicāre   (Cicero *Ver.*)
4 eōdem itinere quō hostēs ierant ad eōs contendit   (Caesar *Gal.*)
5 at quī dextrīs et propiōribus compendiīs ierant   (Tacitus *Ann.*)
6 ex praetōribus, quī in prōvinciās ierant   (Livy)
7 nunc iam illa nōn vult   (Catullus)
8 ille quidem vult plūra loquī   (Ovid *Met.*)
9 ā quō nihil spērēs bonī reī pūblicae quia nōn vult   (Cicero *Att.*)
10 tē rūrsus in bellum resorbēns, unda fretīs tulit aestuōsīs   (Horace *Od.*)
11 ea vōx audīta labōrum prīma tulit fīnem   (Vergil *Aeneid*)
12 sī enim rēctē ambulāvit is quī hanc epistulam tulit   (Cicero *Att.*)

(a) they do not wish this man, so cruel, so wicked, so criminal to be judge
(b) that one indeed wants to say more things
(c) from whom you hope nothing of good for the republic because he does not want
(d) if they avoid (you), they flee, they do not wish to hear about you
(e) this first voice heard brought the end of their labours
(f) the wave carried you to the agitated straits, sweeping you again into battle
(g) now she no longer wants (you)
(h) the people do not care, the leaders do not wish it, I am silent
(i) if indeed he who carried this letter walked correctly
(j) he hastens to them by the same route by which the enemies had gone
(k) of the praetors who had gone to the provinces
(l) but those who had gone by the right and nearer shortcuts

Reading: The Cretan Bull (Labor VII), part 1

Herculēs alium labōrem cōnficere dēbuit. Eurystheus eum nunc in Crētam mīsit, ubi taurus ferōx īnsulam vastābat. Herculēs hunc taurum vīvum in Graeciam ferre dēbēbat. Is nāvem cōnscendit et statim solvit, nam ventus valdē idōneus erat. Quandō nāvis ad īnsulam appropinquābat, tempestās ingēns vītae eius ferē fīnem fēcit. Magnus terror animōs nautārum occupāvit. Omnem spem salūtis dēposuērunt. At Herculēs sōlus nōn perterritus est. Timōrem nōn nōverat, quod tot difficultātēs superāverat.

UNIT 24
Pronominal adjectives

Background

While most 1ˢᵗ–2ⁿᵈ declension adjectives (Unit 6) regularly follow the 1ˢᵗ and 2ⁿᵈ declensions, a small group of 1ˢᵗ–2ⁿᵈ declension adjectives irregularly take genitive and dative singular endings which mimic those of the demonstrative pronouns **ille, illa, illud** and **is, ea, id**.

The nine adjectives are:

alius, alia, aliud other, another
alter, -a, -um the other
neuter, neutra, neutrum neither
nūllus, -a, -um no, none
sōlus, -a, -um alone

tōtus, -a, -um whole, entire, all
ūllus, -a, -um any
ūnus, -a, -um one, alone, single
uter, utra, utrum which of two?

- **alter** and **uter** are both used when discussing a pair:

  Uter vir adveniet?
  Which man will come? ~ Which of the two men will come?

- Note the neuter nominative and accusative singular form **aliud** with an unexpected **-d**.

Using **tōtus, -a, -um** as an example, the forms are:

	Singular			*Plural*		
	Masc.	*Fem.*	*Neut.*	*Masc.*	*Fem.*	*Neut.*
Nom.	tōtus	tōta	tōtum	tōtī	tōtae	tōta
Gen.	tōtīus	tōtīus	tōtīus	tōtōrum	tōtārum	tōtōrum
Dat.	tōtī	tōtī	tōtī	tōtīs	tōtīs	tōtīs
Acc.	tōtum	tōtam	tōtum	tōtōs	tōtās	tōta
Abl.	tōtō	tōtā	tōtō	tōtīs	tōtīs	tōtīs

Latin syntax

Alius and **alter** can both be used correlatively when in adjacent clauses, meaning *the one/some . . . the other(s)*

> **Alius hodiē venit, alius crās veniet.**
> The one comes today, the other tomorrow.

> **Alterī rēgem vident, alterī rēgīnam vident.**
> Some see the king, others see the queen.

When two forms of **alius** occur within the same clause, each may be translated giving a correlative meaning. That is, each may be translated twice!

> **Alius aliud fēcerat.**
> The one had done one thing, the other had done another thing.
> One had done one thing. [literal]

> **Aliī ab aliō inventī sunt.**
> Some were found by one man, others by another man.
> Some were found by another. [literal]

Advanced topics

The genitive singular was often shortened to **-ius** in poetry, especially with the genitive of **alter** (**alterius**).

Dative forms **alterae, nūllō, tūtō,** and **tūtae** do occur in classical prose authors. See Exercise 3 for examples of **alterae.**

There are many compounds consisting of **uter,** which alone is declined:

utercumque, utracumque, utrumcumque whoever of two
uterlibet, utralibet, utrumlibet either one, whichever of the two you please
uterque, utraque, utrumque each of two
utervīs, utravīs, utrumvīs either one, whichever of the two you please

- **alteruter, alterautra, alterumutrum** *the one or the other* declines both parts.

Exercise 1

Translate the following.

1 Utrum librōrum legēs?
2 Tōtus mundus laudāvit ūnam fēminam, rēgīnam pulchram nōbilemque.
3 Amīcus meus ūllum verbum prō rēge negāverat. Ibi stetit et tacuit.
4 Altera castra ā sōlō homine aedificāta sunt.
5 Aliī servī aliōs dominōs vident.
6 Faciētis utrumvīs.
7 Agricolae tōtō in monte vīnum alterīus deī petunt.
8 Nūllum iter longum faciet, quod tempestātēs ferae oppidō tōtī fīnitimōrum nocuērunt.
9 Postquam nāvēs ab īnsulā relīquerant, lūx neutrīus vīsa est et neutra inventa est.
10 Aurēs hōrum animālium sapientium omnēs hominēs audiunt. Id nūllus homō scit.
11 Timōre famis auxilium dē utrāque deā quaerimus.
12 Utrā noxārum incolae illīus īnsulae fugere cōgentur?
13 In silvā malā vīdī ūnam nympham pulchram.
14 Alius mīles aliō gladiō interfectus est.
15 Dīgnus pecūniae es sōlus.
16 Rāmī huius arbōris ingentis omnibus ventīs fortibus totīus mundī in terram ceciderant.
17 Nōlunt īre in ūllum templum, quod eīs pecūnia nōn est.
18 Utrum pinguium taurōrum vir caecō sociō suō parāvit?
19 Properātis ad alteram urbem, ubi sunt amīcī fēlīcēs eōrum.
20 Cīvēs aliud nōmen urbis istīus sciunt.

Exercise 2

Translate the following. Where there is ambiguity in gender, provide all options.

1 Which of the crimes did that damn one do?
2 There was no blood after the crime.
3 The one tooth of the boy fell into the river.
4 Those sailors want to sail around the whole world.
5 The courage of one can bring peace.
6 The enemies had seized neither town.
7 Because they are alone, these children are afraid.
8 He himself read no serious letter.
9 Some came to the town, others went to the island.
10 Which of the jars will you (sg.) drink?

Exercise 3

Each of the following unedited Latin passages contains a pronominal adjective.
Match each passage with the English translation which follows. To assist you,
try to think of English derivatives which stem from some of the Latin words.

 1 prīncipiō nequeunt ūllīus corporis esse sēnsūs   (Lucretius)
 2 celerius tibi hoc rūmor quam ūllīus nostrum litterae
    nūntiārint   (Cicero *Att.*)
 3 neque ego ūllīus cōnsiliī particeps   (Cicero *Att.*)
 4 prōvinciae totī quam maximum potest mīlitum
    numerum imperat   (Caesar *Gal.*)
 5 id etiam totī prōvinciae proderit   (Pliny the Younger)
 6 sēnsērunt totī pāstōria sibila montēs   (Ovid *Met.*)
 7 atque alius ex aliō causam tumultūs quaerit   (Caesar *Gal.*)
 8 alius iam castra capta prōnūntiat   (Caesar *Gal.*)
 9 sī alius ad me prius attulerit   (Plautus *As.*)
10 nē qua legiō alterae legiōnī subsidiō venīre posset   (Caesar *Gal.*)
11 nam huic alterae quae patria sit profectō nesciō   (Plautus *Rud.*)
12 quod alterī praecēperit id ipsum facere nōn posse   (Cicero *Brut.*)

(a) this rumour will have announced to you faster than a letter from any of us
(b) in the beginning the senses cannot exist (without) a body
(c) the one announces the camp is already seized
(d) so that no legion might come to another legion as relief
(e) it will also benefit the whole province
(f) he orders the whole province as great a number of soldiers as it can
(g) for this other one I do not know what really is (her) fatherland
(h) if one carries to me first
(i) and I not a partner of any plan
(j) and one asks another the cause of the confusion
(k) all the mountains felt the shepherd whistling
(l) not able to do that itself, which he commanded to another

Reading: The Cretan Bull (Labor VII), part 2

Mare tranquillus erat, quandō nautae nāvem incolumem ad terram appulērunt.
Herculēs statim ad rēgem Crētae properāvit eumque causam **adventūs** docuit.

Rēgī prōmīsit, "Īnsulam ā perīculō līberābō."

Rēx magnō gaudiō affectus est. Postquam omnia parāta erant, Herculēs ad
eam regiōnem contendit, ubi mōnstrum habitābat. Taurum vīdit. Ad eum cucurrit et cornua eius corripuit. Mōnstrum forte erat, sed **manūs** Herculis id firmē
tenēbant. Herculēs ergō ingentī cum labōre taurum ad nāvem trāxit et laetus
cum praedā in Graeciam rediit.

adventūs of (his) arrival [gen. sg.]   **manūs** hands [nom. pl.]

UNIT 25
Relative clauses

Background

Relative clauses are a type of *subordinate clause.*

A subordinate clause is a clause which cannot stand alone as a full sentence, usually introduced in English by *subordinating conjunctions* like *because, while, since, after, who, whom, that.*

Relative clauses are effectively very fancy adjectives. They, like adjectives, are used to describe a noun. The difference, however, is that they are not a single word describing a noun, but a whole phrase complete with an inflected verb.

Different ways to modify a noun

Adjectives:

*The **tall** man sings*
*The **famous** actress has a large salary.*
*The **happy** cat took a nap.*

Relative clauses:

*The man, **who is tall**, sings.*
*The actress, **who is famous**, has a large salary.*
*The cat, **who is happy**, took a nap.*

Essential components of a relative clause

1 Relative pronoun: *that, who, whom, whose, which*
2 Verb: there must be a verb which follows the relative pronoun

Additionally, outside of the relative clause there must be an:

3 Antecedent: a noun to which the clause refers

Some additional English examples:

*The man, **whose mother I know**, works at the store.*
relative pronoun: *whose*
verb in relative clause: *know*
antecedent: *man*

*The flowers **that John put on the table** withered.*
relative pronoun: *that*
verb in relative clause: *put*
antecedent: *flowers*

Relative clauses in Latin

As in English a relative clause in Latin must have a relative pronoun and a verb.

The relative clause must also refer to a certain antecedent outside of the relative clause.

Since the relative pronoun takes the place of a noun (specifically the antecedent) within the relative clause, it has different forms for gender, case, and number, just like the demonstrative pronouns (Unit 21)

	Singular				*Plural*		
	Masc.	*Fem.*	*Neut.*		*Masc.*	*Fem.*	*Neut.*
Nom.	**quī**	**quae**	**quod**	Nom	**quī**	**quae**	**quae**
Gen.	**cuius**	**cuius**	**cuius**	Gen	**quōrum**	**quārum**	**quōrum**
Dat.	**cui**	**cui**	**cui**	Dat	**quibus**	**quibus**	**quibus**
Acc.	**quem**	**quam**	**quod**	Acc	**quōs**	**quās**	**quae**
Abl.	**quō**	**quā**	**quō**	Abl	**quibus**	**quibus**	**quibus**

How does one determine which of these 14 different forms to use?

1 A relative pronoun gets its *gender and number* from the antecedent it is referring to.
2 It gets its *case* from what grammatical role it is playing in the relative clause.

Vir, *quī cervum vīdit*, in hāc	The man *who saw the stag*
īnsulā habitābat.	was living on this island.

In this sentence the relative clause **quī cervum vīdit** is describing **vir**. Since **vir** is masculine and singular, the relative pronoun that refers to it must also be masculine and singular. To determine which case the relative pronoun is in, we observe what role the relative pronoun is performing in the relative clause. In this instance, **quī** is doing the seeing (**vīdit**), so it is in the nominative. As another example:

| Vir, *cuius māter rēgīna est*, in hāc īnsulā habitat. | The man, *whose mother is the queen*, lives on this island. |

Again the antecedent is **vir**; therefore, again a masculine singular relative pronoun is needed. With respect to case, however, the relative pronoun has the role of a genitive in the relative clause; thus masculine, singular, genitive = **cuius**.

Advanced topic

Relative pronouns are frequently used at the start of sentences in Latin. In such cases the antecedent is in the previous sentence. English uses a pronoun or demonstrative in such situations.

| **Mīlitēs in oppidum advēnērunt.** | ***Quōs** postquam vīdimus, laetī erāmus.* |
| The soldiers arrived in the town. | After we saw **them**, we were happy. |

Exercise 1

Determine the gender, number, and case of each of the English relative pronouns below. Then translate the relative pronoun into Latin. The Latin translation of certain antecedents is provided where the gender is unclear.

1 I saw the man whose dog chased the cat.
2 My brother, who was terrified, ran up a tree.
3 The kings of the island, whom we deposed, were living in a raft now.
4 It snows a lot in winter, which is a very cold month.
　　　　　　　　　　　　　　　　　　　　　　　[**hiems, hiemis** (f.) winter]
5 Memorize the names which are on the tablet.
　　　　　　　　　　　　　　　　　　　　　　　[**nōmen, nōminis** (nt) name]
6 The farmer's daughter, whom I bought a present for, is very beautiful.
7 The love which one has for Rome is unbreakable.
　　　　　　　　　　　　　　　　　　　　　　　[**amor, amōris** (m.) love]
8 The love with which I am possessed feels wonderful.
　　　　　　　　　　　　　　　　　　　　　　　[**amor, amōris** (m.) love]
9 The laws which the senators wrote are thorough.　　[**lēx, lēgis** (f.) law]
10 The laws by which the state is run are thorough.　　[**lēx, lēgis** (f.) law]
11 The war, which lasted five years, was costly.　　[**bellum, -ī** war]
12 Her sons, whose fields are green, are excellent farmers.
13 The gods, whom we offer sacrifices to, protect us.
14 The winds, by which the walls were knocked down, were dangerous.
　　　　　　　　　　　　　　　　　　　　　　　[**ventus, -ī** wind]
15 The names whose letters are unclear are those of gods.
　　　　　　　　　　　　　　　　　　　　　　　[**nōmen, nōminis** (nt.) name]

Exercise 2

Translate the following.

1 Fīlius, cuius pater rēx fuit, agrōs magnōs videt.
2 Servī dominum suum saxīs interfēcērunt, quae in agrīs invēnērant.
3 Poēta, quem omnēs laudant, dīcit istem hominem malum esse.
4 Vulnera, quibus mīlitēs interfectī erant, gravia erant.
5 Cōnsulēs, quibus potestās est, lēgēs populīs scrībunt.
6 Tempestās fortis, quam agricolae vīdērunt, nautās terrēbat.
7 Cūr sīdera, quae in caelō sedent, fulgent?
8 Carcer tenebrārum, in quem est iactus inimīcus noster, tacet.
9 Līberī, quōrum pater vēla dederat, sōlī fuērunt.
10 Pugnam, quam animālia per tōtam silvam excitat, barbarī portant.

Exercise 3

Convert all nouns in Exercise 2 to the opposite number. If the noun is singular, make it plural; if plural, make it singular. Be aware of necessary changes to verbs and relative pronouns and of *pluralia tantum* nouns – nouns which are always plural!

Exercise 4

Translate the following.

1 The daughter of the poet who had found the dog sings well.
2 The storm, which will have arrived, will destroy the towns, which were built on the coasts.
3 Women whose children praise the gods, are happy.
4 You (sg.) ought to give money to the author, whose books were written for everyone.
5 We had sought aid from the king, who did not break our happy spirits and dreams.

Exercise 5

Each of the following unedited Latin passages contains a relative clause. Match each passage with the English translation which follows. To assist you, try to think of English derivatives which stem from some of the Latin words.

1 nāvēs longās quārum et speciēs erat barbarīs inūsitātior   (Caesar *Gal.*)
2 īsdem sublicīs quārum pars inferior integra remanēbat   (Caesar *Gal.*)
3 nōn dubitō quīn tuīs litterīs quārum exemplum lēgī   (Cicero *Deiot.*)
4 ingentem strūxēre pyram cui frondibus ātrīs
    intexunt latera   (Vergil *Aeneid*)
5 quid mihi futūrum est, cui duae ancillae dolent   (Plautus *Truc.*)
6 in hunc cui videō maximās reī pūblicae tempestātēs   (Cicero *Mur.*)
7 catēnās singulāriās istās, māiōrēs, quibus sunt iūnctī   (Plautus *Capt.*)
8 addit equōs et tēla, quibus spoliāverat hostem   (Vergil *Aeneid*)
9 hic eōs quibus erat ignōtus dēcēpit   (Cicero *Pis.*)
10 ad eam partem pervēnit quae nōndum flūmen trānsierat   (Caesar *Gal.*)
11 puella nam mī quae meō sinū fūgit   (Catullus)
12 quī aut ea quae imminent nōn videant   (Cicero *Catil.*)

(a) by the same piles whose lower part remained sound
(b) they heaped up a huge pyre around which they wove
    gloomy leaves
(c) those single chains, the greater ones, by which they are joined
(d) what will happen to me, whom two servants pain?
(e) he came to that part which had not yet crossed the river
(f) onto him with respect to whom I see the greatest storms
    of the republic
(g) or who do not see those things which threaten
(h) I do not doubt that among your letters, a sample of which I read
(i) for my girl who has fled from my love
(j) he increases (his) horses and weapons, for which he
    had plundered the enemy
(k) this (man) deceived those to whom he was unknown
(l) long ships whose appearance was more unusual to the foreigners

Reading: The Man-Eating Horses of Diomedes (Labor VIII), part 1

Postquam Herculēs ex īnsulā Crētā rediit, in Thrāciam missus est. Labor, quī eum ibi manēbat, rūrsus valdē perīculōsus erat. Equōs enim rēgis Diomēdis in patriam suam redūcere dēbēbat. Hī equī ferōcēs erant: carne hominum **vescēbantur**. Diomēdēs omnēs peregrīnōs, quī in rēgnum suum intrāvērunt, equīs obiciēbat. Proptereā Eurystheus **sibi** dīxit, "Herculēs quoque victima equōrum erit." Vir intrepidus magnā celeritāte in Thrāciam cucurrit. Labōrem **quam celerrimē** cōnficere voluit.

    vescēbantur [+ abl.] they were eating   **sibi** to himself
    quam celerrimē as quickly as possible

UNIT 26
Direct questions

Background

A *direct* question is a sentence which seeks to gain information.
In English a direct question is indicated by:

1 A question word

> *How* are you doing?
> *What* did you buy?
> *Where* did you go?

Note that the verb and subject invert their normal position

- additionally, when the verb is *not* a form of the verb *to be* or a *modal verb* (i.e. *can, could, will, would, must, shall, should, may, might*) then a form of the verb *to do* must be inserted after the question word
- linguists term this *do-support* and it is an interesting peculiarity of English
- neither inversion nor *do-support* occur when the question word itself is the subject:

> *Who* spoke?

2 Subject-verb inversion alone (with *do-support* if necessary)

- This type occurs when there is no *question* word
- Since such questions expect a *yes-no* answer, they are also termed *yes-no questions*:

> *Are you* going?
> *Did he* speak?

3 Rising intonation alone

- This also expects a *yes-no* answer:

> *You are going to the park?*

Latin structure

Latin has correspondences of all three types of English sentences, only the first two of which are discussed here. See Exercise 3 for examples of questions dependent on intonation.

Latin question words

The *adverbial question words* of Latin are:

cūr why	**quō modō** how*
quam how*	**ubi** where
quam ob rem why	**unde** from where, whence
quandō when	**ut** how
quō to where, whither	**utrum ... an** [double question]
quō how*	

* There is no difference in meaning between the various forms of *how*

utrum ... an introduces a question which gives choices for the answer

Utrum in bellō pugnābis an in agrō labōrābis?
Will you fight in the battle or work in the field?

Instead of **utrum**, the particle **-ne** or no word/particle at all can be used.
-ne attaches to the end of the first word of the sentence

Līberne es an nōn?
Are you free or not?

Pugnābis an labōrābis?
Will you fight or will you work?

- Further examples:

    Quam ob rem id fēcit?
    Why did s/he do that?

    Quandō mē vīdistis?
    When did you (pl.) see me?

    Unde venīs et quō īs?
    Where are you coming from and where are you going?

The *pronominal question words* of Latin are:

quis who   **quid** what

Since these are pronouns, they – like all pronouns – can be declined:

	Masc./Fem.	Neuter
Nom.	quis	quid
Gen.	cuius	cuius
Dat.	cui	cui
Acc.	quem	quid
Abl.	quō	quō

Though the singular forms account for most occurrences of this pronoun, plural forms exist as well.

The plural forms are identical to those of the relative pronoun, and thus make a three-way gender distinction in the accusative plural (Unit 25). Note that there is no distinction between masculine and feminine in the interrogative pronoun. This makes some sense since more often than not when we use *who* or *whom* in English we do not know the gender of the person we're asking about. The same is true, for example, of French, German, Russian, and Spanish, four languages which have vibrant gender contrasts.

A second interrogative pronoun is **uter**, **utra**, **utrum** *which (of two)*. This pronoun was introduced in Unit 24 along with the other pronominal adjectives which take **-īus** in the genitive sg. and **-ī** in the dative sg.

Examples:

Cuius fīliam in mātrimōnium dūcis?
Whose daughter are you (sg.) marrying?

Quō inimīcōs interfēcistī?
With what did you (sg.) kill the enemies?

Utrī crēdiderātis
Which one had you believed?

The *adjectival question words* of Latin are:

quālis, **quāle** what kind
quantus, **-a**, **-um** how much, how great
quī, **quae**, **quod** which
quot how many

- **quī**, **quae**, **quod** is declined identically to the relative pronoun

  - it most clearly differs from the interrogative pronoun **quis**, **quid** in that, being an adjective, **quī**, **quae**, **quod** must modify a noun

- **quot** is indeclinable

Quālis homō es?
What kind of man are you?

Cuius poētae carmina hodiē legēmus?
The poems of which poet will we read today?

Quibus līberīs dōna dābis?
To which children will you give the gifts?

Quot librōs scrīpsit?
How many books did s/he write?

Latin yes/no-questions

Unlike English these questions are introduced by some question word or particle. The basic *yes/no*-question particle is **-ne**. It attaches to the end of the first word of the sentence regardless of what part of speech it is.

Vēnistīne?   Did you (sg.) come?
Fēminamne vidēs? Do you see (sg.) the woman?

Two additional words which introduce *yes/no*-questions are **nōnne** and **num**. They differ as to whether they anticipate the answer *yes* or *no*.

*   **nōnne** anticipates the answer *yes*
*   **num** anticipates the answer *no*

The best way to translate these into English is as *tag questions*.
    Tag questions consist of forms of *be*, modal verbs, or *do* which are 'tagged' onto the end of a sentence, turning it into a question.
    Note that **num** can also be conveyed by *really*.
    Nōnne translates as a negative *tag*:

Nōnne mīlitēs rēgīnam interfēcērunt?
Did the soldiers not kill the queen?
The soldiers killed the queen, **didn't they**?   [*yes*]

Nōnne venīre potestis?
Are you (pl.) not able to come?
You (pl.) can come, **can't** you?   [*yes*]

Nōnne cōgitābātis eum advenīre?
Were you (pl.) not thinking that he would arrive?
You (pl.) were thinking that he would arrive, **weren't you**?   [*yes*]

Num translates as a positive *tag*, which in English requires the main verb to be negated.

Observe the inserted negative in the translations:

Num mīlitēs rēgīnam interfēcērunt?
Did the soldiers really kill the queen?
The soldiers did**n't** kill the queen, **did they**?   [*no*]

Num venīre potestis?
Are you (pl.) really able to come?
You (pl.) can**'t** come, **can you**?   [*no*]

Num cōgitābātis eum advenīre?
Were you (pl.) really thinking that he would arrive?
You (pl.) were**n't** thinking that he would arrive, **were you**?   [*no*]

To answer *yes* or *no*:

- either the main word of the question is repeated (and negated in the case of *no*)
- or **certē** *certainly*, **etiam** *even so*, **ita** *so*, or **vērō** *truly* is used for *yes*, and **minimē** *by no means*, **nōn** or **nōn ita** for *no*

Exercise 1

Translate the following.

1 Cui vīnum est?
2 Vēnistisne cum eō?
3 Quālia arma inventa erant?
4 Quot mīlitēs nōlunt pugnāre contrā barbarōs?
5 Unde cucurrērunt tristēs puerī? Ubi nunc sunt?
6 Cūr dās praemium laudemque parentibus?
7 Quō amnis it?
8 Quam ob rem bibunt sanguinem ovis illīus?
9 Quandō claudentur portae ingentēs urbis?
10 Nōnne sapiēns est poēta, quī multās epistulās scrīpserat?
11 Quis verba deōrum sacrōrum audīre nōn potest?
12 Quō modō moenia nova is aedificābit?
13 In quō somniō vīderat locum, in cuius templō erant aurum et pecūnia?
14 Quantōs librōs scrīpserit miser auctor?
15 Quam ob rem nōn potuī vulgō canere?
16 Cuius mātrem scītis?
17 Fulgetne sōl hodiē?

18 Cūr dēfessī estis? Quandō dormiētis?
19 Utrum in oppidō cum aliīs manēbis an in urbem cum aliīs ībis?
20 Quō agrum lātum vendidit?

Exercise 2

Translate the following.

1 What frightens the small children?
2 When will you (sg.) give our money to the sailor?
3 Who divided the field?
4 By whom were the gates of the wall broken?
5 Will the soldiers fortify their town?
6 Why are you (pl.) not present? You (pl.) are absent!
7 How does the sun shine through the dark clouds?
8 How many stories will the poet read to the crowd?
9 In whose memory was a kingdom of peace being built here?
10 To where was the sailor setting sail?

Exercise 3

Each of the following unedited Latin passages contains a question. Match each
passage with the English translation which follows. To assist you, try to think
of English derivatives which stem from some of the Latin words.

1 Tuom parasītum nōn nōvistī?   (Plautus *Men.*)
2 linguam vīs meam praeclūdere?   (Phaedrus)
3 Hunc tū vītae splendōrem maculīs adspergis istīs?   (Cicero *Planc.*)
4 Omnisne pecūnia dissolūta est?   (Cicero *Ver.*)
5 Utrum nescīs quam altē ascenderis, an prō nihilō
  id putās?   (Cicero *Fam.*)
6 utrum is clēmēns ac misericors an inhūmānissimus et
  crūdēlissimus esse videātur?   (Cicero *Catil.*)
7 quot vultis esse in ūnō fūrtō peccātōrum gradūs   (Cicero *Ver.*)
8 Quot bella māiōrēs nostrōs et quanta suscēpisse
  arbitrāminī   (Cicero *Ver.*)
9 quālēs et quot et quotiēns lēgātī ad eōs exiērunt   (Cicero *Font.*)
10 Num iūs cīvīle vestrum ex librīs cōgnōscī potest?   (Cicero *Fam.*)
11 Num tibi cum faucēs ūrit sitis, aurea quaeris pōcula? (Horace *S.*)
12 Num negāre audēs?   (Cicero *Catil.*)

(a) What kind and how many and how often did the delegates come out to them?

(b) Do you really seek golden cups when thirst burns your throat?

(c) Is all the money paid up?

(d) Can your civil law really be learnt from books?

(e) Do you really dare deny (it)?

(f) You sprinkle this lustre of a life with those spots?

(g) Do you not know how high you rose, or do you think it for nothing?

(h) How many and how great the wars do you think that our ancestors undertook?

(i) How many steps of sins do you wish there to be in a single theft?

(j) You wish to shut my mouth?

(k) You do not know your own parasite?

(l) May he seem to be merciful and sympathetic or most savage and most cruel?

Reading: The Man-Eating Horses of Diomedes (Labor VIII), part 2

Herculēs rēgem convēnerat, sed Herculēs verbīs suāvibus eī persuādēre nōn potuit. Tum vir fortis īrā commōtus est. Rēgem interfēcit eumque equīs obiēcit. Sīc rēx crūdēlis eōdem modō, quō multōs hominēs innocentēs ipse occīderat, **mortuus est**. Herculēs nōn diū in Thrāciā manēbat. Quī illam regiōnem incolēbant, eum rēgem creāre voluērunt. At Herculēs rēgnum suscipere nōn poterat, nam equōs Eurystheō trādere dēbēbat. Sine morā ē **portū** solvit et paulō post equōs incolumēs in lītus Argolicum exposuit.

mortuus est he died   **portū** harbour [abl. sg.]

UNIT 27
Personal pronouns

Background

Personal pronouns refer to the participants surrounding a verb. They are best understood by imagining a conversation:

- 1st person and 2nd person involve people who are engaged in the conversation.

  - 1st person refers to the person through whose consciousness the world is being viewed: *I, me, we, us*
  - 2nd person refers to a person who is also engaged in the conversation but through whose consciousness the world is not being viewed: *you*

- 3rd person is someone or something who is not engaged in the conversation: *he, him, she, her, it, they, them*

Latin structure

Personal pronouns

Since pronouns take the place of nouns, they too will have forms for the whole gamut of cases.

In Latin personal pronouns exist for *I, you* (sg.), *we* and *you* (pl.).

Unique pronominal forms for the 3rd person (*he, she, it, they*) do not exist but are filled by the demonstrative pronoun **is, ea, id** *this, that* (Unit 21).

		1st *Person*	
	Singular	*Plural*	
Nom.	**ego** I	**nōs**	we
Gen.	**meī** of me	**nostrum ~ nostrī**	of us
Dat.	**mihi** to/for me	**nōbīs**	to/for us
Acc.	**mē** me	**nōs**	us
Abl.	**mē** me	**nōbīs**	us
		2nd *Person*	
	Singular	*Plural*	
Nom.	**tū** you	**vōs**	you
Gen.	**tuī** of you	**vestrum ~ vestrī**	of you
Dat.	**tibi** to/for you	**vōbīs**	to/for you
Acc.	**tē** you	**vōs**	you
Abl.	**tē** you	**vōbīs**	you

Notes

- There are two genitives in the plural which are used in different situations

  - **nostrum** and **vestrum** are used as *partitive genitives*

    - they express the whole of which something is a part

all *of us*	**omnēs nostrum**
some *of you*	**aliquī vestrum**

  - **nostrī** and **vestrī** are used as *objective genitives*

    - they serve as objects of the noun they depend upon

love of us	**amor nostrī**
judgment of you	**iūdicium vestrī**

- The preposition **cum** *with* suffixes itself to the ablative of the personal pronouns, forming a single word.

  Pāx vōbīscum.
  Peace be with you.

- Since the endings on a verb indicate the subject, the nominative forms of the personal pronouns are used for emphasis, contrast or clarity.

  Sed ego veniam.
  But I will go [as opposed to someone else].

Possessive adjectives

To indicate possession, *possessive adjectives* are employed rather than the genitive of the personal pronouns.

The four possessive adjectives are all 1st–2nd declension adjectives:

meus, -a, -um my
tuus, -a, -um your (sg.)
noster, nostra, nostrum our
vester, vestra, vestrum your (pl.)

Examples

Meus **canis magnus est.**   My dog is big.

Ōra *nostrōrum* **canium magna sunt.**
The mouths of our dogs are big.

The genitives of the personal pronouns (**meī, tuī, nostrum, nostrī, vestrum, vestrī**) are used only as *objective genitives* or *partitive genitives*.

Clearly only the plural forms have the ability to serve as *partitive genitives* (see the examples on p. 154).

amor meī   love of me [i.e. someone else's love of me]
amor meus   my love [i.e. my own love]

Reflexive pronouns

A *reflexive pronoun* refers back to the subject of a sentence.

*I see **myself** in the mirror.*
*He bought **himself** a present.*

The English reflexive pronouns are formed by adding *-self* or *-selves* to pronominal forms (e.g. *himself*) or to possessive adjective forms (*ourselves*).

Since by definition a reflexive refers back to the subject, the reflexive does not have a nominative form.

Do not confuse this reflexive use of *-self* with the emphatic use of *-self* seen in Unit 22 while discussing **ipse, ipsa, ipsum**

The reflexive pronouns in Latin are simply identical to the personal pronouns.

Mē videō.
I see myself.

Nōs audīmus.
We hear ourselves.

There are 3rd person reflexive pronominal forms which do not differentiate
between gender or number:

Nom.	---
Gen.	**suī**
Dat.	**sibi**
Acc.	**sē**
Abl.	**sē**

Sē audiunt.
They see themselves.

Sē audit.
He hears himself.
She hears herself.

There is also a 3rd person reflexive possessive adjective: **suus, -a, -um**

Canem *suum* audiunt.
They hear their own dog.

All of the reflexive pronouns can also have the *reciprocal* meaning *each
other*:

Nōs audīmus.   **Sē vident.**
We hear each other.   They see each other.

Exercise 1

Translate the underlined words of each sentence into Latin. The Latin translation and gender of words modified by possessive adjectives are added for your
convenience.

1 When are they going to bring <u>themselves</u>
   over to <u>our</u> country house?   [**vīlla, -ae** *country house*]
2 <u>I</u> hope that <u>we</u> will be able to see <u>your</u> (sg.)
   new dog.   [**canis, canis** (m.) *dog*]
3 <u>You</u> (pl.) are going to give <u>me</u> <u>my</u> book.   [**liber, librī** *book*]
4 Why do <u>I</u> do this to <u>myself</u>?
5 Most of <u>us</u> are coming this weekend.
6 <u>You</u> (sg.) are going to be ignored by <u>me</u>,
   if <u>you</u> (sg.) continue to bother <u>me</u>.

7 He bought <u>himself</u> <u>his own</u> book because <u>we</u> ourselves
   didn't buy one for him.
8 Yesterday <u>your</u> (pl.) mother brought
   <u>you</u> (pl.) to <u>us</u>.   [**māter**, **mātris** (f.) *mother*]
9 <u>You</u> (sg.) talk about <u>yourself</u> to <u>me</u> all the time!
10 When did he bring <u>us</u> from <u>your</u> (pl.)
   country house?   [**vīlla**, **-ae** *country house*]
11 They bought for <u>themselves</u> some of
   <u>our</u> food.   [**cibus**, **-ī** *food*]
12 <u>You</u> (sg.) and <u>I</u> do not like <u>each other</u>.
13 When is he coming to her city to bring
   <u>us</u> <u>our</u> money?   [**pecūnia**, **-ae** *money*]
14 <u>We</u> keep <u>you</u> (sg.) yourself in <u>our</u> memory.   [**memoria**, **-ae** *memory*]
15 He drives <u>his own</u> sheep from their field.   [**ovis**, **ovis** (f.) *sheep*]

Exercise 2

As a review of the pronouns **is**, **ea**, **id** (Unit 21) and **ipse**, **ipsa**, **ipsud** (Unit 22), go back and translate all the non-underlined personal pronouns, emphatic pronouns and possessive adjectives in Exercise 1.

Exercise 3

Translate the following.

1 Tū docēbās multōs nostrum.
2 Invēnit sē in nostrō templō.
3 Rēgīna dābit nōbīs poenam.
4 In iūcundīs litterīs scrīpserat poēta dē amōre vestrī.
5 Mea soror vīdit mē, sed ego ā meō frātre nōn vīsus est.
6 Adulēscentēs nōn sē sed vōs potuerant audīre.
7 Vōs nōs semper iubētis.
8 Nūntiāmus tibi verba rēgis istīus.
9 Cūr vocās mē et meam sorōrem?
10 Sōl sē in flūmine videt.

Exercise 4

Each of the following unedited Latin passages contains a personal or reflexive pronoun. Match each passage with the English translation which follows. To assist you, try to think of English derivatives which stem from some of the Latin words.

1 tam grātum est mihi (Catullus)
2 nīl mihi tam valdē placeat (Catullus)
3 ut mihi quidem videantur dī immortālēs (Cicero *Marc.*)
4 vōs datā facultāte vōbīs cōnsulite (Caesar *Gal.*)
5 vōs carmine compellābō tēque adeō (Catullus)
6 quae vōs fortūna quiētōs sollicitat (Vergil *Aeneid*)
7 isque domum nōbīs isque dedit dominae (Catullus)
8 quae nōbīs nōta sunt (Caesar *Gal.*)
9 iūra, lēgēs, agrōs lībertātem nōbīs relīquērunt (Caesar *Gal.*)
10 fūgit mē ratio (Catullus)
11 tum hōc tempore propter tuum in mē amōrem (Cicero *Fam.*)
12 nōn illī ad mē venīre debuerint (Cicero *Fam.*)

(a) then at this time on account of your love for me
(b) and they ought not come to me
(c) so that the immortal gods seem to me
(d) I will address you with my song and approach you
(e) and he gave a house to us and he gave (it) to (his) mistress
(f) it is so pleasing to me
(g) which are known to us
(h) which fate disturbs you, who are peaceful
(i) an opportunity having been given, you must look out for yourselves
(j) may nothing please me so greatly
(k) they left (our) rights, laws, fields, (and) freedom to us
(l) reasoning fled me

Reading: The Battle with the Amazons (Labor IX), part 1

Gēns Amāzonum omnīnō ex mulieribus cōnstābat. Nēminem timēbant. Etiam cum virīs proelium committere audēbant. Hippolyta, rēgīna eārum, balteum **celeberrimum** habēbat quem ā Marte accēperat. Fīlia rēgis Eurystheī hunc balteum possidēre vehementer cupiēbat. Eurystheus igitur Herculem cum mīlitibus in Asiam mīsit, ubi Amāzōnēs habitābant. "Rēgīna," inquit Herculēs, "Num mē nescīs? Unde vēneram? Herculēs nōmen mihi est. Dominus meus, rēx Eurystheus, vult balteum tuum. Portābō eum mēcum."

Hippolyta, quod Amāzōn erat, lēniter respondit: "Nunc sciō causam **adventūs** tuī. Sī fīliam dominī tuī beātam facere possum, libenter id agam."

celeberrimum most famous **adventūs** of (his) arrival [gen. sg.]

UNIT 28
Imperative mood

Background

Latin possesses three verbal moods:

- *Indicative* – expresses a fact
- *Imperative* – expresses a command
- *Subjunctive* – expresses a variety of things including a wish, unreal situation, result, purpose

Up till now we have only dealt with the *indicative*. The *subjunctive* will be introduced in *Intensive Intermediate Latin*.

The English *imperative* is the base verbal form alone, with no subject expressed. Orthographically the sentence ends with an exclamation point. The negative consists of *do not* placed before the verbal base:

Positive	Negative
Be polite!	*Do not be rude!*
Go the store!	*Do not go to the party!*
Buy lemonade!	*Do not take candy from strangers!*

Since you can really only give a command to someone you are speaking directly to, the imperative is confined to 2nd person forms.

What are often considered 1st and 3rd person 'imperatives' consist of *let* + an object pronoun + the base verbal form:

Let us go!
Let him come!

Besides having only 2nd person forms, the imperative is also confined to the *present*. This makes sense in that a past imperative is logically impossible since an imperative is giving direction towards a present or future activity.

In English the imperative possesses present and future meanings. The future tense itself may even be used with imperative force:

Imagine a parent scolding a child: *You WILL clean your room.*

Latin structure

Like English Latin forms present imperatives which are confined to the 2nd person.

1st and 3rd person *let* forms are translated by the subjunctive (see *Intensive Intermediate Latin*).

Latin possesses both active and passive forms:

Imperative active

- 2nd sg.

  - Drop the **-re** of the infinitive and voilà, you're done:

1st conj.	**amāre**	→	**Amā!**	Love!
2nd conj.	**docēre**	→	**Docē!**	Teach!
3rd conj.	**agere**	→	**Age!**	Drive, Lead!
3rd conj.-*iō*	**capere**	→	**Cape!**	Seize!
4th conj.	**scīre**	→	**Scī!**	Know!

Irregular forms (1)

The following three verbs do not end in the expected vowel:

dīcere	→	**Dīc!**	Say!
dūcere	→	**Dūc!**	Lead!
facere	→	**Fac!**	Do!

The following two verbs also do not end in a vowel, though this is not terribly surprising since their infinitives irregularly lack a vowel to begin with:

esse	→	**Es!**	Be!
ferre	→	**Fer!**	Carry!

- 2nd pl.

  - Drop the **-re** of the infinitive and add **-te**
  - In 3rd conjugation verbs convert the **-e-** to **-i-**

1st conj.	**amāre**	→	**Amāte**	Love!
2nd conj.	**docēre**	→	**Docēte**	Teach!
3rd conj.	**agere**	→	**Agite**	Drive!
3rd conj.-*iō*	**capere**	→	**Capite**	Seize!
4th conj.	**scīre**	→	**Scīte**	Know!

Irregular forms (2)

Two verbs lack a vowel before the ending **-te** though again this is not surprising since there is no vowel present in their infinitives:

| esse | → | **Este!** | Be! |
| **ferre** | → | **Ferte!** | Carry! |

Imperative passive

- 2nd sg.

  - This is identical to the infinitive!

Amāre!	Be loved!
Docēre!	Be taught!
Agere!	Be driven!
Capere!	Be seized!
Scīre!	Be known!

- 2nd pl.

  - This is formed by:

    ○ dropping the **-re** from the infinitive, changing **-e-** to **-i-** in 3rd conjugation verbs and
    ○ adding **-minī**

This form is identical to the *2nd pl. present passive* form (Unit 19).

amāre	→	**Amāminī**	Be loved!
docēre	→	**Docēminī**	Be taught!
agere	→	**Agiminī**	Be driven!
capere	→	**Capiminī**	Be seized!
scīre	→	**Scīminī**	Be known!

Negative imperative

The negative is quite easily formed by:

- **nōlī** in the singular and **nōlīte** in the plural
- followed by the present active or passive infinitive (on the latter, see *Intensive Intermediate Latin*)

| **Nōlī amāre eum!** | Do not love him! |
| **Nōlīte docērī!** | Do not be taught! |

Advanced topics

The *future imperative* (also called the *2nd imperative*) is a rare formation which expresses a future action whose fulfillment is mandated by prior agreements.

Thus it is confined largely to legal documents and recipes.

It has both 2nd and 3rd person forms, though 2nd pl. passive forms are lacking.

- Active

  - Add the following endings to the present stem, with the same vowel changes in the 3rd and 4th conjugations as occur in the present tense (Units 2, 3):

	Singular	Plural
2	-tō	-tōte
3	-tō	-ntō

- Passive

  - Add the following endings to the present stem, with the same vowel changes in the 3rd and 4th conjugations as occur in the present tense:

	Singular	Plural
2	-tor	---
3	-tor	-ntor

Examples

			Active		
2sg.	amātō	docētō	agitō	capitō	scītō
3	amātō	docētō	agitō	capitō	scītō
2pl.	amātōte	docētōte	agitōte	capitōte	scītōte
3	amantō	docentō	aguntō	capiuntō	sciuntō
			Passive		
2sg.	amātor	docētor	agitor	capitor	scītor
3	amātor	docētor	agitor	capitor	scītor
3pl.	amantor	docentor	aguntor	capiuntor	sciuntor

* Note that a long vowel is shortened before the 3rd pl. endings **-ntō** and **-ntor**.

Exercise 1

Translate the following.

1 Ferte cibum hūc!
2 Dīc verba huius rēgīnae rēgī!
3 Nōlīte timēre deōs!
4 Aperīminī, portae!
5 Cane et es fēlīx!
6 Tenēte lupum ferum!
7 Regere ā mē!
8 Tegite sōlem arboribus!
9 Excitāre corpus, quod etiam nunc dēfessus sum!
10 Vidē saxa ingentia, quae dē monte altō cecidērunt!

Exercise 2

The following excerpts from two well-known Christmas carols provide ample examples of imperative. Translate the lines.

1 (a) Adeste fidēlēs!
   (b) Venīte, venīte in Bethlehem!
   (c) Nātum vidēte rēgem angelōrum!

2 (a) Venī, venī Emmanuel!
   (b) Captīvum solvē Israel, quī gemit in exiliō!
   (c) Gaudē, gaudē Emmanuel!
   (d) Noctis dēpelle nebulās dīrāsque noctis tenebrās!
   (e) Rēgna reclūde caelica!
   (f) Fac iter tūtum superum!
   (g) Et claude viās īnferum!

Exercise 3

Each of the following unedited Latin passages contains an imperative. Match each passage with the English translation which follows. To assist you, try to think of English derivatives which stem from some of the Latin words.

1 quidquid habēs bonī malīque, dīc nōbīs   (Catullus)
2 dīc sī quid vīs, nōn nocēbō   (Plautus *Am.*)
3 immō age et ā prīmā dīc, hospes, orīgine
   nōbīs īnsidiās   (Vergil *Aeneid*)
4 sed dīcam vōbīs, vōs porrō dīcite multīs mīlibus   (Catullus)
5 quā, dīcite, nautae, hūc ope pervēnī   (Ovid *Met.*)
6 et mihi quae vōbīs dūdum dīxī dīcite   (Plautus *Poen.*)
7 sī mihi respondēre volēs haec dīcitō   (Cicero *Ver.*)
8 dīcitō potius, quoniam habēs auctōrem idōneum   (Cicero *Ver.*)
9 omnium prīmum salūtem dīcitō mātrī et patrī   (Plautus *Capt.*)
10 et dīxit marī tacē obmūtēsce et cessāvit ventus   (St Jerome *Mark*)
11 tacē et nōlī turbārī sānus   (St Jerome *Tobit*)
12 tacē inquit ante hoc nōvī quam tū nātus es   (Phaedrus)

(a) first of all speak my greeting to (my) mother and father
(b) no, rather do (it) and speak, guest, to us of the treacheries
     from the first beginning
(c) whatever of good and bad you have, tell us!
(d) say, sailors, by what power have I come here
(e) speak whatever if you wish; I will not harm (you)
(f) be silent, o sane one, and do not be disturbed
(g) and tell me what I just now said to you
(h) say rather, since you have a suitable authority
(i) be silent, he says, I knew this before you were born
(j) if you will wish to respond to me, tell (me) this
(k) but I will say to you, speak (it) in turn to many thousands
(l) and he said to the sea, 'be silent, cease,' and the wind stopped

Exercise 4

Return to the listed exercises in previous units and try to locate the following
imperative forms which are ordered in the sequence in which they occur. One
of the forms is an archaic form which does not fit the rules discussed in this
unit. Can you find it?

- Unit 4, Exercise 5: 2nd pl. active, 2nd pl. active
- Unit 5, Exercise 4: 2nd sg. active, 2nd pl. active
- Unit 6, Exercise 4: 2nd sg. active
- Unit 15, Exercise 5: 2nd sg. active
- Unit 19, Exercise 5: 2nd pl. active, 2nd pl. active
- Unit 20, Exercise 4: 2nd pl. active
- Unit 27, Exercise 4: 2nd pl. active

Reading: The Battle with the Amazons (Labor IX), part 2

Quandō hoc audīvit, Iūnō fōrmam Amāzonum sumpsit eāsque contrā Graecōs excitābit. "Estis prūdentēs! Nōlīte hīs virīs crēdere! Ad vōs vēnērunt, quod rēgīnam vestram capere eamque in Graeciam sēcum dūcere volunt."

Mulierēs excitātae sunt et statim aciem īnstrūxērunt et in Graecōs impetum fēcērunt. Herculēs sē rogāvit, "Cūr hoc faciunt Amāzōnēs? Resistere dēbeō."

Diū et ācriter pugnāvērunt. Quandō rēgīna capta erat, Amāzōnēs fugā salūtem petīvērunt. Herculēs, "Mīlitēs," inquit, "nōs, Graecī, numquam contrā mulierēs pugnāmus. Nunc, quod haec pugna fīnīta est, omnibus captīvīs lībertātem dare possumus." Graecī omnēs Amāzōnēs domōs mīsērunt.

Review of units 23–28

A. Translate the following.

1 we will go	3 I was preferring	5 he does not want
2 they carry	4 it is carried	6 you (sg.) want

B. Make the adjective **sōlus, -a, -um** agree with the following nouns. In some instances, there may be more than one answer.

1 **nautārum**	4 **tempestātis**
2 **fīliābus**	5 **mīlitem**
3 **templō**	6 **vīllae**

C. Translate the underlined relative pronouns into Latin.

1 The mother, <u>whose</u> child is playing, is working in the garden.
2 I gave the money to the man, <u>whom</u> I met last week.
3 Because of the children, <u>whom</u> I faintly remember, the school changed its curriculum.

D. Translate the following question words into Latin. Beware that some sentences in English do not require question words.

1 *Why*, *when*, and *how* is he coming?
2 Do you think the storm will end soon?
3 *Which* woman did you meet in the subway?
4 *How much* money does he make?

E. Translate the following personal pronouns/adjectives into Latin.

1 *I* saw *you* (sg.). yesterday afternoon.
2 Some of *us* want to go to *your* (sg.) father.
3 *We* don't like *you* (pl.)

F. Use the following verbs to translate.

amō, **amāre** to love   **capiō**, **capere** to seize
audiō, **audīre** to hear   **dūcō**, **dūcere** to lead

1 Love! (sg.)   3 Do not be seized! (pl.)
2 Be heard! (pl.)   4 Lead! (sg.)

UNIT 29
Vocative and locative

Background

The *vocative* is used to address someone directly:

> **Boys**, come here!
> **Tom**, what are you doing?

It is sometimes preceded by *O* in English:

> **O my God**, *what have I done?*

The *locative* is used to express location, with no movement involved. In English this is achieved via the prepositions *in*, *on*, or *at*:

> *I am* **in the country**.
> *You are* **on Crete**.
> *He's* **at the house**.

Latin structure

The *vocative* and *locative* are Latin's two minor cases.
Unique forms exist only for a subset of nouns.

Vocative

It is *identical to the nominative* for all declensions except for the singular of 2nd declension masculine nouns which end in **-us**.

- Nouns ending in **-us** replace this with **-e**

amīcus	→	**amīce**	*friend*
dominus	→	**domine**	*master*

- Nouns endings in **-ius** replace this with **-ī**:

  fīlius → **fīlī** *friend*

- Exceptionally, the masculine form of the adjective **meus, -a, -um** is **mī** in the vocative sg.

  Mī fīlī, labōrā!   **Mea fīlia, labōrā!**
  My son, work!   My daughter, work!

- The word **deus** *god* does not have a vocative singular.

  Deus, auxilium mihi dā!
  God, give me aid!

Locative

The preposition **in** *in, on* is used to express location for most nouns in Latin.

  in Circō Maximō
  in the Circus Maximus

  in oppidō
  in the town

In the following five situations, however, a special *locative* case is used:

- names of towns
- names of cities
- names of small islands
- **domus, -ūs** (f.) *home*   (for its declension, see Unit 36)
- **rūs, rūris** (nt.) *country*

The endings are as follows:

	Singular	*Plural*
1st declension:	**-ae**	**-īs**
2nd declension:	**-ī**	**-īs**
3rd declension:	**-e ~ -ī**	**-ibus**
domus	domī	domibus
rūs	rūrī	rūribus

Examples:

1st declension

Rōma, -ae Rome   **Rōmae** at Rome
Athēnae, -ārum Athens   **Athēnīs** at Athens

2nd declension

Rhodus, -ī Rhodes (small island) **Rhodī** on Rhodes
Delphī, -ōrum Delphi   **Delphīs** at Delphi

3rd declension

Carthāgō, Carthāginis (f.) Carthage **Carthāgine ~ Carthāginī** at Carthage
Gādēs, Gādium (f.) Cadiz   **Gādibus** at Cadiz

Notes

- Some place names are always plural: **Athēnae, Delphī, Gādēs**
- The locative plural is always identical to the ablative plural.
- The 1st and 2nd declension singulars are identical to genitive singulars.
- **domus, -ūs** is a 4th declension noun (Unit 36) with some 2nd declension forms, most notably **domō** (dat. sg.), **domum** (acc. sg.), and **domōs** (acc. pl.).

Advanced topics

Traces of locatives can occasionally be found in other simple nouns such as:

humī on the ground
domī mīlitiaeque in peace and war
   literally: at home and in service   [**mīlitia, -ae** military service]
bellī domīque in peace and war
   literally: in war and at home   [**bellum, -ī** war]

A noun which is in apposition with a noun in the locative is placed in the *ablative*.

Apposition is a further description of a noun, almost as an afterthought. It is usually set off by commas in English, as in the translation below:

Mīlitēs Albae cōnstitērunt *in urbe opportūnā* (Cicero *Phil.* IV 2.6)
   The soldiers stopped at Alba, <u>a suitable city</u>

Domī, however, is modified by the genitive of the possessive adjective

Domī *suae* senex est mortuus.
The old man died at his own house.

Exercise 1

Translate the following.

1 Puer, ubi es tuus frāter?
2 Mīlitēs, venīte ad mē!
3 Serve mī, cūr nihil fēcistī?
4 Rūrī villa eius est.
5 Aedificābimus templum novum Rōmae.
6 Puellae, portāte mihi mītem cibum, quem volō.
7 Carthāgine potest vidēre multa sīdera, quae in caelīs fulgent.
8 Frātrēs, agite gregem ovium in nāvem!
9 Petimus auxilium bellī domīque ā deā pulchrā.
10 Veniēmus ad servum deī, quī est Rhodī.
11 Aquilam, quae humī fuit, invēnimus.
12 Agrī lātī sunt nōbīs Athēnīs.
13 Sociī, cūr mē nōn vīs?
14 Domī meae mānserant amīcī.
15 Dūcite barbarum in carcerem, virī!
16 Tange, fīlī, portam sacrī templī!
17 Poēta, scrībe novum librum!
18 Audīte mē, animālia!
19 Frequēntia oppida inveniuntur Rhodī.
20 Mulier, ī mēcum perīculō ad illud antrum!

Exercise 2

Each of the following unedited Latin passages contains a vocative or locative. Match each passage with the English translation which follows. To assist you, try to think of English derivatives which stem from some of the Latin words.

1	fōrmam quidem ipsam, Marce fīlī, et tamquam faciem honestī vīdēs	(Cicero *Off.*)
2	habēs ā patre mūnus, Marce fīlī, meā quidem sententiā magnum	(Cicero *Off.*)
3	officia dūcerentur ab honestāte, Marce fīlī, atque ab omnī genere virtūtis	(Cicero *Off.*)
4	neque sōlum domī, sed etiam apud fīnitimās cīvitātēs	(Caesar *Gal.*)
5	reliquī, quī domī mānsērunt, sē atque illōs alunt	(Caesar *Gal.*)
6	summō locō nātus adulēscēns et summae domī potentiae	(Caesar *Gal.*)
7	Rōmae diērum vīgintī supplicātiō redditur	(Caesar *Gal.*)
8	adeō ut et pānis Rōmae saepe dēficeret	(Suetonius *Cal.*)
9	statuam eius Rōmae īnsignis aquila circumplexa	(Suetonius *Dom.*)
10	nōn soleō, mī Brūte, quod tibi nōtum esse arbitror	(Cicero *Brut.*)
11	quā rē omnī studiō ā tē, mī Brūte, contendō	(Cicero *Brut.*)
12	mī Brūte, velim quam plūrimum tēcum habeās	(Cicero *Brut.*)

(a) and not only at home but also among the neighbouring states

(b) a distinguished eagle surrounded his statue at Rome

(c) the duties are led by integrity, Marcus my son, and from every kind of virtue

(d) I am not in the habit, my Brutus, as I think it is known to you

(e) I would wish, my Brutus, that you may have (him) with you as much as possible

(f) because of which thing, I entreat you, my Brutus, with all my spirit

(g) you have, Marcus my son, from your father a gift – indeed a great one in my opinion

(h) the rest, who stayed at home, support themselves and those ones

(i) so that bread was often lacking at Rome

(j) thanksgiving of twenty days is rendered at Rome

(k) you see indeed the shape itself, Marcus my son, as if the face of goodness

(l) a young man born into the highest rank and at home of the highest power

Reading: Cacus Steals the Oxen (Labor X), part 1

Herculēs bovēs Gēryonis per Hispāniam et Ītaliam ēgit. Cum eīs ad **Tiberim** vēnit. "Itinere dēfessus sum," inquit. "Mihi **diēs** quiētī dantur. Hīc manēbō." Haud procul ā flūmine erat antrum in quō Cācus, mōnstrum horribile, habitābat. Ex ōre ignem spīrābat. Hoc mōnstrum nocte, dum Herculēs dormiēbat, quattuor bovēs abripuit. Hōs caudīs in antrum trāxit. Posterō **diē** simul atque ē somnō excitātus est, Herculēs fūrtum animadvertit. Herculēs vestīgia eōrum nōn cōgnōscere poterat. Bovēs frūstrā quaerēbat, quod vestīgiīs falsīs dēceptus est.

Tiberim Tiber [acc.sg.]   **diēs** days [nom. pl.]   **diē** day [abl. sg. masc.]

UNIT 30
Uses of the accusative

Background

In addition to indicating the direct object and the object of certain prepositions (Unit 7), the accusative has a range of other more adverbial meanings.

Latin structure

I Accusative of duration of time

The accusative is used to express *how long* the event expressed by a verb lasts. The preposition **per** *through* may be used.

Vīgintī annōs ibi mānsit.
He remained there 20 years.

In vīllā eius *multōs diēs* vīvēmus.
We will live in his country house many days.

II Accusative of extent of space

The accusative expresses *how long* a physical distance is.

agrī *vīgintī pedēs* lātī
fields 20 feet wide

puella *septem passūs* cucurrerat.
The girl had run seven paces.

III Accusative of limit of motion

The preposition **ad** + the accusative expresses the endpoint towards which someone or something is moving.

In the following five situations, however, the accusative alone without the aid of a preposition can express the limit of motion:

- names of towns
- names of cities
- names of small islands
- **domus, -ūs** (f.) *house*   (for its declension, see Unit 36)
- **rūs, rūris** (nt.) *country*

Note that these are the same five types of nouns which take special locative forms (Unit 29).

> **Domum** **crās ībimus.**
> We will go home tomorrow.

> **Quandō** *Athēnās* **venīs?**   (**Athēnae, -ārum** Athens)
> When are you coming to Athens?

IV Greek accusative

A body part in the accusative can express where the description of an adjective or the action of a verb applies. This construction is largely confined to poetry and later Latin, and as the name suggests it is due to Greek influence.

In Classical prose it is usually replaced by the *ablative of respect* (Unit 8).

> **Mīles** *oculōs* **vulnerātus est.**
> The soldier has been wounded in the eyes.

> **Nūdī** *pectora* **erant hominēs.**
> The men were bare with respect to their chests.

V Accusative of exclamation

The accusative, modified by an adjective, occurs in exclamations.

> **Crūdēlēs deōs!**
> Cruel gods!

> **Mē prosperum!**
> Fortunate me!

VI Adverbial accusative

Certain neuter adjectives have become fossilized with certain adverbial meanings. The main such fossilized forms are:

aliquid somewhat   **plērumque** generally
multum much   **plūrimum** very greatly
nihil not at all   **quid** why?
                         tantum only

Nihil **carmina rēgī canere possunt.**
They are not at all able to sing the songs for the king.

Plērumque **hīc sunt multae fēminae et suae puellae.**
Generally there are many women and their daughters here.

Exercise 1

Determine which type of accusative the underlined portions would be if translated into Latin.

1 O <u>unlucky you</u>! What will you do?
2 He <u>generally</u> sleeps all day.
3 <u>How many miles</u> did you walk last weekend?
4 They are going to <u>Philadelphia</u>.
5 The little boy trembles <u>at his lips</u> as he stands in front of the class.
6 It will take me <u>five years</u> to read all these books!
7 <u>How long</u> did it last?
8 She likes his cooking <u>somewhat</u>.
9 They sat down because they were tired <u>in their legs</u>.
10 <u>Damn weather</u>! We wanted a picnic today.
11 When do you think she will arrive <u>home</u>?
12 The trees in the forest are <u>70 feet</u> high.
13 He does not speak <u>much</u>.
14 Dried <u>with respect to her hands</u> she went back inside.
15 The fence encloses the yard of <u>8 square miles</u>.

Exercise 2

Each of the following unedited Latin passages contains an accusative. Match each passage with the English translation which follows. To assist you, try to think of English derivatives which stem from some of the Latin words.

1 percussa novā mentem formīdine (Vergil *G.*)
2 ego rūs ībō atque ibi manēbō (Terence *Eu.*)
3 est mēcum per diem tōtum (Pliny the Younger)
4 aggerem lātum pedēs trecentōs trīgintā
  altum pedēs octōgintā (Caesar *Gal.*)
5 trabēs dīstantēs inter sē bīnōs pedēs (Caesar *Gal.*)
6 sedet aeternumque sedēbit īnfēlīx (Vergil *Aeneid*)
7 ō miserās hominum mentēs (Lucretius)
8 mē caecum quī haec ante nōn vīderim (Cicero *Att.*)
9 maximam partem lacte et pecore vīvunt (Caesar *Gal.*)
10 Rōmam ad senātum profectus (Caesar *Gal.*)
11 Rōmam ad senātum vēnisse auxilium postulātum (Caesar *Gal.*)
12 Rōmam praetrepidus rediit (Suetonius *Nero*)

(a) a rampart 330 feet wide, 80 feet high
(b) he, unhappy, sits there and will sit there forever
(c) he went to Rome to the senate to demand aid
(d) he returned very nervous to Rome
(e) o wretched minds of men
(f) I, blind, who had not seen these things before
(g) struck by a new terror in the mind
(h) beams being apart from each other by two feet each
(i) for the most part they live on milk and cattle
(j) he set out to Rome to the senate
(k) he is with me the entire day
(l) I will go to the country and will stay there

Reading: Cacus Steals the Oxen (Labor X), part 2

Quandō relinquere cōnstituit, ūnus ex bōbus suīs mūgīre coepit. Subitō quattuor in antrō inclūsī mūgītum reddidērunt. Sīc Herculēs locum, quō quattuor bovēs cēlābantur, scīvit. Ille vehementer īrātus ad antrum cucurrit. At intrāre nōn potuit, quod saxum ingēns ā Cācō in **introitū** positum erat. "Quid facere dēbeō?" sē interrogāvit. Breve tempus magnā vī saxum āmōvit. Quod antrum fūmō replētum est, Herculēs Cācum vidēre nōn potuit. In antrum ergō irruit et collum mōnstrī corripuit. Ille sē nūllō modō līberāre potuit atque mox mortuus in terram cecidit.

introitū entrance [abl. sg.]

UNIT 31
Indefinite pronouns

Background

An *indefinite pronoun* refers to a non-specific entity.
The following are examples of indefinite pronouns:

Someone is walking across the street.
No one likes that movie.
He doesn't like anything.
A certain one is coming.
Whoever comes down the street, we'll see her.
Each one is coming this evening.

The adjectival correlates of the pronouns above simply have a noun immediately following them. They are:

Some man is walking across the street.
No student likes that movie.
He doesn't like any film.
A certain professor is coming.
Whichever lady comes down the street, we'll see her.
Each student is coming this evening.

Latin structure

The indefinite pronouns of Latin are:

Masc/Fem.	Nt.	
aliquis	**aliquid**	someone, something
quisquam	**quidquam**	anyone, anything
quisque	**quidque**	each one, each thing
Masc./Fem.	*Nt.*	
quīdam/quaedam	**quiddam**	a certain (one), a certain (thing)
quīcumque/quaecumque	**quidcumque**	whoever, whatever

- These translate as *someone, anyone, each (one), a certain (one)*, and *whoever* in the masculine and feminine.
- They translate as *something, anything, each (thing), a certain (thing)* and *whatever* in the neuter.
- **quisque, quidque** primarily means *each*, with *everyone, everything* being translated by **omnis, omne**.

Aliquis, quisquam, quisque

The first group of three pronouns, **aliquis, quisquam, quisque**, is built using the *interrogative pronoun* **quis, quid** (Unit 26).

There is no gender distinction between the masculine and feminine.

Only the **quis, quid** element is declined. Since these are indefinites and the exact identity and number of people involved are unknown, singular forms alone occur. Observe the following:

	someone	*something*	*anyone*	*anything*
Nom.	**aliquis**	**aliquid**	**quisquam**	**quidquam**
Gen.	**alicuius**	**alicuius**	**cuiusquam**	**cuiusquam**
Dat.	**alicui**	**alicui**	**cuiquam**	**cuiquam**
Acc.	**aliquem**	**aliquid**	**quemquam**	**quidquam**
Abl.	**aliquō**	**aliquō**	**quōquam**	**quōquam**
	each one	*each thing*		
Nom.	**quisque**	**quidque**		
Gen.	**cuiusque**	**cuiusque**		
Dat.	**cuique**	**cuique**		
Acc.	**quemque**	**quidque**		
Abl.	**quōque**	**quōque**		

Aliquis aliquem videt.
Someone sees someone.

Aliquid ab aliquō vidēbātur.
Something was being seen by someone.

Quidque amō!
I love each thing!

Quisque alicui crēdidit.
Each one believed something/someone.

Vix quidquam vīdī.
I hardly saw anything.

Apparent plural forms of **quisque** such as **quōsque** in the following are actually the relative pronoun, here **quōs**, plus the enclitic **-que** *and*.

quibus illī agrōs dedērunt *quōsque* **posteā . . . recēpērunt**   (Caesar *Gal.*)
to whom they gave fields and whom they afterwards received

Quīdam, quīcumque

The remaining two indefinites, **quīdam** and **quīcumque**, are derived from the *relative pronoun* (Unit 25) and as such they have a three-way gender contrast.

	certain		
Nom.	**quīdam**	**quaedam**	**quiddam**
Gen.	**cuiusdam**	**cuiusdam**	**cuiusdam**
Dat.	**cuidam**	**cuidam**	**cuidam**
Acc.	**quendam**	**quandam**	**quiddam**
Abl.	**quōdam**	**quādam**	**quōdam**
	whoever, whatever		
Nom.	**quīcumque**	**quaecumque**	**quidcumque**
Gen.	**cuiuscumque**	**cuiuscumque**	**cuiuscumque**
Dat.	**cuicumque**	**cuicumque**	**cuicumque**
Acc.	**quemcumque**	**quamcumque**	**quidcumque**
Abl.	**quōcumque**	**quācumque**	**quōcumque**

Notes

- Note the occurrence of **quid-** and not **quod** (as in the relative pronoun) in the neuter nom. and acc. sg. of both forms.
- In **quīdam** note as well **quen-** and **quan-** in the accusative instead of expected **quem** and **quam**.

  - This change of **-m-** to **-n-** happens for expected phonetic reasons; specifically, the **-m-** changes its place of articulation (lips) to agree with that of the following **-d-** (behind upper front teeth). The same phenomenon was seen in certain forms of **īdem, eadem, idem** *same* in Unit 22.

Examples

Quīcumque hodiē advenit, fēlīx erit.
Whoever comes today, will be happy.

Quaedam fēlīx est.
A certain (woman) is happy.

Finally, *nobody, nothing* is expressed via:

- the nouns

nēmō, nēminis (m./f.)   no one
nihil   nothing
nīl   nothing

Nihil and **nīl** are indeclinable; that is, they never change their form regardless of what case they should be in.

Occasionally the dative/ablative form **nihilō** is seen:

Utrum nescīs quam altē ascenderis, an prō nihilō id putās?
(Cicero *Fam.*)
Do you not know how high you rose, or do you think it for nothing?

Outside of the nominative and the accusative, Classical Latin prefers using forms of **nūllus** (see Unit 24) to express *no one*, making the paradigm:

Nom. **nēmō**
Gen. **nūllīus**
Dat. **nūllī**
Acc. **nēminem**
Abl. **nūllō**

Advanced topics

Aliquis, aliquid loses its **ali-** when it follows **sī** *if*, **nisī** *if not*, **num** *whether*, or **nē** *not*.

Sī, nisī, nē will be encountered in *Intensive Intermediate Latin*.

Nōn videō num *quis* adveniat.
I do not see whether someone is coming.

Exercise 1

Translate the following.

1 Quidcumque vidēs, nōlī timēre!
2 Aliquis mihi aliquid dedit, sed nōn sciō quem.
3 Cuique est aliquis, quī eum amat.
4 Nēminī pecūnia fuit. Rēgīna sōla dīves erat.
5 Nihil bibī. Bibam quidquam.
6 Illī currunt ā quōque.
7 Quaecumque istem hominem videt, ea scit eum deum esse.
8 Mittō cuiquam nīl, quod quīdam meam pecūniam invēnit.
9 Vīllae Carthāgine ab lūnā sunt iactae in lūcem, quod nūlla nūbēs in caelō erat. Quisque erat caecus.
10 Sciō nēminem, quī hīc vīvit.
11 Quidque terret meum amīcum.
12 Ab aliquō territus est meus amīcus.
13 Dīvidite quidque et date cuique aliquid!
14 Cavē canem! Cavē animālia omnia! Cavē quidque!
15 Aliquis mihi litterās scrīpsit. Quīcumque eās scrīpsit, ille auctor bonus est.
16 Quandō inimīcī nōs pugnant, nēmō valet.
17 Cūr nīl tū facis? Dēbēs aliquid nōbīs facere.
18 Quandō venet quaedam, quae ā barbarīs capta erat?
19 Quis hoc fēcit? Rogābimus quendam, quī hīc erat.
20 Quidcumque, quod noxae est, interficere possumus.

Exercise 2

Translate the following.

1 Someone closed that gate.
2 We were not able to decide anything.
3 Kill (pl.) whatever you see!

4 Someone fell from the high tree.
5 A certain (woman) remembers me.
6 When she touches anything, each thing turns into gold.
7 The king divided the wolf for each.
8 Whatever makes wine good, we ought to learn.
9 No one had fed the animals.
10 He saw nothing, when he stood here with me.

Exercise 3

Each of the following unedited Latin passages contains an indefinite pronoun.
Match each passage with the English translation which follows. To assist you,
try to think of English derivatives which stem from some of the Latin words.

1 quod nōn alicui venustum esse videātur (Cicero *Fam.*)
2 quod nōn alicui prōmissum iam sit (Cicero *Phil.*)
3 alicui quī tē ignōret vērum esse videātur (Cicero *Ver.*)
4 quōscumque adit ex cīvitāte ad suam
   sententiam perdūcit (Caesar *Gal.*)
5 quōscumque velīs adiungere ad amīcitiam (Q. Tullius Cicero)
6 sed eōrum ad quōscumque illīus morte vēnissent (Cicero *Ver.*)
7 sī quidquam ab hīs praesidī spērent (Caesar *Gal.*)
8 tamquam ad rem attineat quidquam (Horace *S.*)
9 neque senātuī quidquam manēre (Tacitus *Ann.*)
10 trium mēnsum molita cibāria sibi quemque
   domō efferre iubent (Caesar *Gal.*)
11 sua quemque fraus et suus terror maximē vexat (Cicero *S. Rosc.*)
12 nōminē quemque vocāns (Vergil *Aeneid*)

(a) they ordered each to carry out of the home for themselves ground
    provisions of three months
(b) as if anything may pertain to the thing
(c) whomever you wish to attach to friendship
(d) but theirs to whomever they had come because of that one's death
(e) he brings to his own opinion whomever he approaches
    from the state
(f) and not anything remains to the senate
(g) his own deceit and his own fright especially troubles each
(h) if they should hope for anything of support from them
(i) that it not seem to be charming to someone
(j) calling each by name
(k) it may seem to be true to someone who is not acquainted with you
(l) which has not already been promised to someone

Herculēs ab Eurystheō ad extrēmam partem mundī missus est. Pōma aurea Hesperidum abripere dēbēbat. Nesciēbat hortum, in quō pōma cūstōdiēbantur. Iter per multās regiōnēs fēcit et ad locum vēnit ubi Atlās Terram in umerō tenēbat. Hic locus Ōceanō propinquus erat. "Hortum quaerō," Herculēs inquit, "multās terrās peragrāvī, cāre senex. Hūc vēnī quod ā tē iuvābor. Tū enim sōlus mē iuvāre potes. Tē patrem Hesperidum esse sciō. Lībenter facient quaecumque ab eīs petēs, quod Hesperidēs fīliae tuae sunt. Iuvā mē!"

"Amīce," respondit senex, "vērum est Hesperidēs fīliās meās esse. Ego sōlus mortālis sum quī locum hortī nōvit. Lībenter tē iuvābō, sī prō mē Terram tenēbis."

UNIT 32
Indefinite adjectives

Background

The last unit introduced *indefinite pronouns*. This unit deals with their close relatives: *indefinite adjectives*.

The following are examples of indefinite pronouns:

***Someone** is walking across the street.*
***No one** likes that movie.*
*He doesn't like **anything**.*
*A **certain** one is coming.*
***Whoever** comes down the street, we'll see her.*
***Each one** is coming this evening.*

The adjectival correlates of the pronouns above are:

***Some** man is walking across the street.*
***No** student likes that movie.*
*He doesn't like **any** film.*
*A **certain** professor is coming.*
***Whichever** lady comes down the street, we'll see her.*
***Each** student is coming this evening.*

Latin structure

The indefinite adjectives of Latin are:

Masc.	Fem.	Neut.	
aliquī	aliqua	aliquod	some
quīque	quaeque	quodque	each, every
quīdam	quaedam	quoddam	a certain
quīcumque	quaecumque	quodcumque	whichever
ūllus	ūlla	ūllum	any
nūllus	nūlla	nūllum	no, none

Ūllus and nūllus are pronominal adjectives which were introduced in Unit 24.

They are declined like *1st–2nd declension* adjectives aside from their genitive singulars (ūllīus, nūllīus) and dative singulars (ūllī, nūllī).

The remaining four indefinite adjectives are all declined similarly.

- **aliquī** and **quīdam** illustrate:

some

		Masc.	Fem.	Neut.
sg.	Nom.	aliquī	aliqua	aliquod
	Gen.	alicuius	alicuius	alicuius
	Dat.	alicui	alicui	alicui
	Acc.	aliquem	aliquam	aliquod
	Abl.	aliquō	aliquā	aliquō
		Masc.	Fem.	Neut.
pl.	Nom.	aliquī	aliquae	aliqua
	Gen.	aliquōrum	aliquārum	aliquōrum
	Dat.	aliquibus	aliquibus	aliquibus
	Acc.	aliquōs	aliquās	aliqua
	Abl.	aliquibus	aliquibus	aliquibus

a certain

		Masc.	*Fem.*	*Neut.*
sg.	Nom.	quīdam	quaedam	quoddam
	Gen.	cuiusdam	cuiusdam	cuiusdam
	Dat.	cuidam	cuidam	cuidam
	Acc.	quendam	quandam	quoddam
	Abl.	quōdam	quādam	quōdam
		Masc.	*Fem.*	*Neut.*
pl.	Nom.	quīdam	quaedam	quaedam
	Gen.	quōrundam	quārundam	quōrundam
	Dat.	quibusdam	quibusdam	quibusdam
	Acc.	quōsdam	quāsdam	quaedam
	Abl.	quibusdam	quibusdam	quibusdam

Notes

Aliquī, quīque, quīdam, quīcumque all contain the relative pronoun **quī, quae, quod** (Unit 25) and are declined identically to it with the following two slight modifications:

- In **aliquī, -qua** occurs in place of expected **-quae** in:
  - fem. nominative sg.: **aliqua**
  - nt. nominative and accusative pl.: **aliqua**
- In **quīdam** an expected **-m-** becomes **-n-**
  - accusative sg.: **quendam, quandam**
  - genitive pl.: **quōrundam, quārundam**

Examples

Aliquī virī aliquem ferum canem interfēcērunt.
Some men killed some wild dog.

Quaeque fēmina oppidae hīc est.
Each woman of the town is here.

Quīcumque hominēs ā mē videntur, eīs pecūniam dō.
Whichever men are seen by me, I give them money.

Exercise 1

Translate the underlined words. Latin words whose genders are not apparent from the English translation are included in parentheses.

1 <u>Some</u> farmers never find anything for themselves.
2 Do you (sg.) know <u>a certain</u> woman, who lives here by herself?
3 <u>Whichever</u> door you (pl.) find, open it!   [**porta**, **-ae** door]
4 Did you (pl.) see <u>any</u> camps?   [**castra,-ōrum** camp]
5 We ought to praise <u>each</u> ally, who risked their own lives to save us.
6 Ride <u>no</u> horse without asking me first.   [**equus**, **-ī** horse]
7 The world was made by <u>certain</u> gods, who fight with each other.
8 They set sail for <u>some</u> island.   [**īnsula**, **-ae** island]
9 Be happy with <u>whichever</u> gift he will give you (sg.).   [**dōnum**, **-ī** gift]
10 The wolf was killed by <u>some</u> arrow of <u>some</u> soldier.   [**sagitta**, **-ae** arrow]

Exercise 2

Go back to Exercise 1 and translate all the pronouns.

Exercise 3

Translate the following.

1 Quaedam tempestās veniet.
2 Scītisne ūlla perīcula, quae inimīcī nōbīs facient?
3 Quodque saxum dē monte aliquō cecidit.
4 Apertus erat quaedam porta ab servō īnfēlīcī.
5 Senēs nōn cupiunt ūllum somnium immortāle.
6 Commūnia verba audiēbantur in aliquā urbe.
7 Nōn mihi sunt ūllī honōrēs.
8 Alicuius fēminae puer cucurrit ab templō sacrō.
9 Quodcumque vīnum bibēs, id etiam bibam.
10 Utrum praemium eī ferēs an eum in aliquem antrum tenebrārum dūcēs?
11 Nōlīte flēre! Est nūlla noxa.
12 Quaecumque scelera gravia illī fēcērunt, dēbēmus nōn timēre.
13 Rēx cuiusque urbis rēgit cum laetitiā.
14 Quibusdam antīquīs nōn crēdimus.
15 Aliquī miser meum dextrum bracchium frēgerit.
16 Manēre hīc nōn vult, quod nōn habet ūllam fortūnam bonam.
17 Mittitisne eīs quemcumque taurum, quī ā vōbīs captus erat?

18 Quīdam fīnitimī suōs gladiōs vendunt, quod nūlla pugna est.
19 Quīque cīvis cuiusque urbis hunc librum auctōris illīus legere dēbet.
20 Quandō aliquī mīlitēs nōs servābunt?

Exercise 4

Each of the following unedited Latin passages contains an indefinite adjective.
Match each passage with the English translation which follows. To assist you,
try to think of English derivatives which stem from some of the Latin words.

1	et quaecumque pars castrōrum nūdāta dēfēnsōribus premī vidēbātur	(Caesar *Gal.*)
2	quaecumque fortūna eius fuerit	(Cicero *Att.*)
3	quaecumque morā fluidōque calōre corpora tābēscunt	(Ovid *Met.*)
4	quōsque gregēs pecorum, quae sēcum armenta trahēbat	(Ovid *Met.*)
5	et rōbustissimōs quōsque in exercitū	(St Jerome)
6	sed persequiminī hostēs et extrēmōs quōsque fugientium caedite	(St Jerome)
7	quendam mūnicipem meum dē tuō volō ponte īre	(Catullus)
8	sed audiō māiōrem quendam in urbe timōrem esse	(Cicero *Att.*)
9	intellegimus in istīs subscrīptiōnibus ventum quendam populārēm esse quaesītum	(Cicero *Clu.*)
10	cum est ūsus atque aliquod bellum incidit	(Caesar *Gal.*)
11	adferet aliquod scelerātī hominis exemplum	(Cicero *Phil.*)
12	ut sī in circō aut theātrō ludicrum aliquod postulārent	(Tacitus *Hist.*)

(a) each herd of cattle which, the cattle, he was taking with himself
(b) as if they might demand something playful in the racecourse
    or in the theatre
(c) whichever bodies decay in time by means of such flowing heat
(d) I want a certain citizen of mine to go from your bridge
(e) whichever fortune might be his
(f) but pursue the enemies and kill every last of them fleeing
(g) and whichever part of the camp, bare with respect to defenders,
    seemed to be pressed
(h) we understand that in those notes of censors a certain popular
    wind was sought
(i) but I hear there is a certain greater fear in the city
(j) when there is use and some war occurs
(k) and every strongest one in the army
(l) he will present some example of a wicked man

Reading: The Golden Apples of the Hesperides (Labor XI), part 2

Hoc audīvit Herculēs et magnō gaudiō affectus est. Nōn frūstrā ad extrēmam partem mundī vēnerat.

"Pōne Terram," inquit, "in umerō meō! Properā ad fīliās tuās! Nōlī sine pōmīs redīre!" Postquam Herculēs haec dīxerat, Atlās Terram in umerō eius posuit. Senex statim ad hortum cucurrit. Fīliābus persuāsit. At puellae voluntātem deae Iūnōnis violāre nōlēbant. Diū resistēbant. Sed dēmum pōma patrī trādidērunt. Nunc Atlās sine morā ad Herculem rediit, quod pōma eī trādere volēbat. Herculēs magnō cum gaudiō senem vīdit. At Herculēs vir callidus erat. "Cāre senex," inquit, "lībenter Terram tenēbō. Sed tenē eam paulum. Aliquid in umerō meō pōnere volō, quod Terra tam dūra est."

Herculēs Terram Atlantī trādidit. Senex eam tenuit. Herculēs pōma cēpit et laetō cum **vultū** ait: "Senex, grātiās tibi agō. Prōh dolor, in Graeciam redīre dēbeō. Valē!"

vultū face [abl. sg.]

UNIT 33
Participles

Background

A participle is a *verbal adjective*. That is, it is a verb that is *used as an adjective*. Below, each participle is modifying a noun (*man, dog*) just as adjectives do.

verb	participle	
walk →	*walking*	*the <u>walking</u> man*
bark →	*barking*	*the <u>barking</u> dog*

English possesses several participles beyond the present active in *-ing*.

	Active	**Passive**
Present	*loving*	*being loved*
Past	*having loved*	*having been loved*
Future	*going to love*	*going to be loved*

- note that in all of these, *-ing* indicates that we are dealing with a participle
- a form of the verb *be* indicates the participle is passive
- a form of *have* indicates the participle is past

Since participles are still verbal, they may take modifying adverbs and prepositional phrases as well as direct objects.

A *participial phrase* is the group of words which are directly concerned with the participle:

*The dog, **having been loved by us**, had to be given away.*

Here, the participle *having been loved* is modified by the prepositional phrase *by us*. The two together form a participial phrase.

*The dog, **having bitten the mailman**, went back inside.*

Here, the participle *having bitten* takes the direct object *the mailman*. Together they constitute a participial phrase.

English participles are often usurped by various types of subordinate clauses introduced by certain subordinating conjunctions which themselves add to the meaning:

*The dog, **which was loved by us**, had to be given away.*

(relative clause)

*The dog, **although it was loved by us**, had to be given away.*

(concessive clause)

*The dog, **which had bitten the mailman**, went back inside.*

(relative clause)

*The dog, **when it had bitten the mailman**, went back inside.*

(temporal clause)

Latin structure

Latin is simpler than English in that – for whatever reason – it only has *four participles.*

There is neither a *present passive* nor a *perfect active.*

amō, amāre, amāvī, amātus to love

	Active	*Passive*
Present	**amāns**	-------
Perfect	-------	**amātus**
Future	**amātūrus**	**amandus**

The future passive participle is known as the *gerundive* and will be discussed in *Intensive Intermediate Latin.*

Present participle

- To form the present active participle drop **-re** from the infinitive
- Convert the stem to the stem used in the imperfect
- Add the ending **-ns**

amāre	→	**amā-**			→	**amāns**	loving
vidēre	→	**vidē-**			→	**vidēns**	seeing
dūcere	→	**dūce-**	→	**dūcē-**	→	**dūcēns**	leading
capere (capiō)	→	**cape-**	→	**capiē-**	→	**capiēns**	seizing
audīre	→	**audī**	→	**audiē**	→	**audiēns**	hearing

Since participles are verbal adjectives they will be declined for *number*, *case*, and *gender*. They are declined like 3rd declension adjectives of 1 termination (Unit 17).

Note the stem ends in **-nt-** which shortens the long vowel of the nom. sg.

	Singular		*Plural*	
	Masc/Fem.	*Neuter*	*Masc/Fem.*	*Neuter*
Nom.	**amāns**	**amāns**	**amantēs**	**amantia**
Gen.	**amantis**	**amantis**	**amantium**	**amantium**
Dat.	**amantī**	**amantī**	**amantibus**	**amantibus**
Acc.	**amantem**	**amāns**	**amantēs**	**amantia**
Abl.	**amante**	**amante**	**amantibus**	**amantibus**
	~ **amantī**	~ **amantī**		

- The ablative in **-ī** is used when the participle is directly modifying a noun.
- The ablative in **-e** is used when the participle is substantive (i.e. acting as a noun)

Līberī ab *amantī* mātre spectantur.
The children are being watched by the loving mother.

Līberī ab *amante* spectantur.
The children are being watched by the loving (one).

The present participle does *not* indicate an action occurring in the present. Rather, it indicates an action which is occurring or occurred at the *same time* as that of the main verb. So in the following, the *mother* was *loving* at the same time as the *seeing*:

Līberī ab *amantī* mātre vīsī sunt.
The children were seen by the loving mother.

Perfect participle

Its formation is easy. It is simply the fourth principal part:

amō, amāre, amāvī, *amātus* loved
videō, vidēre, vīdī, *vīsus* seen
dūcō, dūcere, dūxī, *ductus* led
capiō, capere, cēpī, *captus* seized
audio, audīre, audīvī, *audītus* heard

- This participle is only *passive* in meaning.
- It is a 1ˢᵗ–2ⁿᵈ declension adjective (Unit 6).
- It is used to describe a situation which occurred prior to that of the main verb.

> **Canis territus ex antrō cucurrit.**
> The (having been) frightened dog ran out of the cave.

- The act of becoming frightened occurred *prior* to the running.

> **Canis territus ex antrō currit.**
> The dog, (having been) frightened, runs out of the cave.

Future active participle

This is formed by replacing the **-us** of the fourth principal part with **-ūrus**

amātus	→	**amātūrus**	going to love
vīsus	→	**vīsūrus**	going to see
ductus	→	**ductūrus**	going to lead
captus	→	**captūrus**	going to seize
audītus	→	**audītūrus**	going to hear

- This participle is a 1ˢᵗ–2ⁿᵈ declension adjective (Unit 6).
- It expresses an action which occurs subsequent to that of the main verb.

> **Vir itūrus līberōs vīdit.**
> The man, about to go, saw his children.

> **Vir itūrus līberōs spectat.**
> The man, about to go, sees his children.

Uses of the participles

As mentioned in the background section of this unit, English participles are often replaced by various types of subordinate clauses introduced by a litany of various subordinating conjunctions (e.g. *since, because, although, if, when*).

The Latin participles may be translated in English in any one of these possible ways. Context will determine which is the most appropriate translation and specifically which English subordinating conjunction should be inserted.

Mīlitēs pugnantēs oppidum discessērunt.
The fighting soldiers left the town.
The soldiers, who were fighting, left the town.
Although the soldiers were fighting, they left the town.
Since the soldiers were fighting, they left the town.
Because the soldiers were fighting, they left the town.
When the soldiers were fighting, they left the town.
If the soldiers were fighting, they left the town.

At the beginning stage, however, the most conservative approach is to simply translate the participles literally as English participles as in the first option above.

Exercise 1

Classify the following participles by *tense*, *voice*, *gender*, *number*, and *case*. Some words may have more than one possibility.

1	cernentēs	6	tentūrae
2	vocātī	7	interfectā
3	imperātūrum	8	flente
4	cupītōrum	9	missam
5	pāstō	10	nocentem

Which form above cannot be used with a noun? What would need to happen for it to occur with a noun?

Exercise 2

Link up each participle on the left with a noun on the right with which it agrees. Use each noun only once.

1	amātūrō	virī	[**vir, virī** man]
2	mānsā	ovem	[**ovis, ovis** (f.) sheep]
3	trāctum	tempestātēs	[**tempestās, tempestātis** (f.) storm]
4	iactōrum	nāvī	[**nāvis, nāvis** (f.) ship]
5	flentēs	sīdera	[**sīdus, sīderis** (nt.) star, constellation]
6	ventae	caput	[**caput, capitis** (nt.) head]

7	rēctārum	frātre	[**soror, sorōris** (f.) sister]
8	fulgentia	sēminum	[**sēmen, sēminis** (nt.) seed]
9	scrīptō	urbium	[**urbs, urbis** (f.) city]
10	fugientem	rūmōre	[**rūmor, rūmōris** (m.). rumour]

Exercise 3

Translate the following.

1 Quis bibēns vīnum nihil nōbīs portāvit?
2 Virum fīliam suam tenentem videō.
3 Tempestās ventūra terret nōs.
4 Deus ā cīvibus laudātus omnia eīs dabit.
5 Portam moenium claudentēs ibi mīlitēs stēterant.
6 Ramō frāctō interfectus est clārus poëta.
7 Verba audīta auctor scrībet.
8 Amīcus rīdēns incipiet hoc opus.
9 Puerī cursūrī in antrum sunt.
10 Petentī puellae auxilium rēgīnae dabunt.

Exercise 4

Each of the following unedited Latin passages contains a participle. Match each passage with the English translation which follows. To assist you, try to think of English derivatives which stem from some of the Latin words.

1 ā quō numquam mē cōnsule dormientēs opprimēminī (Cicero *Mur.*)
2 et vēnit at invēnit eōs dormientēs (St Jerome)
3 maribus animīs et vīribus alacribus dormientēs
  aggrēdiāmur (Apuleius *Met.*)
4 captae superāvimus urbī (Vergil *Aeneid*)
5 urbis utī captae cāsum convulsaque vīdit
  līmina tēctōrum (Vergil *Aeneid*)
6 in prīmō tumultū captae urbis (Livy)
7 ita dēmum firmiter ac diūtissimē imperātūrum (Suetonius *Vit.*)
8 flēns animal cēterīs imperātūrum (Pliny the Elder)
9 cum comperisset imperātūrum eum vērum in senectā (Suetonius *Gal.*)
10 ultrōque vocant venientia fāta (Ovid *Met.*)
11 et quaecumque procul venientia lintea vīdī (Ovid *Ep.*)
12 prōspexit venientia vēla (Ovid *Tr.*)

(a) and they voluntarily call the coming fates
(b) that we may attack them, sleeping, with our masculine courage and ready strength
(c) when he had learned that he would be commanding, to be sure, in old age
(d) she watched the coming sails
(e) we outlived our captured city
(f) as he saw the misfortune of his captured city and the shattered doorways of homes
(g) and whatever sails I saw coming at a distance
(h) the animal, weeping, about to command the others
(i) and he came and found them sleeping
(j) so at last, him, going to rule firmly and for a very long time
(k) in the first confusion of the captured city
(l) with me as consul you, sleeping, will never be overwhelmed by that

Reading: Bringing Cerberus out of the Underworld (Labor XII), part 1

Postquam pōma aurea ad Eurystheum relāta sunt, ūnus modo ē duodecim labōribus relinquēbātur. Rēx Herculem magnopere timēbat. Proptereā eum in locum perīculōsum mittere volēbat. Erat locus unde numquam redīre poterit. Eī imperāvit canem Cerberum ex Orcō in lūcem trahere. Hoc opus tam difficile erat. Nēmō id perficere potuerat. Mercuriō duce Herculēs in Orcum dēscendit. Prīmum ad rīpam flūminis Stygis vēnit, quō rēgnum Plūtōnis continēbātur. Hoc trānsīre necesse erat. Erat nūllus pōns in hōc flūmine. Umbrae mortuōrum ā Charonte ad rīpam ulteriōrem nāve trāductae sunt. Hic senex ab Hercule adeō territus est. Herculem nūllō modō trādūcere volēbat. At Herculēs eum hoc facere coēgit.

UNIT 34
Ablative absolute

Background

There are two general types of clauses in both English and Latin: *main clauses* and *subordinate clauses*.

Both types of clauses have at the very least a subject and a verb.

They differ structurally in that:

- a *main clause* can stand alone as a complete sentence.

    Bill bought a cat.

- a *subordinate clause* cannot stand alone as a complete sentence. It serves as a modifier of the main clause, either further describing a particular noun mentioned in it, qualifying in what ways the main clause is true, or providing background context.

    Since Bill bought a cat, *he needs to buy cat food once a week.*

Relative clauses (Unit 25) are one type of subordinate clause.

    The cat, **which Bill bought**, *is cute.*

In English most subordinate clauses are introduced by a *subordinating conjunction* such as: *since, because, when, after, although, despite, that.*

    Bill is happy, **_when_** **he's brushing his new cat.**
    Although **Bill had little money**, *he bought a cat.*
    I think **_that_** **Bill bought a cat.**

English does allow a participial phrase to serve as a clause despite not having a subordinating conjunction to introduce it.

    Seeing the cat in the store, *Bill went in and bought it.*

When the noun doing the action of the participle is also in the participial phrase, a *nominative absolute* is produced.

Bill seeing the cat in the store, *the owner gave him a good deal.*

The presence of *Bill* in the participial phrase makes this an *absolute* construction.

Latin structure

Latin has a plethora of different types of subordinate clauses, most of which will be presented in *Intensive Intermediate Latin*. A key step in improving one's confidence in reading Latin is conquering its various subordinate clause types.

Latin, again like English, also has an *absolute* construction which is not introduced by a subordinating conjunction. It consists of a noun or pronoun in the *ablative* accompanied by an agreeing *participle*. Unsurprisingly this construction is termed an *ablative absolute*.

Any of Latin's four participles may be used (see the previous unit for discussion) but it is primarily confined to the *present participle* and *perfect participle*.

The only limit on the construction is that the ablative noun or pronoun may not be the subject or object of the main clause.

Mīlitibus pugnantibus, **cīvēs oppidī fūgērunt.**
The soldiers fighting, the citizens of the town fled.

Recall that the present participle indicates that the action of the participle occurs *at the same time* as that of the main verb and not necessarily in the present time.

In translating Latin ablative absolutes, any one of the following subordinate conjunctions may be inserted depending on the context: *since, because, when, if, although.*

Since the soldiers were fighting, the citizens of the town fled.
Because the soldiers were fighting, the citizens of the town fled.
When the soldiers were fighting, the citizens of the town fled.
If the soldiers were fighting, the citizens of the town fled.
Although the soldiers were fighting, the citizens of the town fled.

The past participle indicates that the action took place *prior to* that of the main verb.

Oppidō incēnsō, **cīvēs fūgērunt.**
The town had burned down, the citizens fled.
Since the town burned down, the citizens fled.
Although the town had burned down, the citizens fled.
etc.

1 Being verbal, participles can take direct objects and can be modified by adverbs or various types of adverbial phrases.

Mīlitibus ācriter inimīcōs pugnantibus, cīvēs oppidī fūgērunt.
The soldiers fiercely fighting the enemies, the citizens of the town fled.
Since the soldiers were fiercely fighting the enemies, the citizens of the town fled.
etc.

Oppidō ab inimīcīs incēnsō, cīvēs fūgērunt.
The town having been burned down by the enemies, the citizens fled.
Since the town had been burned down by the enemies, the citizens fled.
etc.

2 Since the verb **sum** has no present participle, it may be understood when two ablative nouns or an ablative noun and adjective come together.

Rēge salvō, cīvēs patriae fuērunt fēlīcissimī.
The king being safe, the citizens of the country were very happy.
Since the king was safe, the citizens of the country were very happy.
etc.

3 The present participle uses its ablative form in **-e** when in an ablative absolute and not its alternative form in **-ī**.

Populō senātōribus crēdente, patria bellum geret.
The people believing the senators, the country will wage war.
Since the people believe the senators, the country will wage war.
etc.

4 Since Latin does not possess a past active participle, clauses that are active in English must be reworded as a passive when translating into a Latin ablative absolute.

Since the soldiers had destroyed the city, the citizens fled.   →
Since the city had been destroyed by the soldiers, the citizens fled.   →
Urbe ā mīlitibus dēlētā, cīvēs fūgērunt.

• Deponent verbs though, having passive forms with active meanings, are capable of forming ablative absolutes with a past active meaning (*Intensive Intermediate Latin*).

Senātōre fātō, populus audīvit.
When the senator spoke, the people listened.

Exercise 1

Translate the following.

1 Verbīs poētae audītīs, puerī fēlīcēs erant.
2 Tempestāte grave, nāvis ad īnsulam portāta est.
3 Rēgīnā perīculum vidente, mīlitēs templum eius dēlēvērunt.
4 Saxīs nōn parvīs, moenia hodiē aedificantur.
5 Eō flente, erat nihil, quod potuerāmus facere.
6 Librō populō scrīptō, omnēs nōbilēs auctōrem laudant.
7 Tempōre brevī, in pāce vīvere dēbētis.
8 Ignōtīs currentibus, perīculum lupōrum nūntiātur.
9 Inimīcīs suō cum rēge per viās terrae euntīs, populī oppidōrum urbiumque
   tacuērunt.
10 Mē valente, puerī meī nōn timent tenebrās.
11 Aliquis ad āram templī nōs dūcet, auxiliō dē deīs petītō.
12 Praedā istīus agricolae inventā, agrī tibi erunt.
13 Crēdimus quibuscumque rēx nōbīs dīcit, nostrō oppidō pulchrō et nōn
   frequentī.
14 Negōtiō factō, nunc domī sumus.
15 Līberīs ab leōne fugientibus, pedēs in pāce noctis audītae erant.
16 Nūllā lūce in carcere, nēminem vidēre poterit.
17 Quid agētur, dīgnīs fīliīs patriae interfectīs?
18 Eīs vīnum bonum bibentibus, omnēs in somnum cecidērunt.
19 Mīlitibus castra mūnientibus, servābimur.
20 Multa optō annō novō inceptō.

Exercise 2

Translate the following.

1 Since the gate was opened, the soldiers came into the country house.
2 When will you (pl.) go to that wretched town, although no one lives there?
3 When the food was prepared by her mother, the brothers were carrying
   branches.
4 While the fire is strong, they sleep.
5 Because the inhabitants of the island were killed by arrows, there is no one
   who can save the animals.
6 His name being bad, no one says anything to him.
7 While the sheep were standing in the countryside, black clouds filled the sky.
8 Because our fatherland is beautiful, many men want to come here.

9 A cruel ambush having been commanded, the legion did not want to remain near the enemies.

10 Although the smell of blood is sensed, the parents do not leave the garden.

Exercise 3

Each of the following unedited Latin passages contains an ablative absolute. Match each passage with the English translation which follows. To assist you, try to think of English derivatives which stem from some of the Latin words.

1	rēgnō occupātō	(Caesar *Gal.*)
2	diē cōnstitūtā causae dictiōnis	(Caesar *Gal.*)
3	omnibus rēbus ad profectiōnem comparātīs	(Caesar *Gal.*)
4	eō opere perfectō	(Caesar *Gal.*)
5	sē invītō	(Caesar *Gal.*)
6	ratibusque complūribus factīs	(Caesar *Gal.*)
7	locīs superiōribus occupātīs	(Caesar *Gal.*)
8	omnibus fortūnīs sociōrum cōnsūmptīs	(Caesar *Gal.*)
9	hōc proeliō factō	(Caesar *Gal.*)
10	plūribus praesentibus	(Caesar *Gal.*)
11	rūrsus nūllō veniente	(Ovid *Met.*)
12	aquilā veniente	(Vergil *Ecl.*)
13	magnō veniente fragōre	(Vergil *Aeneid*)
14	veniente diē	(Vergil *G.*)
15	veniente columbā	(Lucretius)

(a) the kingdom having been seized
(b) all the fortunes of the allies having been spent
(c) many being present
(d) with day coming
(e) a day having been established for the sake of speaking
(f) an eagle coming
(g) all things for a departure having been purchased
(h) a great coming crash
(i) several rafts having been made
(j) his being unwilling
(k) a coming dove
(l) this task having been completed
(m) this battle having been made
(n) no one coming again
(o) higher ground having been seized

Reading: Bringing Cerberus out of the Underworld (Labor XII),
part 2

Sīc ad rīpam ulteriōrem trāductus Herculēs ad sēdem Plūtōnis ipsīus contendit.
Rēx ad portās urbis stāns virum fortem prohibuit. Herculēs nōn potuit rēgnum
intrāre voluntāte rēgis. At sagittā Herculis vulnerātus sententiam mūtāvit et
benīgnē verba Herculis audīvit. Hic Cerberum invēnit et Plūtōnem interrogāvit
"Licetne mihi Cerberum auferre?" Rēx mortuōrum respondit, "Hoc lībenter
permittam, sed post labōrem tuum Cerberus in Orcum redūcerētur." Herculēs
cōnsēnsit. Deinde Cerberum nōn sine magnō perīculō prehēnsum ad urbem
Eurystheī trāxit. Mōnstrō vīsō, tantus timor animum rēgis occupāvit. Herculēs
multīs cum lacrimīs rogāvit, "Nōlī tenēre mōnstrum in urbe." Herculēs ergō
Cerberum in Orcum redūxit. Sīc contrā opiniōnem omnium duodecim labōrēs,
quōs Eurystheus praecēperat, intrā duodecim annōs cōnfectī sunt. Herculēs
servitūte rēgis līberātus magnō cum gaudiō Thēbās rediit. Nunc sine cūrīs ibi vīvit.

Review of units 29–34

A. Provide the locative for the following words.

1 **Rōma, -ae**   2 **Carthāgō, Carthāginis**   3 **domus, -ūs**

B. Provide the vocative for the following nominatives. Keep the number constant.

1 **fīliī**   2 **rēx**   3 **deus**   4 **socius**

C. Which types of accusative would the underlined phrases be rendered into Latin as?

1 He walked <u>five miles</u> after waiting at home for <u>five hours</u>.
2 They had bitten him <u>at his nose</u>.
3 <u>Great Zeus</u>, <u>why</u> do you do such a thing?

D. Rewrite the following Latin sentences replacing every noun with the correct form of the indefinite pronoun **aliquis, aliquid**. If a noun is plural, then render it singular. Then, go back and add the indefinite adjective **aliquī, aliqua, aliquod** as a modifier of each noun.

1 Puer mātrem amat.   3 Sagittīs virum interficiam.
2 Poēta rēgīnae litterās mittit.   4 Rēgī līberī sunt.

E. Use the following verbs to translate the italicized participles.

amō, amāre to love	**capiō, capere** to seize
audiō, audīre to hear	**dūcō, dūcere** to lead

1 I saw the *loving* mother.
2 I could not believe the words (**verbum, -ī**), *heard* by me.
3 He gave money to the boy, who was *about to lead* the donkey to town.
4 Have you visited the towns (**oppidum, -ī**), *seized* by the enemies?

F. Translate the following as Latin ablative absolutes.

1 after the man was heard
2 since the young men were building the camp
3 the cave having been seen because of the flames

UNIT 35
Verbs that take the dative

Background

It has already been seen that the accusative case is used for direct objects and the dative case for indirect objects.

While being largely true this is not, however, a watertight statement. There are specific verbs which mandate that their object always be in the dative case. There are two such classes of verbs:

* Intransitive verbs
* Prefixed verbs

Intransitive verbs

An *intransitive verb* is one which can*not* take a direct object.

A *transitive verb*, on the other hand, *can* take a direct object. For instance:

Intransitive	Transitive
I sleep.	*I catch the ball.*
We lay down.	*I sing the aria.*
They come.	*We see him over there.*

Some verbs may be both intransitive and transitive:

Intransitive	Transitive
I am walking.	*I am walking the dog.*

Latin and English largely agree in having the same verbs be intransitive or transitive.

Intransitive	Transitive
Venimus.	**Eum interficiō.**
We are coming.	*I kill him.*

Some English verbs are made intransitive by placing what effectively is the direct object into a prepositional phrase:

*I am **angry at** him.*
*We **yield to** the leaders.*

Latin does exactly the same thing with some of the same verbs. However, rather than use a preposition as in English, the object is put into the bare dative case:

Sample verbs

cēdō, -ere, cessī, cessus to yield to
concēdō, -ere, concessī, concessus to yield to
īrāscor (1) to be angry at

• **īrāscor** is a deponent verb (see *Intensive Intermediate Latin*)

Examples

Eī īrāscor.
I am angry at him/her.

Prīncipibus cēdimus.
We yield to the leaders.

• Latin possesses dozens of other intransitive verbs which belong to this class which take dative objects. A handful are given here. As you can see from the translations, these verbs are fully transitive in English:

crēdō, -ere, crēdidī, crēditus
 to believe
faveō, -ēre, fāvī, fautus to favour
fīdō, -ere, fīsus sum to trust
cōnfīdō, -ere, cōnfīsus sum
 to trust
diffīdō, -ere, diffīsus sum
 to distrust
īgnōscō, -ere, īgnōvī, īgnōtus
 to forgive
imperō (1) to command
indulgeō, -ēre, indulsī, --- to
 indulge, grant
invideō, -ēre, invīdī, invīsus
 to envy

minitor (1) to threaten
minor (1) to threaten
noceō, -ēre, nocuī, nocitus to harm
parcō, -ere, pepercī, parsus
 to spare
pāreō, -ēre, pāruī, pāritus
 to obey
persuādeō, -ēre, persuāsī, persuāsus
 to persuade
placeō, -ēre, placuī, placitus to please
resistō, -ere, restitī, --- to resist
serviō, -īre, servīvī, servītus
 to serve
studeō, -ēre, studuī, --- to be eager for

Populus rēgī invidēbat.
The people were envying the king.

Imperātor mīlitibus persuāsit oppida victa esse.
The emperor persuaded the soldiers that the towns had been captured.

Quis nōbis nocet?
Who harms us?

Notes

- These verbs may form *impersonal passives*, in which the subject is the 3rd neuter sg. *it* referring to nothing specific (for more on impersonal verbs see *Intensive Intermediate Latin*).

  - The dative object stays in the dative:

    Rēgī ā populō invīsum est.
    The king was envied by the people.
    (*literally*: It was envied with reference to the king by the people.)

    Mīlitibus ā imperātōre persuādētur.
    The soldiers are being persuaded by the emperor.
    (*literally*: It is being persuaded with reference to the soldiers by the emperor.)

- Other intransitive verbs, which do not take dative objects, may also occur in the passive. This is used to stress the verbal action and not the agent.

  - This construction is non-existent in English.

    In viīs curritur.
    There is running in the streets.
    (*literally*: It is being run in the streets).

Compound verbs

Latin has a large group of verbs which occur with prepositional prefixes.
    This is similar to English verbs like <u>understand</u> or <u>overachieve</u>.
    When a verb possesses one of the following 12 prepositional prefixes, it takes a dative object to complete the meaning of the preposition:

ad-	ante-	circum-	con-
in-	inter-	ob-	post-
prae-	prō-	sub-	super-

- If the verbs are transitive, they may take an accusative direct object in addition to their dative object, but crucially these verbs cannot occur with an accusative direct object alone. The dative object must be expressed.

Sample verbs

iniciō, -ere, iniēcī, iniectus to throw in
praesum, praeesse, praefuī, --- to be at the head of
praeficiō, -ere, praefēcī, praefectus to put in command of

Examples

Terrōrem nōbīs iniēcit.
He threw fear into us.

Castrīs praeest.
He is at the head of the camp.

Novum hominem mīlitibus praefēcī.
I placed the new man in command of the soldiers.

Advanced topics

The dative with such compound verbs was used to refer to a non-physical, figurative motion. So in the examples above, there is no actual physical location to which the datives refer.

A prepositional phrase would be needed to express movement or transfer to a physical location:

In gladium eius incumbuit.
He fell upon his (someone else's) sword.

In the development of Latin, however, the bare dative came to be used to refer to physical location as well (from Livy 2.53):

porta, cui sīgna intulerat
the gate against which he had advanced the standards

The accusative is used with verbs prefixed by **trā(ns)-**.

Agricolae equōs agrōs trādūcunt.
The farmers lead the horses across the fields.

Exercise 1

Translate the following.

1 Cui crēditis?
2 Līberī suīs parentibus placēre nōlunt.
3 Deus tempestātum nāvibus nautārum aliquōrum nocuit.
4 Legiōnī iuvenem praeficiet senātus.
5 Quīcumque dominō servit, ille nōn liber est.
6 Māter nūllī suārum fīliārum favet.
7 Rēge sagittīs interfectō, rēgīna nōn poterat virō ibi stantī īgnōscere.
8 Crūdēlēs fīnitimī mihi imperāvērunt in oppidum aurum ferre.
9 Eī mihi imperāvērunt rūrī manēre.
10 Homō īnfēlīx fēlīcī mulierī suae invīdit.
11 Parce nōbīs gravem labōrem!
12 Canis ferus nōn pāret mīlitibus.
13 Nōbīs barbarōrum rēx nōn fīdit, quod amīcum eius interfēcimus.
14 Nēmō poētae, quī verba pulchra cuique scrībēbat, succurret.
15 Dēbētis pugnae eōrum ā manibus ipsibus resistere.
16 Cornua taurī nocēbunt nēminī quī in agrō erit.
17 Vātēs eīs imperāvit dōna deābus portāre.
18 Quis omnibus deīs praefuit?
19 Bellum pācī immortālī antepōnit.
20 Ignem castrīs inimīcīs iniēcimus.

Exercise 2

Translate the following.

1 When will the nymphs of the deep sea favour the sailors?
2 The king commands us to obey our mothers.
3 She prefers the crown itself to joy.
4 She will grant the sailors strong winds.
5 The gods favour the man, who does good for the world.
6 The boys envied the farmer's son, who had found the reward.
7 Whom will the emperor put in command of the crowd of people?
8 I will not serve you (sg.), who has seized everything from me.
9 Whoever is eager for peace, he will find it.
10 Why do you (pl.) trust someone, whom you do not know?

Exercise 3

Each of the following unedited Latin passages contains a verb which takes the
dative. Match each passage with the English translation which follows. To assist
you, try to think of English derivatives which stem from some of the Latin words.

1   nēmō umquam ūllī artium validius fāvit   (Pliny the Elder)
2   candidiorque diēs sēcrētō fāvit amōrī   (Petronius)
3   hīs fāvit nātūra locīs   (Statius *Silv.*)
4   dicta placent paucīs   (Ovid *Met.*)
5   haec tibi serta placent   (Ovid *Met.*)
6   tuae mihi turbae nōn placent   (Plautus *Mil.*)
7   sī anteposuit suam salūtem meae   (Cicero *Pis.*)
8   ignōtissimum quaestūrae candidātum nōbilissimīs
    anteposuit   (Suetonius *Tib.*)
9   nam stultē anteposuit exiliī lībertātem domesticae
    servitūtī   (Cicero *Tusc.*)
10 quae virtūs voluptātī resistere vidētur   (Cicero *Att.*)
11 possum vōbīs, Quīritēs, auctōribus improbitātī hominis
    resistere   (Cicero *Agr.*)
12 huic autem barbarae superstitiōnī resistere sevēritātis   (Cicero *Flac.*)

(a) he preferred the most unknown candidate for the
     quaestorship to the most noble
(b) if he placed his own health before mine
(c) your riots do not please me
(d) indeed did he foolishly prefer the freedom of banishment
     to domestic slavery?
(e) moreover to resist this barbarous superstition was of such strictness
(f) the words are pleasing to a few
(g) nature favoured these places
(h) which seems to be a virtue to resist pleasure
(i) these garlands please you?
(j) I am able with you, Roman citizens, to resist the authors of the
     wickedness of man
(k) and a brighter day favoured their secret love
(l) no one ever favoured any of the arts more strongly

Reading: Hercules and His Friend Admetus, part 1

Virō intrepidō in Thessaliā iter faciente, quōdam **diē** domum rēgis Admētī Herculēs intrāvit. Rēx et hospes amīcī bonī erant. Admētō eum hospitāliter excipiente, vir fortis animadvertit rēgem valdē tristem esse.

"Quid accidit?"

"Nihil," respondit Admētus. "Quaedam mulier peregrīna **mortua est**."

"Tē, amīce, turbāre nōlō. In domō alīus amīcī pernoctābō. Grātiās maximās tibi agō."

"Nōn sīc, cāre amīce. Numquam permittam tē hoc facere. Mēcum manēbis. In extrēmā parte vīllae dolor noster tē minimē turbābit."

Quod Herculēs amīcum bonum offendere nōluit, in domō eius mānsit.

diē day [abl. sg.]   **mortua est** she has died

UNIT 36
4th and 5th declensions

Background

Like the 1st declension (Unit 4) and the 2nd declension (Unit 5) the 4th and 5th declensions are characterized by specific nominative singular endings:

- 4th declension
    - masculine: **-us**
    - neuter: **-ū**
- 5th declension: **-ēs**

Additionally, also like the 1st and 2nd declensions, the choice of genders in the 4th and 5th declensions is rather limited:

- 4th declension: masculine and neuter
- 5th declension: feminine
    - there is one notable masculine fifth declension noun, however.

Latin structure

- 4th declension
    - The endings of the 4th declension are:

		Masculine	*Neuter*
sg.	Nom.	-us	-ū
	Gen.	-ūs	-ūs
	Dat.	-uī	-ū
	Acc.	-um	-ū
	Abl.	-ū	-ū
pl.	Nom.	-ūs	-ua
	Gen.	-uum	-uum
	Dat.	-ibus	-ibus
	Acc.	-ūs	-ua
	Abl.	-ibus	-ibus

Example

		Masculine	*Neuter*
sg.	Nom.	frūctus fruit	cornū horn
	Gen.	frūctūs	cornūs
	Dat.	frūctuī	cornū
	Acc.	frūctum	cornū
	Abl.	frūctū	cornū
pl.	Nom.	frūctūs	cornua
	Gen.	frūctuum	cornuum
	Dat.	frūctibus	cornibus
	Acc.	frūctūs	cornua
	Abl.	frūctibus	cornibus

- 5th declension

  - The endings of the 5th declension are:

	singular	*plural*
Nom.	-ēs	-ēs
Gen.	-eī ~ -ēī	-ērum
Dat.	-eī ~ -ēī	-ēbus
Acc.	-em	-ēs
Abl.	-ē	-ēbus

Notes

The alternative endings in the gen. and dat. singulars are partitioned as follows:

- if the stem ends in a vowel, then the ending -ēī is selected

  - for example: **di-** from **diēs** *day* gives **diēī**

- if the stem ends in a consonant, then the ending -eī is selected

  - for example: **fid-** from **fidēs** *faith* gives **fideī**

    o the stem is found by dropping the nominative sg. ending -ēs

5th declension nouns are feminine.

- The noun **diēs** *day* and derivatives of it (e.g. **merīdiēs** *midday*) are exceptionally masculine.

Example

sg.	Nom.	**fidēs** faith	**diēs** day
	Gen.	**fideī**	**diēī**
	Dat.	**fideī**	**diēī**
	Acc.	**fidem**	**diem**
	Abl.	**fidē**	**diē**
pl.	Nom.	**fidēs**	**diēs**
	Gen.	**fidērum**	**diērum**
	Dat.	**fidēbus**	**diēbus**
	Acc.	**fidēs**	**diēs**
	Abl.	**fidēbus**	**diēbus**

Advanced topics

The noun **domus** *house* belongs to the 4th declension but:

- it is feminine
- it has a few 2nd declension forms (in bold below)

Nom.	domus	domūs
Gen.	**domī** ~ domūs	**domōrum**
Dat.	domuī	domibus
Acc.	domum	**domōs** ~ domūs
Abl.	**domō**	domibus

- it's locative sg. is **domī**

4th declension nouns whose nominative ends in **-cus** allow a dat. and abl. pl. in **-ubus**

- **lacubus** ~ **lacibus**   from **lacus, -ūs** *lake*

Exercise 1

Determine which case, number, and gender the following adjectives are in. Then make the nouns listed below agree with each adjective. Unpredictable genders are listed in parentheses. Not every noun will be able to agree with every adjective, since the latter are already marked for gender!

domus, -ūs (f.) home	**fidēs, -eī** faith	**cornū, -ūs** horn
senātus, -ūs senate	**diēs, -ēī (m.)** day	**faciēs, -ēī** form; face

1 difficile   [**difficilis, difficile** difficult]
2 plēnīs   [**plēnus, -a, -um** full]
3 terribilibus   [**terribilis, terribile** terrifying]
4 brevis   [**brevis, breve** short]
5 cōpiōsās   [**cōpiōsus, -a, -um** rich, abundant]
6 pulchrō   [**pulcher, pulchra, pulchrum** beautiful]
7 malōs   [**malus, -a, -um** bad, evil]
8 īnfēlicēs   [**īnfēlix, īnfēlicis** unhappy]
9 ācre   [**ācer, ācris, ācre** sharp, keen]
10 commūnium   [**commūnis, commūne** common]

Exercise 2

Translate the following.

1 Exercitūs ē castrīs ad oppidum aliquod ab rēge ductī sunt.
2 Sagittae ab arcū eius reliquentēs impetum incipient.
3 Quālia animālia in hōc lacū vīvunt?
4 Rēgīnā lūctū implētā nēmō quidquam facere poterat.
5 Pulchrōs versūs scrīpserit poēta nōbilis caecusque.
6 Senātus et rēgēs contrā sē pugnant et semper pugnābunt.
7 Fidē populī frāctā, rēgīnae non iam est potestās.
8 Tōtum diem mānsit quisque in carcere.
9 Capite cornua illīus taurī ferī!
10 Manibus parvīs portābō dōnum ad templum vātis.
11 Vīdistīsne vultum istīus rēgīnae, cui nūllum honōrem dabimus?
12 Gregem pecūque nōn vult hodiē pāscere agricola.
13 Omnia domūs urbis frequentis exercitū dēlētae erant.
14 Genua eius fortiōra sunt quam mea.
15 Moenibus aedificātīs spēs salūtis crēscet.
16 Cūr impetus ab inimīcīs barbarīs contrā vōs fertur?
17 Properā domum rē inceptā.
18 Faciēs multae sunt nūbibus.
19 Poetā versūs scrībente nympha auctōrī auxilium dat.
20 Senātuī aquila deōrum pāret.

Exercise 3

Translate the following into Latin.

1 I had envied the bow of the strong soldier.
2 We do not wish to remember our grief.
3 His faith was similar to that one's hope.
4 The nearest army made an attack against the wretched senate.
5 She is strong in her knees.
6 The pastures stood between the house and the town before the war.
7 When the sun shines high in the sky, the days are long.
8 Whatever things you (sg.) find, you ought to keep them.
9 The horns of the bull having been touched, the animal ran.
10 That lake was built by hands alone.

Exercise 4

Each of the following unedited Latin passages contains a 4th or 5th declension noun. Match each passage with the English translation which follows. To assist you, try to think of English derivatives which stem from some of the Latin words.

 1 hic servō spē lībertātis magnīsque persuādet praemiīs   (Caesar *Gal.*)
 2 cētera quae ad mē eīsdem litterīs scrībis dē nostrā spē   (Cicero *Att.*)
 3 nam saepe senex spē carminis ambō lūserat   (Vergil *Ecl.*)
 4 ita mihi saepe occurrit vultus eius querentis   (Cicero *Att.*)
 5 ūnus erat tōtō natūrae vultus in orbe   (Ovid *Met.*)
 6 istī color immūtātus est, vultus, ōrātiō, mēns
      dēnique excidit   (Cicero *Ver.*)
 7 quem timor prohibēbat cuiusquam fideī suam
      committere salūtem   (Caesar *Gal.*)
 8 cuius fideī līberōs tuōs tē tūtō committere putārēs   (Cicero *Fam.*)
 9 suās cīvitātisque fortūnās eius fideī permissūrum   (Caesar *Gal.*)
10 addis cornua pauperī   (Horace *Od.*)
11 candentis vaccae media inter cornua fundit   (Vergil *Aeneid*)
12 ut duōbus ictibus quasi cornua efficeret   (Suetonius *Dom.*)

(a) (he) would give up his own fortunes and that of the state to his faith
(b) he persuades the slave with hope of freedom and great rewards
(c) you increase the horns of a poor man
(d) the one face of nature was in the entire world
(e) the rest which you write to me with the same letter about our hope
(f) the colour changed of that one, his face, his speech, and finally
     his mind failed him
(g) so the face of him complaining often occurs to me
(h) he might accomplish them in two blows as if horns
(i) indeed the old man often ridiculed them both out of hope of a song
(j) she pours between in the middle of the horns of the shining white cow
(k) to whose trust you might think yourself safe to commit your children
(l) whom fear prevented from committing his own safety to anyone's trust

Reading: Hercules and His Friend Admetus, part 2

Sōlus ad mēnsam sedēbat. Servī dīligenter labōrāre dēbēbant. Hospes eōrum magnam cōpiam cibī vīnīque cōnsumpsit. Subitō Herculēs cantāre incēpit. Servī hospitem cantantem perterritī spectābant.
　　"Quid spectātis? Venīte et bibite mēcum!"
　　"Nōs bibere nōn possumus," dīxērunt servī.

"Cūr nōn potestis bibere?" interrogāvit Herculēs. "Quod fēmina peregrīna **mortua est**?"

"Fēmina peregrīna? Quis hoc tibi dīxit?"

"Admētus ipse. Rēx mendāx esse nōn potest."

"Ita est. Sed Admētus hospitālis esse voluit."

"Cūr vōs omnēs tam tristēs estis? Respondēte! Dīcite mihi. Quis est illa fēmina?"

"Alcestis, rēgīna nostra."

mortua est she has died

UNIT 37
Comparatives

Background

Adjectives occur in 3 *degrees*:

- *positive*:   big   small   beautiful
- *comparative*:   bigger   smaller   more beautiful
- *superlative*:   biggest   smallest   most beautiful

Up till now we have only dealt with adjectives in the positive degree (Units 6 and 17). This unit deals with *comparatives* and the next with *superlatives*.

As the name suggests comparatives are used to compare two things:

*Susan is **taller** than Jessica.*
*This comedian is **more humorous** than the officer.*

English *comparatives* are formed either by adding an *-er* suffix (*bigger, smaller*) or by placing *more* in front of the adjective (*more beautiful, more cheerful*).

As a general rule of thumb adjectives that are one syllable *or* two syllables and end in *-y* take *-er*. Otherwise they take *more*.

The thing being compared to is introduced by *than*.

Latin structure

In order to form the comparative in Latin, first go to the adjective stem.

- You get to the stem of 1st–2nd declension adjectives by dropping the *-a* of the feminine:

      pulcher, pulchra, pulchrum beautiful → **pulchr-**
      dēfessus, dēfessa, dēfessum tired → **dēfess-**
      vīvus, vīva, vīvum alive → **vīv-**

- You get to the stem of 3rd declension adjectives by dropping the *-is* of the genitive:

  3-terminations

  ācer, ācris, ācre sharp, fierce → **ācr-**

  2-terminations

  fortis, forte strong → **fort-**

  1-termination

  ingēns, ingentis huge → **ingent-**

To the stem, add the suffix **-ior** for masculine and feminine and **-ius** for neuter:

		M./F.	Nt.	
pulchr-	→	**pulchrior**	**pulchrius**	more beautiful
dēfess-	→	**dēfessior**	**dēfessius**	more tired
vīv-	→	**vīvior**	**vīvius**	more alive
ācr-	→	**ācrior**	**ācrius**	sharper, fiercer
fort-	→	**fortior**	**fortius**	stronger
ingent-	→	**ingentior**	**ingentius**	more huge

The comparatives are declined as 3rd declension adjectives.

Unlike *positive* 3rd declension adjectives, they do NOT take *i-stem* endings aside from the ablative singular where it is optional. So, they have genitive plural **-um** and neuter nominative and accusative plural **-a**.

The ablative in **-ī** is common among poets and older and classical prose.

		Masculine/Feminine	Neuter
Sing.	Nom.	**ingentior**	**ingentius**
	Gen.	**ingentiōris**	**ingentiōris**
	Dat.	**ingentiōrī**	**ingentiōrī**
	Acc.	**ingentiōrem**	**ingentius**
	Abl.	**ingentiōre** *or*	**ingentiōre** *or*
		ingentiōrī	**ingentiōrī**
Pl.	Nom.	**ingentiōrēs**	**ingentiōra**
	Gen.	**ingentiōrum**	**ingentiōrum**
	Dat.	**ingentiōribus**	**ingentiōribus**
	Acc.	**ingentiōrēs**	**ingentiōra**
	Abl.	**ingentiōribus**	**ingentiōribus**

Syntax of the comparative

The *than*-part of a comparison is expressed by **quam**. What follows **quam** is in the *same case* as what it is being compared to.

Vir fortior est quam puer.   (nominative)
A man is stronger than a boy.

Moenia urbis altiōra sunt quam vīllae.   (genitive)
The city's walls are taller than the villa's.

Cōgitō puellam hanc dēfessiōrem esse quam illam.   (accusative)
I think this girl is more tired than that one.

A bare ablative can replace **quam**. This is the *ablative of comparison.*

Vir fortior est *puerō*.
A man is stronger than a boy.

Cōgitō puellam hanc dēfessiōrem esse *illā*.
I think this girl is more tired than that one.

An ablative may also be used to express just how much the two things/ people being compared actually differ. This is the *ablative of degree of difference.*

Vir fortior multō est puerō.
A man is stronger than a boy by much.

Quantō *by how much* in unison with **tantō** *by so much* expresses *the more X . . . the more X*:

Quantō pulchrior tempestās erat, tantō fēlīciōrēs erāmus.
The more beautiful the weather was, the happier we were.

- **quō . . . hōc** is an alternative to this construction

    Quō pulchrior tempestās erat, hōc fēlīciōrēs erāmus.
    The more beautiful the weather was, the happier we were.

When no notion of comparison is discernible, a comparative can simply be translated as *rather.*

Vir fortior est.
The man is rather strong.

Exercise 1

Convert the following adjectives from the *positive* degree to the *comparative*, while keeping *case*, *gender*, and *number* constant. Some may have multiple possibilities.

1 difficile   [**difficilis, difficile** *difficult*]
2 longīs   [**longus, -a, -um** *long*]
3 terribilibus   [**terribilis, terribile** *terrifying*]
4 brevis   [**brevis, breve** *short*]
5 cōpiōsās   [**cōpiōsus, -a, -um** *rich, abundant*]
6 pulchrārum   [**pulcher, pulchra, pulchrum** *beautiful*]
7 iūcundōs   [**iūcundus, -a, -um** *joyful*]
8 sacrī   [**sacer, sacra, sacrum** *holy, sacred*]
9 fēlīx   [**fēlīx, fēlīcis** *happy*]
10 sapientium   [**sapiēns, sapientis** *wise*]

Exercise 2

Translate the following.

1 Quantō gravius bellum est, tantō territior populus oppidī est.
2 Vir fortior nōn capiētur et interficiētur.
3 Cucurrērunt per silvam nocte animālia ingentiōra.
4 Saxīs in viīs leniōrēs sunt legiōnēs exercitūs.
5 Fīnitimī nostrī amīciōrēs sunt vestrīs.
6 Itinere factō bibimus vīnum mītius, quod mulier hospitis nōbīs dederat.
7 Cuius vultus pulchrior vidētur?
8 Vidī nūbem candidiōrem, quae in caelō fulsit.
9 Ager hic agricolae huius nōn est lātior quam ille istīus.
10 Dēfessiōribus somnō captīs legiōnī nūlla potestās fuit.
11 Quō clārior poēta est, hōc pulchriōrēs versūs scrībit.
12 Lupī celeriōrēs canibus sunt.
13 Vult rēx īnsulae moenia altiōra quam templum manibus populī aedificāre.
14 Circum flūmen dea crūdēlior equōs, quī aquam prope rīpam bibunt, capit.
15 Urbs frequentior est quam rūs.
16 Cibus, quī factus ā senī virō est, erat dulcior quam cibus iuvenis virī.
17 Studēmus carnī feriōris et pinguiōris animālis.
18 Quantō graviōra vulnera nautae sunt, tantō īnfēliciōrēs amīcī eius sunt.
19 Opera pulchriōra auctōris clāriōris legere dēbuimus.
20 Saeviorne dea est quam illa?

Exercise 3

Translate the following.

1 When will you (sg.) receive a freer life?
2 The cloud is blacker than the darkness of the cave.
3 The more wretched you (sg.) are, the more unhappy the life is, which you lead. You will have all the grief of the world.
4 The sail having been set, the sailors were seeking a more sacred animal.
5 Which guardian will find the more cruel danger?
6 The slower soldiers remained in the camp.
7 We desire the fatter sheep.
8 His arms are stronger than his head.
9 The waves, harsher by much, will destroy the trees of the island and their branches.
10 We prefer a stronger sword to a newer arrow.

Exercise 4

Each of the following unedited Latin passages contains a comparative adjective. Match each passage with the English translation which follows. To assist you, try to think of English derivatives which stem from some of the Latin words.

1 sed antīquiōrēs litterae quam ruere coepit   (Cicero *Att.*)
2 litterāsque antīquiōrēs altiōrēsque penetrāverat   (Gellius)
3 iūnior sum tempore vōs autem antīquiōrēs   (St Jerome *Job*)
4 ad altiōra et nōn concessa tendere   (Livy)
5 in loca altiōra collēsque impedītiōrēs equitī   (Livy)
6 nox prōvecta et nox altior et dein concubia altiōra   (Apuleius *Met.*)
7 sunt etiam iūdicēs quīdam tristiōrēs   (Quintilian *Inst.*)
8 quōrum in voltū habitant oculī meī tristiōrēs vidēbam (Cicero *Phil.*)
9 tristiōrēs autem sine maximō dolōre audīre nōn possint (Cicero *Dom.*)
10 sed breviōrem mē duae rēs faciunt   (Cicero *Fam.*)
11 brevitās tuārum litterārum mē quoque breviōrem in
   scrībendō facit   (Cicero *Fam.*)
12 ūnam breviōrem, alteram efficit partem longiōrem   (Vitruvius)

(a) onto higher places and hills more impassable for the cavalry
(b) he entered into older and higher literature
(c) advanced sleep and a deeper night and then a deeper bedtime
(d) it makes the one side shorter, the other longer
(e) in whose face my eyes lived, I was seeing them as sadder

(f) moreover sadder men might not be able to hear without
    very great sorrow
(g) there are even certain, rather sad judges
(h) but two things make me more brief
(i) the conciseness of your letter makes me also briefer in writing
(j) I am younger in time, you, moreover, are older
(k) to aim for higher and non-granted things
(l) but the letter is older than when he began to go to ruin

Reading: Hercules and His Friend Admetus, part 3

"O mē miserum! Ego, hospes, in hāc domō dolōris cantāvī. Quid prō meō amīcō fidēlī facere possum?"

In silentiō profundō paulum cōgitāvit. Deinde repentē surrēxit.

"Mortem cōgam. Admētō rēgīnam reddam."

Cēnā relictā, ad sepulcrum cucurrit. Mors fortiter restitit. Tamen Herculēs eam vīcit. Alcestis līberāta est. Admētus tristis domum redit. Herculēs amīcum intrantem salūtāvit. Alcestis cum virō magnī corporis in portā stābat.

"Nōvistīne hanc fēminam, Admēte?"

"Haec est fraus," exclāmāvit Admētus.

"Haec nōn est fraus. Est uxor tua, quae **mortua erat**. Rūrsus vīvit. Ā Morte eam pugnā recēpī. Ecce Alcestis, cāra uxor tua."

Sīc Herculēs sē amīcum fidēlem praebuit.

mortua erat she had died

UNIT 38
Superlatives

Background

The *superlative* is used to express an unsurpassed level. For instance:

*John is the **fastest** swimmer.*
*I liked the **most engaging** professor.*
*Tonight has to be the **coldest** it has been all year!*

In a sense while comparatives compare *two* persons or things, a superlative compares *one* person or thing to *every other* person or thing within a certain defined sphere:

John is faster than Paul.	(comparative: comparing *John* and Paul)
John is the fastest runner on the team.	(superlative: comparing *John* to every member on the team)
Susan is the most beautiful woman.	(superlative: comparing *Susan* to every woman in the world)

Superlatives are formed by adding the suffix *-est* (*biggest, smallest*) or by placing *most* (*most beautiful, most cheerful*) in front of the adjective.

As with comparatives, adjectives either of one syllable or of two syllables and ending in *-y* take *-est*. Otherwise they take *most*.

Latin structure

In order to form the superlative in Latin, first go to the stem. (See the previous unit to refresh your memory on how to locate the stem.)

Add the endings **-issimus, -a, -um**:

dēfessus, -a, -um	→ **dēfessissimus, -a, -um**	most tired
vīvus, -a, -um	→ **vīvissimus, -a, -um**	most alive
fortis, forte	→ **fortissimus, -a, -um**	strongest
ingēns, ingentis	→ **ingentissimus, -a, -um**	most huge

There are two small exceptions to the rule above:

- Exception 1: If the masculine singular dictionary form of the adjective ends in **-er**, then add **-rimus, -a, -um** directly to the dictionary form:

  pulcher, pulchra, pulchrum → **pulcherrimus, -a, -um** most beautiful
  ācer, ācris, ācre → **ācerrimus, -a, -um** sharpest, fiercest

- Exception 2: The following 6 adjectives take **-limus, -a, -um**:

facilis, facile easy	→	**facil-limus, -a, -um**
difficilis, difficile difficult	→	**difficil-limus, -a, -um**
similis, simile similar	→	**simil-limus, -a, -um**
dissimilis, dissimile dissimilar	→	**dissimil-limus, -a, -um**
gracilis, gracile slender	→	**gracil-limus, -a, -um**
humilis, humile humble, low	→	**humil-limus, -a, -um**

Syntax of the superlative

The *genitive* is used to express the defined set of which a person or thing possesses an unsurpassed quality. This is an instance of the *partitive genitive* (see Unit 12):

Rēgīna pulcherrima fēminārum erat.
The queen was the most beautiful of women.

Cōgitō eum celerrimum nūntiōrum esse.
I think him to be the fastest of messengers.

The *ablative of degree of difference* (Unit 37) may also be used with the superlative.

Vir fortissimus multō est.
The man is the strongest by much.

Quam + the superlative = *as . . . as possible*

Rēgīna quam pulcherrima est.
The queen is as beautiful as possible.

Cōgitō eum quam celerrimum esse.
I think him to be as fast as possible.

When an idea of comparison is not discernible, a superlative can simply translate as *very*.

Rēgīna pulcherrima est.
The queen is very beautiful.

Irregular comparison

A handful of adjectives do not form their comparatives and superlatives according to the rules laid out in this and the previous unit. Rather, the stems to which the endings are added are different from the stem of the positive degree – an instance of *suppletion*.

* the stems may be *partially suppletive*, adding or transforming one sound unpredictably *or*
* they may be *totally suppletive*, using a wholly different stem.
  All the irregular adjectives are examples of total suppletion.

Total suppletion		
Positive	*Comparative*	*Superlative*
bonus, -a, -um well	**melior, melius** better	**optimus, -a, -um** best
malus, -a, -um bad	**peior, peius** worse	**pessimus, -a, -um** worst
magnus, -a, -um great	**māior, māius** greater	**maximus, -a, -um** greatest
parvus, -a, -um small	**minus, minor** smaller	**minimus, -a, -um** smallest
multus, -a, -um much	**plūs** more	**plūrimus, -a, -um** most

Notes

* **plūs** is only neuter and is used substantivally (i.e. like a noun), taking a *partitive genitive*

  Plūs īnsulārum invēnimus.
  We found more islands.
  (*literally*: We found more of islands.)

- **Plūs** is interchangeable with its plural forms **plūrēs, plūra** which function as normal adjectives and thus agree with a noun in gender, number, and case.

    Plūrēs īnsulās invēnimus.
    We found more islands.

- The comparatives are declined as expected: **melior, meliōris, meliōrī, meliōrem . . .**

Exercise 1

Convert the following adjectives from the *positive* degree to the *superlative*, while keeping *case*, *gender*, and *number* constant. Some may have more than one possibility.

1	dulcī	[**dulcis, dulce** *sweet*]
2	immortālium	[**immortālis, immortāle** *immortal*]
3	bonam	[**bonus, -a, -um** *good*]
4	longō	[**longus, -a, -um** *long*]
5	sacrīs	[**sacer, sacra, sacrum** *holy, sacred*]
6	parvārum	[**parvus, -a, -um** *small*]
7	lātī	[**lātus, -a, -um** *wide*]
8	sapiēns	[**sapiēns, sapientis** *wise*]
9	facilibus	[**facilis, facile** *easy*]
10	senem	[**senex, senis** *old*]

Exercise 2

Translate the following.

1 Pulcherrima fīlia rēgis capiētur ab inimīcīs nautīs.
2 Apud parentēs meōs bibam vīnum dulcissimum.
3 Prīnceps senātūs dēbet esse quam nōbilissimus.
4 Plūrimōs diēs huius annī nihil fēcimus.
5 Māiōrem laudem et immortālem pācem dē vāte deōrum petīverint.
6 Optima legiō, quae oppida īnsulae servāverat, crēdidit imperātōrī.
7 In silvā nēmō vīdit candidissimum celerrimumque equum.
8 Exercitū turpissimō mīlitēs ab urbe sine victōriā cucurrērunt.

9　Maximumne est templum, quod umquam vīdistī?

10　Pessimīs impetibus cīvibus nūllus cibus erat.

11　Agricola sēmina in terram firmissimam iēcit.

12　Versūs quam pulcherrimōs scrīpsit poēta clārissimus.

13　Nōn possunt servī veterēs novissimō hominī placēre.

14　Flēns puer in āram sacerrimam pōnētur.

15　Nōn fīdimus huic, quī in monte altissimō habitat.

16　Timētisne mortem miserrimam?

17　Mel est semper dulcissimum cibōrum omnium, quī in vīllā sunt.

18　Vōcem tristissimam equitis audīvimus.

19　Vēnistis ad urbem maximam tōtīus orbis terrārum.

20　Ferissima animālia silvae possunt hominibus fēminīsque illīus oppidī nocēre.

Exercise 3

Translate the following.

1　What will you (sg.) do, after the strongest storm will have come?

2　No one does a very wicked crime.

3　Whichever tree is better, we will find it.

4　While the farmer drives the flock of sheep, the slowest clouds stood in the sky.

5　Why do you (pl.) ask the most aid from the servants of the very swift god?

6　No one is more worthy than him. He is the most worthy citizen of Rome.

7　Do not indulge (sg.) the happiest and most joyful children!

8　The most wretched queen persuaded us to go.

9　The highest walls having been destroyed, the enemies threw soldiers into the camp.

10　Though the sun shines in the sky, the cave is as dark as possible.

Exercise 4

Each of the following unedited Latin passages contains a superlative adjective or an irregular comparative. Match each passage with the English translation which follows. To assist you, try to think of English derivatives which stem from some of the Latin words.

1 in fortūnās optimī cuiusque ērumperent	(Cicero *Mur.*)
2 ad supplēmentum longē optimī generis mīlitum habēbat	(Livy)
3 ut optimī statūs auctor dīcar	(Suetonius *Aug.*)
4 vidēte nunc quam versa et mūtāta in peiōrem partem sint omnia	(Cicero *S. Rosc.*)
5 certē equidem puerum peiōrem quam tē nōvī nēminem	(Plautus *Per.*)
6 nam ego sī iūrātus peiōrem hominem quaererem	(Plautus *Ps.*)
7 prōcēdit in tumulum facillimum vīsū īnsidiantibus	(Sallust *Jug.*)
8 petō ā tē, id quod facillimum factū	(Cicero *Fam.*)
9 facillimum erit ab eō tibi ipsī impetrāre	(Cicero *Fam.*)
10 quī nūntiārent superiōre nocte maximā coortā tempestāte	(Caesar *Gal.*)
11 tum enim erāmus in maximā spē	(Cicero *Att.*)
12 prō hāc nōbilitāte pars maxima cīvitātis in armīs fuit	(Cicero *S. Rosc.*)

(a) then indeed we were in the greatest hope
(b) it will be very easy for you yourself to obtain (them) from him
(c) who announced that the preceding night, with the greatest storm having arisen
(d) he had for reinforcements the best kind of soldiers by far
(e) that I may be said to be the author of the best standing
(f) see now that everything is turned and changed into a worse part
(g) he proceeded to the mound, very easily seen by those waiting in ambush
(h) for I, if having taken an oath, may seek a worse man
(i) certainly, indeed, I know no boy worse than you
(j) I ask from you that which is very easily done
(k) they would have burst into the fortunes of every very good man
(l) for this nobility the greatest part of the state was in arms

Reading: The Death of Hercules, part 1

Quōdam diē sacrificium Herculēs facere dēbēbat. Vestem albam induit. Nessus, quem ōlim Herculēs interfēcerat, moriēns sanguinem suum uxōrī Herculis dedit. Nessus dīxerat sanguinem sacrum esse. Sanguis crēvit amōrem, quem virī uxōribus suīs habēbant. Fēmina Herculis, quae amōrem marītī sibi servāre voluit, sanguine mortiferō Nessī imbuit vestem. Herculēs, veste indūtā, brevī dolōrem ācerrimum tōtō corpore sēnsit. Eam dētrahere **cōnātus est**, at nūlla spēs sibi erat. Herculēs quasi furōre impulsus in montem Oetam sē contulit. Parātus mortem convenīre, rogum summā celeritāte exstrūxit.

cōnātus est he tried

UNIT 39
Adverbs

Background

Adverbs are closely related to adjectives. While the latter modify *nouns*, adverbs modify *verbs*, *adjectives*, or other *adverbs*.

*He spoke very **quickly**.*   (modifying the verb *spoke*)
*He spoke **very** quickly.*   (modifying the adverb *quickly*)
*The **impeccably** dressed man spoke*   (modifying the adjective *dressed*).
   very quickly.

Since adjectives and adverbs are close kin, it should be unsurprising that aside from some very common adverbs (e.g. *well, very, often, again*) many are formed from adjectives by simply adding *–ly*.

lately	*happily*	*terribly*	*rudely*	*rapidly*
(late)	*(happy)*	*(terrible)*	*(rude)*	*(rapid)*

Adverbs also form *comparatives* and *superlatives*.
Comparative adverbs in English consist of *more* + the adverb, while *superlative adverbs* consist of *most* + the adverb.

Positive	Comparative	Superlative
intelligently	*more intelligently*	*most intelligently*
quickly	*more quickly*	*most quickly*

As with comparative adjectives, *than* often accompanies comparative adverbs.
As opposed to comparative adjectives which contrast two *people or things*, comparative adverbs usually contrast two *actions* or *qualities*.

John bikes more quickly that he runs.
Theresa thinks more radically than Chris does.
That dress is more amazingly gorgeous than that yellow one.

- The first example is comparing the actions *biking* with *running* and the second example the actions *Theresa's thinking* with *Chris's thinking*.
- The third example is comparing the qualities of being *amazingly gorgeous*.

Latin structure

Adverbs are formed by adding **-ē** to the stem of 1st–2nd declension adjectives and **-iter/-ter** to the stem of 3rd-declension adjectives.

-ter is used with those adjectives whose nominative ends in **-ns**.

pulcher, pulchra, pulchrum	→ **pulchrē**	beautifully
ācer, ācris, ācre	→ **ācriter**	sharply/fiercely
sapiēns, sapientis	→ **sapienter**	wisely

There are plenty of adverbs, however, which do not follow these rules, a very small sampling of which are:

clam secretly	**iam** already	**modo** only
multum much	**paulātim** gradually	**prīmum** at first

The *comparative* adds the ending **-ius** to the adjectival stem.

It is identical to the neuter nom./acc. sg. of the comparative adjective.

pulcher, pulchra, pulchrum	→ **pulchrius**	more beautifully
ācer, ācris, ācre	→ **ācrius**	more sharply/fiercely
incrēdibilis, incrēdibile	→ **incrēdibilius**	more incredibly

The *superlative* adds the ending **-issimē** to the adjectival stem.

Those adjectives that formed the superlative adjective with **-rimus** or **-limus** likewise take **-rimē** or **-limē** respectively as their superlative adverbial forms.

incrēdibilis, incrēdibile	→ **incrēdibilissimē**	most incredibly
pulcher, pulchra, pulchrum	→ **pulcherrimē**	most beautifully
facilis, facile	→ **facillimē**	most easily

Some of the same syntactic constructions apply to adverbs as to adjectives, including

- the *ablative of degree of difference*
- **quam** or the *ablative of comparison* with comparatives
- **quam** + superlative expressing *as . . . as possible*

> **Rēgīna pulchrius *multō* canit *quam rēx*.**
> The queen sings more beautifully by much than the king.

Rēgīna pulchrius *multō* canit *rēge*.
The queen sings more beautifully by much than the king.

Puerī *quam celerrimē* cucurrērunt.
The boys ran as quickly as possible.

Irregular comparison

A handful of adverbs do not form their comparatives and superlatives according to the rules laid out in the last section.

Partial suppletion		
Positive	*Comparative*	*Superlative*
diū for a long time	**diūtius** longer (time)	**diūtissimē** longest (time)
magnopere greatly	**magis** more	**maximē** most
---	**prius** previously, before	**prīmum** first
prope near	**propius** nearer	**proximē** nearest, next
Total suppletion		
Positive	*Comparative*	*Superlative*
bene well	**melius** better	**optimē** best
male badly	**peius** worse	**pessimē** worst
multum much	**plūs** more	**plūrimum** most
parum little	**minus** less	**minimē** least

Notes

* **prius** has no positive degree since its root meaning *previous* implies a comparison
* observe that **prīmum** and **plūrimum** do not end in -**ē**

Exercise 1

Form the *positive*, *comparative*, and *superlative* adverbs from the following adjectives.

1 amīcus, -a, -um *friendly*
2 celer, celeris, celere *swift*
3 pulcher, pulchra, pulchrum *beautiful*
4 iūcundus, -a, -um *joyful*
5 brevis, breve *short*
6 levis, leve *light*
7 asper, aspera, asperum *rough, harsh*
8 lātus, -a, -um *wide*
9 difficilis, difficile *difficult*
10 dignus, -a, -um *worthy*

Exercise 2

Translate the following.

1 Canit pulchrius quam ego.
2 Vēla dant quam celerrimē.
3 Saevē hominēs, quī in carcere erant, rēgīna interfēcit.
4 Vulnerātō ōre, respondet nunc lentius.
5 Domī mānsimus fēlīciter.
6 Sagittās mīlitēs ferē iaciēbant.
7 Legiō urbem senātūs causā turpiter dēlēvit.
8 Bene doctus canis puerum captum in antrō servāvit.
9 Hīc diū vīximus.
10 Nōlīte facere peius quam eī.
11 Prīmum ad īnsulam nāvibus nāvigāre dēbētis.
12 Quod animal labōrat in agrīs plūrimum?
13 Ad castra propius venient exercitūs inimīcī.
14 Nēmō sapientius cōgitat quam ille.
15 Deīs nōs mītius pugnat tempestās.
16 Amīcē mihi pater meus īgnōscit.
17 Quam facillimē parentibus pārēbō.
18 Eī rēx crūdēlis persuāsit facilius quam rēgīna sapiēns.
19 Clam paulātimque it caecus auctor ad vīllam istīus virī dīvitis.
20 Bellō inceptō prō rēge humiliter dūx inimīcōrum stat.

Exercise 3

Translate the following.

1 We drink joyfully, because the children saved their own dog.
2 The horse firmly takes the big branches of the tree with its wide mouth.
3 I only had to drag the bull, which had been killed.
4 Why did she do all those things secretly?
5 The winds of the storm will strike the small town as fiercely as possible.
6 The holy nymphs sing more beautifully than the farmers.
7 The old make laws more wisely than do the young.
8 A bow and arrows were found recently in the forest.
9 He falls into a dream as quickly as possible.
10 The sun was shining in the sky as radiantly as possible.

Exercise 4

Each of the following unedited Latin passages contains an adverb. Match each passage with the English translation which follows. To assist you, try to think of English derivatives which stem from some of the Latin words.

1 nēmō melius iūdicāre potest quam tū   (Cicero *ad Brut.*)
2 tibi verō ipsī certē nēmō melius dabit   (Cicero *Fam.*)
3 melius lūgēbitis ambō   (Ovid *Met.*)
4 ubi sē diūtius dūcī intellēxit   (Caesar *Gal.*)
5 nōlō tē iactārī diūtius   (Plautus *Trin.*)
6 dubitābitis etiam diūtius, iūdicēs   (Cicero *Font.*)
7 quam sapienter aut quam fortiter nihil attinet ā disputārī   (Cicero *Fam.*)
8 quī deōrum mūneribus sapienter ūtī   (Horace *Od.*)
9 illīc indignissimum cāsum sapienter tolerāns   (Tacitus *Ann.*)
10 sīc lētālis hiems paulātim in pectora vēnit   (Ovid *Met.*)
11 paulātim sēsē tollit mare et altius undās ērigit   (Vergil *Aeneid*)
12 sī paulātim haec cōnsuetūdō serpere ac prōdīre coeperit   (Cicero *Div. Caec.*)

(a) how wisely or how strongly nothing is of importance by being discussed
(b) I do not wish you to be flung any longer
(c) no one is able to judge better than you
(d) who use the gifts of the gods wisely
(e) certainly in fact no one will give better to you yourself
(f) in this way deadly winter came gradually into (her) chest
(g) better that you both mourn
(h) he enduring wisely his most unworthy misfortune there
(i) will you still doubt longer, judges?
(j) when he understood that he was being led for a rather long time
(k) the sea gradually lifts itself up and raises its waves up higher
(l) if this habit begins to crawl and progress gradually

Reading: The Death of Hercules, part 2

Deinde vidēns eōs, quī adstābant, rogāvit, "Potestis rogum accendere?"

At omnēs recūsābant, "Tāle scelus numquam committēmus."

Dēmum quīdam pāstor ignem rogō subdidit. Statim fūmus omnia implēvit et Herculēs dēnsā nūbe opertus ā Iove in Olympum abreptus est. Hic erat fīnis vītae Herculis, ūnīus ex clārissimīs virīs Graeciae. Erat homō multārum virtūtum vitiōrumque. Vitia expiāre voluerat. Duodecim labōrēs difficilēs eī datī erant. Sed prō virtūtibus magnīs deī eum dīgnum putāvērunt. In caelum sublātus est.

UNIT 40
Uses of the ablative II

Background

Unit 8 presented several uses of the ablative case – the catch-all case of Latin.

Since Unit 8 other uses of the ablative have been presented. This unit has two goals:

- to catalogue in one place the uses of the ablative which have been introduced since Unit 8
- to present a few more uses of the ablative

Uses of the ablative since Unit 8

I Ablative of personal agent (Unit 19)

- An ablative preceded by the preposition **ā/ab** is used to express the human agent of a passive verb.

  Mīles *ab illō homine* interfectus erat.
  The soldier had been killed by that man.

II Ablative of means

- This use must be contrasted with the *ablative of means* (Unit 8) which is used to express the non-human agent of a passive verb.

  - It is a bare ablative without an accompanying preposition.

    Agricola *sagittīs* interfectus erat.
    The farmer had been killed by arrows.

III Ablative absolute (Unit 34)

- A participle (Unit 33) in the ablative in unison with a noun in the ablative expresses a subordinate clause which provides background information to the main clause.

- The noun in the ablative absolute can be neither the subject nor the direct object of the main clause.

    Agricolā canente, **labor multus celeriter factus est.**
    The farmer singing, much work was done quickly.

IV Ablative of comparison (Unit 37)

- A bare ablative can express the person or thing to whom something or someone is being compared.

    - **quam** + a noun in the same case as the person or thing being compared to is an alternative construction.

        Mīlitēs exercitūs nostrī sunt fortiōrēs *hostibus*.
        The soldiers of our army are stronger than the enemies.

V Ablative of degree of difference (Unit 37)

- A bare ablative is used to express to what degree the two compared things differ.

    Mīlitēs exercitūs nostrī *multō* fortiōrēs sunt.
    The soldiers of our army are stronger by much.

New uses of the ablative

VI Ablative of separation

- The ablative is used to express something which is lacking, deprived, or separated.

    - The prepositions **ā/ab, ē/ex,** and **dē** may be used.
- The verbs used in this construction are:

    careō, -ēre, caruī, caritus to lack
    egeō, -ēre, eguī to be wanting
    līberō (1) to free
    prīvō (1) to deprive
    solvō, -ere, solvī, solūtus to free, release

Examples

    Carēsne *aurō* et *argentō*?
    Do you lack gold and silver?

Eōs *perīculō* **līberābimus.**
We will free them from danger.

Bellum eum *spē* **prīvāvit.**
The war deprived him of hope.

VII Ablative of source

- The ablative can be used to express descent or origin.
- It is very common with the following two past participles:

  - **nātus, -a, -um** born
  - **ortus, -a, -um** arisen

    rēge **deōrum ortus**
    arisen from the king of gods

    parientibus bonīs **nāta**
    born of good parents

VIII Ablative of time

- The ablative of a time word expresses *when* something occurred.

  Eā nocte **nēmō hīc mānsit.**
  That night no one remained here.

  Illō mēnse **pugnābam contrā meōs fīnitimōs.**
  That month I was fighting against my neighbours.

- The ablative of a time word with a future verb expresses *when* or *within how much time* something will take place.

  Septem diēbus **venient mīlitēs.**
  Within seven days the soldiers will come.

  Proximō diē **bellum inceptum erit.**
  The next day battle will have begun.

IX Ablative of place from which

- The ablative commanded by the prepositions **ā/ab** and **ē/ex** indicates the origin of movement.
- When, however, one is leaving a *specific town, city, small island,* or either **domus, -ūs** (f.) *house* or **rūs, rūris** (nt.) *countryside,* the bare ablative is used.

  - For the 2nd declension forms interspersed in the declension of **domus**, see Unit 36.

■ This is the same class of nouns which form a locative (Unit 29) and which can use a bare accusative to indicate direction towards a place (Unit 30).

Īmus *rūre* Rōmam.
We are going from the countryside to Rome.

***Domō* veniet.**
S/he will come from home.

X Ablative with verbs

• Aside from the verbs which take an *ablative of separation* a few other verbal expressions take an ablative.

■ **opus est** it is necessary

this takes:

■ an ablative indicating what is necessary
■ a dative indicating for whom the noun expressed in the ablative is necessary

***Pāce* nōbīs opus est.**
We need peace.
Literally: It is necessary to us with respect to peace.

■ A class of *deponent verbs* takes ablative objects.

○ A deponent verb is a verb which only possesses passive forms though they have active meanings.

Deponent verbs are discussed in *Intensive Intermediate Latin*.

○ The list of verbs is:

fruor, -ī, frūctus sum to enjoy
fungor, -ī, fūnctus sum to perform
potior, -īrī, potītus sum to gain possession of
ūtor, -ī, ūsus sum to use
vēscor, -ī to eat

Examples

***Pāce* fruimur.**
We enjoy peace.

***Agrīs* rēgis rēgīnaeque potientur.**
They will gain possession of the fields of the king and queen.

***Quō* ūsī estis?**
What did you (pl.) use?

Exercise 1

Determine what type of ablative the underlined portions would be if translated into Latin.

1 We noticed that Frank was slower <u>than Elizabeth</u>.
2 My friend is coming <u>from Cardiff</u>.
3 The politicians enjoy <u>kickbacks</u>.
4 She was born <u>to a grateful family</u>.
5 That show was rather funny <u>by a long shot</u>.
6 The mouse was caught <u>by the trap.</u>
7 The mouse was caught <u>by my mother</u>.
8 <u>In five months</u> we will be done school!
9 <u>What</u> are you lacking now?
10 <u>The storm</u> having missed the town, the citizens were jubilant.
11 Tomorrow <u>night</u> there is a party.
12 They freed the men <u>from prison</u>.
13 The cake was eaten <u>by the boy</u>.
14 Risen <u>from the sea</u> the whale dove back into the water.
15 After so much <u>work</u> was done on our day off, we're happy to go out <u>from our home</u>.

Exercise 2

Each of the following unedited Latin passages contains an ablative. Match each passage with the English translation which follows. To assist you, try to think of English derivatives which stem from some of the Latin words.

1 arāneās dēiciam dē pariete   (Plautus *St.*)
2 omnia domō eius abstulit   (Cicero *Ver.*)
3 omnium rērum nātūrā cognitā līberāmur mortis metū   (Cicero *Fin.*)
4 cui vīgintī hīs annīs supplicātiō dēcrēta est   (Cicero *Phil.*)
5 amplissimā familiā nātī adulēscentēs   (Caesar *Gal.*)
6 dīcitur oculīs sē prīvāsse   (Cicero *Fin.*)
7 novō cōnsiliō mihi nunc opus est   (Plautus *Ps.*)
8 lūx quā fruimur ā deō nōbīs datur   (Cicero *S. Rosc.*)
9 multīs annīs nōn vēnit   (Cicero *S. Rosc.*)
10 amīcitia . . . nūllō locō exclūditur   (Cicero *Amic.*)
11 nōn opus est verbīs sed fūstibus   (Cicero *Pis.*)
12 nōn sōlum domō, dē quā cognōstis, sed tōtā urbe careō   (Cicero *Dom.*)

(a) he did not come for many years
(b) the light which we enjoy is given to us by a god
(c) young men born of the most distinguished family
(d) he carried away everything from his house
(e) it is said he deprived himself of eyes
(f) friendship is shut out from no place
(g) I will knock down the spider webs from the wall
(h) with the nature of all things being known, we are freed from the fear of death
(i) for whom in the last twenty years has a thanksgiving been decreed?
(j) I need now a new plan
(k) there is no need of words but of clubs
(l) not only do I lack my home, about which you know, but the whole city

Reading: Excerpt from Caesar's Gallic Wars

Note that subordinate clauses, such as relative clauses and *quod*-clauses, are indented. The level of indentation indicates which clause each subordinate phrase immediately depends on for its meaning. In the first sentence, for instance, lines 2–4 all depend on line 1, whereas lines 5 and 6 depend on line 4.

Gallia est omnis dīvīsa in partēs trēs,
    quārum ūnam incolunt Belgae,
    aliam Aquitānī,
    tertiam
        quī ipsōrum linguā Celtae,
        nostrā Gallī appellantur.

Hī omnēs linguā, īnstitūtīs, lēgibus inter sē differunt.

Gallōs ab Aquitānīs Garumna flūmen,
ā Belgīs Matrona et Sēquana **dīvidit**.

Hōrum omnium fortissimī sunt Belgae,
    proptereā quod ā cultū atque hūmānitāte prōvinciae longissimē absunt,
    proximīque sunt Germānīs,
        quī trāns Rhēnum incolunt,
        quibuscum continenter bellum gerunt.

Note **dīvidit** for grammatically expected **dīvidunt**.

Review of units 35–40

A. Determine whether the following verbs take a dative object because they are intransitives or because they have a prefix. Which verb does *not* take a dative object?

1 **īrāscor**	3 **crēdō**	5 **circumplector**
2 **trādūcō**	4 **praeficiō**	6 **placeō**

B. Determine the case and number of each of the following nouns. Some may have multiple possibilities.

1 **diēbus**	3 **cornūs**	5 **cornua**
2 **faciēs**	4 **fidērum**	6 **senātuī**

C. Make the adjectives **pulchrior, pulchrius** *more beautiful* and **pulcherrimus, -a, -um** agree with each of the following nouns.

1 **templum**	4 **somniōrum**
2 **nautam**	5 **fīliīs**
3 **fīliās**	6 **vīllae**

D. Form adverbs from the following adjectives.

1 **laetus, -a, -um**	4 **ācer, ācris, ācre**
2 **laetior, laetius**	5 **ācrior, ācrius**
3 **laetissimus, -a, -um**	6 **ācerrimus, -a, -um**

E. Which types of ablative would the following be rendered into Latin as?

1 She is faster than him *by much*.
2 *The storm having passed*, we all went outside.
3 Born *of the big kangaroo*, the newborn was healthy.
4 You will be there *within a week*.

Key to exercises

UNIT 1

1 1 nauta: two syllables; diphthong 2 poēta: long vowel 3 nātūra: long vowel
4 via: two syllables 5 vīta: two syllables; long vowel 6 pugna: two syllables; two
consonants 7 adulēscentis: two consonants 8 imperātōre: long vowel 9 rēx only
syllable 10 lībertās: two consonants 11 mīles: two syllables; long vowel 12 senātus:
long vowel 13 quibus: two syllables 14 quisque: two syllables; two consonants

2 1 haec: only syllable 2 tempestātem: long vowel 3 ambulāvissem: two consonants 4 hiemis: penult. cannot hold it 5 negōtium: penult. cannot hold it
6 īnsidiae: penult. cannot hold it 7 īnsidiārum: long vowel 8 proelium: penult.
cannot hold it 9 amantium: penult. cannot hold it 10 pāx: only syllable
11 equitātuum: penult. cannot hold it 12 quem: only one syllable 13 aliquis: penult.
cannot hold it 14 speciēs: penult. cannot hold it 15 passūs: only two syllables;
two consonants 16 vallēs: two syllables; two consonants 17 removeō: penult.
cannot hold it 18 rīdeō: penult. cannot hold it 19 Rōmānus: long vowel
20 interficiō: penult. cannot hold it

UNIT 2

1 1 1, we hasten 2 4, they come 3 1, I build 4 1, they stand 5 2, you (sg.)
remain 6 1, s/he, it lives 7 2, you (pl.) move 8 1, you (pl.) carry 9 2, they have
10 2, I hold 11 2, s/he, it is silent 12 4, s/he, it feels 13 1, I think 14 1, we love
15 1, s/he, it desires 16 2, they are strong 17 2, they are afraid 18 4, you (sg.)
open 19 2, s/he, it extends 20 2, we burn 21 2, you (pl.) shine 22 4, s/he, it
sleeps 23 1, they excite 24 1, I prepare 25 4, you (pl.) fortify 26 1, we save
27 1, they give 28 2, I see 29 4, they know 30 1, you (sg.) think 31 2, we laugh
32 2, s/he, it is eager 33 2, you (sg.) frighten 34 2, you (pl.) harm 35 1, s/he, it
fights 36 2, s/he, it owes 37 1, you (sg.) announce 38 2, I respond 39 1, you
(pl.) ask 40 2, they warn 41 1, s/he, it stands 42 1, we command 43 1, I deny
44 1, s/he, it calls 45 4, they hear 46 4, you (sg.) do not know 47 2, we teach
48 2, you (pl.) order 49 2, they beware 50 2, you (pl.) weep

2 1 properō 2 venit 3 aedificāmus 4 stat 5 manētis 6 habitant 7 movēs 8 portās 9 habet 10 tenēmus 11 tacent 12 sentiunt 13 cōgitāmus 14 amō 15 optant 16 valet 17 timet 18 aperītis 19 patent 20 ārdeō 21 fulgēs 22 dormiunt 23 excitat 24 parāmus 25 mūnīs 26 servō 27 dat 28 vidēmus 29 scit 30 putātis 31 rīdeō 32 student 33 terrētis 34 nocēs 35 pugnant 36 dēbent 37 nūntiātis 38 respondēmus 39 rogās 40 monet 41 stant 42 imperō 43 negāmus 44 vocant 45 audit 46 nescītis 47 doceō 48 iubēs 49 cavet 50 flēs

3 1 optāmus 2 dormiunt 3 rīdēs 4 ārdet 5 portāmus 6 venīmus 7 nocet 8 patet 9 terreō 10 valent 11 monet 12 scīmus 13 rogātis 14 negō 15 docent 16 studet 17 amās 18 pugnāmus 19 fulget 20 putō 21 invenit 22 timeō 23 audiunt 24 properāmus 25 stat 26 nūntiat 27 aperītis 28 flent 29 imperat 30 nescīmus

4 1 B 2 K 3 I 4 L 5 D 6 M 7 F 8 A 9 G 10 C 11 E 12 J

UNIT 3

1 1 3rd-reg.; you (sg.) seek 2 3rd-iō; s/he, it flees 3 3rd-reg.; we touch 4 3rd-reg.; you (pl.) lead 5 3rd-reg.; I drive 6 3rd-iō; they throw 7 3rd-reg.; s/he, it drinks 8 3rd-reg.; you (sg.) buy 9 3rd-reg.; you (pl.) close 10 3rd-reg.; we press 11 3rd-reg.; I cover 12 3rd-reg.; s/he it breaks 13 3rd-reg.; they sing 14 3rd-reg.; you (sg.) learn 15 3rd-reg.; you (pl.) read 16 3rd-reg.; I run 17 3rd-reg.; you (pl.) fall 18 3rd-reg.; you (sg.) conduct 19 3rd-reg.; they send 20 3rd-reg.; s/he, it drives 21 3rd-reg.; I put 22 3rd-iō; we seize 23 3rd-reg.; you (sg.) leave 24 3rd-reg.; they live 25 3rd-reg.; s/he, it rules 26 3rd-iō; I do 27 3rd-reg.; I say 28 3rd-reg.; you (pl.) decide 29 3rd-reg.; you (sg.) believe 30 3rd-reg.; we write 31 3rd-reg.; they believe 32 3rd-reg.; I descend 33 3rd-reg.; s/he, it drags 34 3rd-reg.; you (sg.) depart 35 3rd-reg.; they force 36 3rd-reg.; you (pl.) join 37 3rd-iō; they begin 38 3rd-reg.; I turn 39 3rd-reg.; we grow 40 3rd-reg.; s/he, it divides 41 3rd-iō; I kill 42 3rd-reg.; you (pl.) inquire 43 3rd-reg.; you (pl.) understand 44 3rd-reg.; they learn 45 3rd-iō; they desire

2 1 petitis 2 fugiunt 3 tangō 4 dūcis 5 pellimus 6 iacit 7 bibunt 8 emitis 9 claudis 10 premō 11 tegimus 12 frangunt 13 canit 14 nōscitis 15 legis 16 currimus 17 cadis 18 geritis 19 mittit 20 agunt 21 pōnimus 22 capiō 23 relinquitis 24 vīvit 25 rēgunt 26 facimus 27 dīcimus 28 cernis 29 crēditis 30 scrībō 31 crēdit 32 dēscendimus 33 trahunt 34 discēditis 35 cōgit 36 iungis 37 incipit 38 vertimus 39 crēscō 40 dīvidunt 41 interficimus 42 quaeris 43 intellegis 44 discit 45 cupit

3 1 dīvidis 2 dīcō 3 mittitis 4 quaerimus 5 pōnunt 6 bibit 7 legit 8 cupit 9 emimus 10 frangunt 11 interficit 12 scrībimus 13 crēditis 14 discēdunt 15 incipit 16 regit 17 claudit 18 facimus 19 canō 20 crēscunt 21 dūcis

4 1 D 2 J 3 G 4 B 5 C 6 I 7 A 8 H 9 L 10 E 11 F 12 K

5 vērum – true; deum – god; pāce – peace; ante – before; ancorās – anchors;
quattuor – four

UNIT 4

1 1 laetitiae *joys* 2 noxa *(the) harm;* noxārum *of (the) harms;* noxīs *to a/the
harm* 3 fēminae *to a/the woman;* fēminā *by a/the woman* 4 amīcitiīs *by (the)
friendships* 5 lacrimae *of a/the tear* 6 agricolās *(the) farmers* 7 deam *(the)
goddess* 8 vītīs *by means of (the) lives* 9 īnsidiae *to a/the ambush;* īnsidiā *by
means of a/the ambush* 10 cōpiae *of a/the supply* 11 comae *(the) hair* 12 turba
(the) mob; turbārum *of (the) mobs;* turbīs *to (the) crowds*

2 fēmina, aquilam 2 fēminae, fābulam, puellīs 3 rēgīna, īnsulae, servās 4 nauta,
aquilam, sagittā 5 turba, laetitiā 6 agricolae, prōvinciae, terram, tenebrārum
7 turba, fābulam, fīliae, rēgīnae 8 dea, corōnam, victōriae, incolae, patriae
9 rīpa, viam 10 linguā, poēta fābulam 11 agricolae, fīliae, pugnam 12 noxam,
īnsulae 13 fortūnā, fīlia, deae, silvam 14 dea, īnsulam, undīs 15 agricola, umbram,
portae 16 īra, deae, memoriam 17 poena, aquam, nymphīs 18 stellīs, lūnā,
praedam, vīllā 19 animam, flammīs, ārae 20 fābulam, iniūriae, litterīs

3 [Note that *a(n)* (e.g. *a boy*) or nothing (e.g. *boys, wine*) can be replaced by
the in the following translations (e.g. *the boy, the boys, the wine*) and vice versa]
1 A woman carries the crown of the queen into the country house. *or* A woman
carries the crown for the queen into the country house. 2 The inhabitants of the
islands sing because of joy. 3 The daughters of the sailor and poet do not remain
in darkness but they run into the forest. 4 I do not find the loot because of
the shadow of the moon. 5 An eagle sees dinner in the water. 6 We believe the
report of the inhabitants about the goddess. 7 When are you (pl.) coming to
the island? 8 The arrows of the nymphs fall onto the riverbank. 9 We love the
stories of the country and of the island. 10 Inhabitants fear the anger of the
goddess.

4 1 Fēminae corōnās rēgīnārum in vīllīs portant. 2 Incola īnsulae laetitiīs canat.
3 Fīlia nautārum poētārumque nōn in tenebrīs manet sed in silvās currit. 4 Umbrīs
lūnārum praedās nōn inveniō. 5 Aquilae in aquīs cēnās vident. 6 Fāmīs incolae
dē deīs crēdimus. 7 Quandō ad īnsulās venītis? 8 Sagitta nymphae in rīpās cadit.
9 Fābulam patriārum īnsulārumque amāmus. 10 Incola īrās deārum timet.

5 1 A 2 L 3 K 4 D 5 H 6 G 7 B 8 E 9 I 10 J 11 F 12 C

6 aurās (Unit 2, sentence 6); fossae (3, 4); concordiā (3, 5); ancorās (3, 11)

REVIEW OF UNITS 1–4

A   1 **intexunt** – the penult because it is followed by *x*; 2 **īnfandum** – the penult because it is followed by two consonants; 3 **lacrimīs** – the antepenult because the penult is light; 4 **procul** – penult; 5 **vīribus** – antepenult because the penult is light; 6 **dēlēcta** – penult because it has a long vowel; 7 **reditū** – antepenult because the penult is light; 8 **nōtissima** – antepenult because the penult is light; 9 **suspecta** – penult because it is followed by two consonants; 10 **ecce** – penult; 11 **amor** – penult; 12 **refūgit** – penult because it has a long vowel; 13 **comitante** – penult because it is followed by two consonants; 14 **obtulerat** – antepenult because the penult is light; 15 **īnsonuēre** – penult because it has a long vowel

B   1 we love 2 they love 3 you teach 4 s/he, it comes 5 veniunt 6 doceō 7 amat 8 docētis

C   1 you seize 2 you lead 3 they lead 4 capiunt 5 dūcis 6 capimus

D   1 genitive plural 2 accusative singular 3 genitive singular, dative singular, nominative plural 4 dative plural, ablative plural 5 accusative plural 6 ablative singular

UNIT 5

1   1 deus *god*; deōrum *of the gods* 2 somnium *dream* 3 aurīs *to objects made of gold; by means of objects made of gold* 4 vēlōrum *of the sails* 5 templa *temples* 6 mundō *to the world; by the world* 7 ventus *wind*; ventōrum *of the winds* 8 campī *plains* 9 somnīs *to the sleeps; by the sleeps* 10 caelī *of heaven* 11 pontī *seas* 12 antrō *to the cave; by the cave*

2   [Note that *a(n)* (e.g. *a boy*) or nothing (e.g. *boys*, *wine*) can be replaced by *the* in the following translations (e.g. *the boy*, *the boys*, *the wine*) and vice versa] 1 They throw rocks against the walls of iron. 2 Branches remain in the streets. 3 The son of a sailor announces a story about the garden of the gods and goddesses. *or* The son announces a story about the garden of the gods and goddesses to the sailor. 4 A sailor always brings food to the horses. *or* A sailor always brings food by means of the horses. 5 Today we drink wine! 6 Bulls move into the field of a farmer and they stand there. 7 The wolf of the forest kills a bull and a horse. 8 The queen gives food to the crowds and the men divide the food for (their) sons and daughters. 9 The people of the island live in caves and sleep there. 10 The boys of the allies of the island hear the words of the goddess and they are not afraid. 11 A servant flees out of the country house of the master and he hastens to the land of the neighbours. 12 When the inhabitants of the island see the barbarians, the women and men take weapons and swords of iron. 13 The eyes and hair of the god shine, the arms of the god are strong, and the mind of the god burns. 14 S/he holds hatred of barbarians in memory. 15 The queen gives tasks to the crowd. 16 The people build walls around the camp by means of slaves. 17 The barbarian wages war against the inhabitants of the town. 18 The crowd seeks the aid of the gods because of the danger of war. 19 Because of (his) help the people give a reward to the boy. 20 A number of children sing for the queen in the place.

3 1 Portās mūrī fīnitimī claudunt. 2 Līberī odiō barbarōrum flent. 3 Ventus valet et pontus nautās ad īnsulam portat. 4 Fīlius deae aquilam in caelō invenit et taurum gladiō interficit. 5 Rēgīna imperat vulgum ad antra currere. 6 Crēdimus verbīs nymphae. 7 Somnus animum capit quandō vir bibit. 8 Vēlīs et auxiliō rēgīnae populus discēdit. 9 Poēta fābulās līberīs oppidī scrībit. 10 Incolae mūrum ferrī aurīque aedificant circum agrum.

4 1 C 2 L 3 B 4 A 5 I 6 G 7 F 8 H 9 K 10 D 11 E 12 J

5 asȳlum (Unit 2, sentence 1); dōna (2, 4); iussa and verba (2, 6); deum (3, 3); ōtiō (3, 9); volturiōs (3, 10); pontō (3, 12); cōnsōlandō and minandō (4, 1); gaudium (4, 2); stabula (4, 4); tēlōrum (4, 7); armōrum and studiō (4, 8)

Reading: *Hercules and the Serpents I*

Hercules, son of Alcmena, lives in Greece. He is a strong man. Juno, the queen of the gods, hates Alcmena. She wants to kill the song of Alcmena. The goddess therefore sends two serpents into the home of Alcmena.

In the middle of the night they come into the bedroom, where Hercules sleeps. Alcmena does not place (her) son in bed, but in a big shield.

UNIT 6

1 1 magna 2 magnō 3 magnam 4 magnīs 5 magnī (gen. sg. and nom. pl.), magnō (dat. sg.) 6 magnī 7 magnus 8 magnās 9 magnōrum 10 magnā 11 magnō 12 magnum

2 [Note that *a(n)* (e.g. *a boy*) or nothing (e.g. *boys*, *wine*) can be replaced by *the* in the following translations (e.g. *the boy*, *the boys*, *the wine*) and vice versa] 1 We find high sails in the deep sea. 2 The friends build wide and high walls for the people of the town. 3 Why do you come (sg.) to the small country house? 4 The man seizes by means of (his) long arms eagles for the crowd. 5 Many barbarians run onto the island and they fight against the prosperous inhabitants. 6 A sole boy places a long branch onto the altar of the beautiful goddess. 7 The tired sailors seek firm land. 8 The black hair of the daughter of

the queen does not move by means of the slow wind of the sky. 9 The poet writes about a white bull and a radiant nymph. 10 Stars do not shine in the dark cave. 11 People grow a public garden. 12 The teacher teaches about ancient people. 13 The neighbours buy new, strong horses. 14 The great town extends into the good field. 15 An enemy kills the queen by means of bad wine. 16 S/he seizes the free girls by means of treachery and sells (them) to barbarians. 17 Boys and girls do not know the unknown and blind poet of many letters. 18 S/he sends to the famous queen black horses, gold, and radiant iron. 19 The joyful people sing with joy in the holy and pure place to the worthy master. 20 The wrathful goddess makes wild winds, a rough sea, high waves, and black darkness for the wretched sailors.

3 1 Laetitiā populum īnsulae magnae rēgīna bona rēgit. 2 Sociī prosperī auxilium fīliō miserō nautae malī dant. 3 Umbra tenebrārum implet locum īrā deōrum. 4 Lupī ferī candidīque ē silvā profundā discēdunt. 5 In campō lātō in tenebrīs flammā aurum inveniunt. 6 Dēfessī sōlīque (dēfessae sōlaeque *if women*) cibum et arma petimus ā nostrīs fīnitimīs. 7 Cūr litterās longās pulchrae fīliae rēgīnae scrībis? 8 Virī taurum malum interficiunt et in templum trahunt. 9 Quandō vīta nova incipit incolīs miserī oppidī? 10 Fābulam dīgnam nōn dīcit vulgō iūcundō.

4 1 F 2 E 3 I 4 H 5 B 6 G 7 D 8 A 9 K 10 J 11 L 12 C

5 mea (Unit 2, sentence 5); rīdicula (2, 8); nūdō (2, 10); vērum (3, 1); parvum (3, 2); cava (3, 4); parvae (3, 5); contermina and alta (4, 4); praecipuō (4, 8); vānīs (5, 4); candidā (5, 7)

Reading: *Hercules and the Serpents II*

The serpents secretly approach the shield. Then Hercules moves the shield, because he comes out of sleep. Hercules is not afraid. He holds the serpents with (his) small hands and squeezes (their) necks. The boy is stronger than animals. He kills them.

UNIT 7

1 1 dē caelō obscūrō 2 in pontum 3 ā castrīs lātīs 4 apud nostram fīliam 5 prope mūrum altum vīllae 6 sine auxiliō incolārum dēfessōrum 7 per viam in oppidum 8 dē fābulā poētae clārī 9 intrā hortum pulchrum 10 ante bellum inimīcum 11 ob/propter prētium aurī 12 laetitiae familiae meae causā/grātiā 13 contrā barbarōs ferōs 14 ex aquā et ā rīpā 15 Stellae circum prōvinciam quiētam fulgent. 16 Propter/Ob somnium puerī sacrī timēmus. 17 Antīquī ursae magnae in caelō aureō crēdunt. 18 Cibum in antrō obscūrō prope nostrum oppidum invenīs. 19 Populī bonī causā/grātiā canunt līberī iūcundī. 20 Cum armīs terram lātam regimus.

2 1 N 2 A 3 G 4 J 5 T 6 E 7 H 8 L 9 M 10 D 11 F 12 S 13 B 14 I 15 V 16 Y 17 K 18 C 19 U 20 O 21 W 22 P 23 R 24 X 25 Q

3 **eōrum** – their; **eius** – his; **eī** – to him; **fīnibus** – borders; **erat** – there was; **potentissimōs** – most powerful; **firmissimōs** – most stable; **trēs** – three

Reading: *Hercules and the Serpents III*

Alcmena, the mother of the boy, hears the noise and arouses (her) husband from sleep. He snatches a sword and hastens into the bedroom. When he enters, he sees Hercules. The boy is laughing and shows with joyful eyes the dead serpents. This is the first story of the Greek poets about the life of Hercules.

UNIT 8

1 1 Manner 2 Price 3 Cause 4 Respect 5 Manner 6 Respect 7 Means 8 Price 9 Description 10 Respect 11 Description 12 Cause 13 Means 14 Manner 15 Respect 16 Respect 17 Description 18 Cause 19 Means 20 Price

2 1 G 2 H 3 E 4 L 5 I 6 J 7 A 8 B 9 C 10 K 11 F 12 D

3 -e

Reading: *Hercules Kills His Family I*

The young Hercules defends Thebes from enemies. The king of the town adorns Hercules with great rewards. He gives his own daughter to him in marriage. Hercules leads a happy life with (his) wife, but after a few years he suddenly falls into anger. With (his) own hands he kills (his) three sons.

UNIT 9

1 1 nūntiābās 2 cavēbat 3 nocēbant 4 dīcēbam 5 audiēbāmus 6 crēscēbant 7 cupiēbam 8 tenēbās 9 habitābat 10 tegēbātis 11 bibēbāmus 12 vidēbās 13 veniēbant 14 properābās 15 flēbātis 16 pugnābat 17 currēbant 18 gerēbātis 19 interficiēbātis 20 vīvēbam 21 canēbātis 22 fugiēbāmus 23 terrēbam 24 scrībebat 25 dābās 26 tacēbant 27 amābam 28 claudēbam 29 crēdēbātis 30 sciēbātis

2 1 They were fortifying the high walls of the camp. 2 The small children of the men and women were afraid because of the anger of the queen. 3 A fortunate inhabitant was finding gold in the field. 4 On account of the bad and wild battle of the neighbours we were leaving our towns. 5 Onto the holy altar a worthy servant girl was placing a branch of the forest. 6 When were you (pl.) reading joyful stories of the unknown poet? 7 Between the tired horse and small wolf a great bull was standing. 8 Enemies were sailing to our country. We were afraid. 9 Out of the beautiful garden we were calling the slow master. 10 You (sg.) were hastening into the cave. What were you (sg.) doing there?

3 1 Mundum deus regēbat. 2 Post pugnam magister līberōrum flēbat. 3 Auxilium dominī petēbat. 4 Poēta ignōtus scrībēbat epistulās amīcās novāsque populō dīgnō. 5 Agrum lātum et asperum agricolae emēbāmus.

4 1 C 2 L 3 K 4 J 5 D 6 B 7 I 8 H 9 E 10 F 11 A 12 G

5 miscēbant (Unit 4, sentence 2); tendēbant (4, 5); dūcēbās (4, 10)

Reading: *Hercules Kills His Family II*

Note **From Units 9 through 12 the translations of the past tense verbs are clunky since the student has not yet learned the perfect tense.**

On account of this most cruel deed Hercules was living with great sadness. He wanted to atone for this greatest fault. He decided therefore to go to the famous Delphic oracle. There in the temple the wife of Apollo, Pythia by name, gave advice to men. Apollo moreover was teaching (his) wife. Pythia knew the wishes of Apollo and was announcing them to men.

UNIT 10

1 1 you (sg.) will teach 2 I will be strong 3 s/he, it will burn 4 they prepare 5 you (pl.) will depart 6 s/he, it will think 7 we will desire 8 I will decide 9 s/he, it falls 10 s/he, it will flee 11 s/he, it will sing 12 they will believe 13 you (pl.) harm 14 we will drink 15 s/he, it will turn 16 they depart 17 s/he, it will save 18 we will laugh 19 s/he, it will fight 20 you (pl.) will feel 21 we will see 22 s/he, it seizes 23 s/he, it will break 24 you (sg.) will leave 25 s/he, it warns 26 s/he, it will run 27 I will open 28 we will close 29 you (sg.) will buy 30 I will think

2 4 parābunt 9 cadet 13 nocēbitis 16 discēdent 22 capiet 25 monēbit

3 1 We will find the gold of the queen. 2 Today I know. Tomorrow I will not know. 3 After the war we will build a new wall of iron. 4 When will you (sg.) run through the forests into the waves of the water? 5 The gods will give a cruel punishment to the hostile inhabitants out of anger. 6 Great branches press against the country house. 7 Because of the injury of the eyes the unfriendly poet will never see. 8 I will fight with the enemies, and I alone will rule the island with great joy. 9 The sailors are afraid because of the darkness of the deep sea. 10 Before the dinner the daughters of the man will feed the horses on the riverbank.

4 1 Inimīcōs ferōs sagittīs parvum in antrum premēs. 2 Viam ad oppidum aedificābō. 3 Nostrōs fīnitimōs miserōs servābit dea. 4 Cēnam vulgō parābunt. 5 Crās fulgēbit stēlla.

5 1 C 2 I 3 G 4 E 5 K 6 D 7 F 8 J 9 L 10 A 11 B 12 H

Reading: *Hercules Kills His Family III*

Pythia was hearing the words of Hercules. When the sad man was making (his) story, Pythia was saying: "You will arrive to the city of Tiryns. There you will remain and you will seek Eurystheus, king of the town. When you will find him, he will order you. You will atone for your fault."

When Hercules was hearing the words of Pythia, he hastened to the city. There he was making himself servant to Eurystheus. He was serving Eurystheus for twelve years and was accomplishing twelve tasks. He was only atoning for the greatest and most cruel fault by the tasks.

REVIEW OF UNITS 5–10

A 1 nominative singular, accusative singular 2 genitive singular, nominative plural 3 genitive plural 4 dative plural, ablative plural 5 nominative singular 6 nominative plural, accusative plural

B 1 meum 2 meum 3 meās 4 meōrum 5 meīs 6 meae

C trāns, ante, prō, cum, causā, sine

D 1 means 2 means and cause 3 manner and price

E 1 you were teaching 2 s/he, it will seize 3 you will love 4 we were coming 5 they will lead 6 amābat 7 capiēbant 8 docēbitis 9 dūcēbam 10 veniēmus

UNIT 11

1 1 possunt 2 sunt, possunt 3 potēs 4 sum 5 est 6 potest 7 estis 8 possunt 9 possunt 10 sunt

2 1 poterant; poterunt 2 erant, poterant; erunt, poterunt 3 poterās; poteris
4 eram; erō 5 erat; erit 6 poterat; poterit 7 erātis; eritis 8 poterant; poterunt
9 poterant; poterunt 10 erant; erunt

3 1 H 2 I 3 K 4 C 5 B 6 D 7 G 8 J 9 L 10 E 11 F 12 A

Reading: *The Nemean Lion (Labor I), part 1*

A terrifying lion was rendering dangerous a field near the town Nemea. Eurystheus
was ordering Hercules to kill this wild animal. The brave man was entering the
forests. In these forests the lion was living. In vain for hours Hercules was
searching the wild beast. Finally after hours the monster appeared. It was walking on a narrow path. Hercules wanted to wound the wild beast out of the dense
forest, but he was not catching it. The arrows of Hercules were falling onto the
ground, because the monster indeed had rough skin.

UNIT 12

1 1 verb (remembering) 2 description 3 value 4 material 5 objective [could
be subjective if *his family* is doing the loving] 6 partitive; verb (accusing)
7 verb (forgetting) 8 characteristic 9 material 10 verb (accusing) 11 subjective
12 partitive 13 description 14 value 15 characteristic 16 objective [could be
subjective if the *city* is doing the attacking] 17 verb (forgetting) 18 verb (accusing)
19 possession 20 subjective

2 1 C 2 J 3 H 4 A 5 E 6 F 7 L 8 I 9 B 10 K 11 G 12 D

3 1 -is 2 -ērum

Reading: *The Nemean Lion (Labor I), part 2*

The lion with anger was now observing the man behind the trees. Quickly it
was running to him. The wild animal wanted to tear the man to pieces. Hercules
was throwing arrows into the ground. With a great (piece of) wood, which he
always carried, he wanted to dash the head of the wild animal to pieces. But in
vain! Then the strongest man was seizing the neck and was squeezing (it). The
lion was opening (its) great mouth, which wanted to devour Hercules. But the
hands of Hercules were strong, and the wild animal fell onto the earth dead.

UNIT 13

1 1 rēxistis 2 crēdidimus 3 amāvit 4 nōvī 5 cōnsuēvistis 6 docuērunt 7 cēpit
8 meministī 9 ōdimus 10 parāvistis 11 vīdit 12 portāvī 13 audīvistī 14 negāvērunt
15 cecinimus

2 1 Why do you (pl.) not remember the ancient battles? You will learn. 2 The new ally bought a horse for a good price. 3 The sailors set sail for the new land. 4 They killed the unknown blind man with a sword of iron. 5 We sang to the god of the deep sea. 6 I left, because I feared. 7 I felt a cruel danger in my sleep. 8 Why did you (pl.) remain with the inhabitants in the cave of great darkness? 9 The inhabitants placed onto the altar the golden crown of the beautiful queen. 10 They are accustomed to build a high wall between gardens and fields.

3 1 Quandō deum ventōrum vīdistī? 2 Cūr fābulae poētae caecī nōn meministis? 3 Litterās servī nōn lēgit vulgus. 4 Ad rīpam laetitiā cucurrimus. 5 Dē oppidō per portās mūrōrum altōrum equī dēscendērunt.

4 1 G 2 I 3 A 4 E 5 B 6 J 7 H 8 K 9 F 10 C 11 D 12 L

5 coepērunt (Unit 2, sentence 11); īnstituistī (2, 12); vīdī (4, 4); disiēcit (5, 6); ēvertit (5, 6); coepit (6, 6); fuit (6, 11); commīsērunt (7, 20); ēmit (8, 5); vendidī (8, 9); mūtāvit (8, 12); fēcistī (10, 12); fuit (12, 2)

Reading: *The Nemean Lion (Labor I), part 3*

Hercules now carried the wild beast back into the town on (his) shoulders. Many men and women inhabited the town.

They were greatly rejoicing, when they saw Hercules with the monster. Now they were free from the dangerous monster. They gave great rewards to Hercules. Hercules moreover carried the skin of the wild animal for a close friend.

UNIT 14

1 1 valuerās 2 posuerit 3 properāverō 4 incēperātis 5 ōderint 6 habuerit 7 aperuerant 8 mūnīverimus 9 dīxerāmus 10 fulserant 11 responderitis 12 nōverāmus 13 relīquerat 14 patuerit 15 cecinerat 16 coēgerint

2 1 After the boys had come, we were happy. 2 When will you (sg.) have built a new country house? 3 Good food had been on the broad altar of the cave. 4 The inhabitants of the island remembered the fields within the fatherland. 5 They will not sail when a bad wind will have begun through the waves of the deep sea. 6 Why had you (pl.) written a joyful letter to the queen? She will not respond. 7 The slow and tired wolves had not given harm to our neighbours. 8 The son of the female slave and of the male slave will have seen the long hair of the beautiful and free girl. 9 The crowd had fought against the barbarians, when they killed the horses of the queen by means of swords of iron. 10 In the ancient world many poets had been blind and unknown.

3 1 A 2 F 3 C 4 G 5 K 6 E 7 D 8 B 9 H 10 I 11 L 12 J

4 serv<u>om</u>

Reading: *The Lernean Hydra (Labor II), part 1*

A short time afterwards Eurystheus ordered Hercules to kill the Hydra. It was
another monster, Hydra by name.

It was devastating the fields around Lerna. The monster had nine mortal heads.
The tenth head moreover was immortal. Hercules went by means of a chariot to
the place, where Hydra was living. The brave man aroused the monster with arrows.
It approached Hercules with terrifying sounds. He was hardly scared. He snatched
the neck with (his) left hand and cut away the nine heads one after another. But
he was working in vain. Two new heads grew in the place of each head.

UNIT 15

1 [*the* may be dropped in all of these answers] 1 guests 2 by means of peace
3 for the flowers; by means of flowers 4 sea 5 names 6 women 7 for the head
8 of the star 9 of praises 10 for the laws; by means of laws 11 journeys 12 of
feet 13 work 14 for the herd 15 by the age 16 for brothers; by means of brothers
17 courage 18 of time 19 air 20 air 21 chest 22 for the wound 23 of the fathers
24 mouths 25 weather 26 horsemen 27 of the sun 28 legion 29 lion 30 by means
of a seed

2 1 hospes, hospitem 2 pācibus 3 flōrī, flōre 4 aequora 5 nōmen 6 mulier,
mulierem 7 capitibus 8 sīderum 9 laudis 10 lēgī, lēge 11 iter 12 pēdis 13 opera
14 gregibus 15 aetātibus 16 frātrī, frātre 17 virtūtēs 18 temporum 19 āerēs
20 āerēs 21 pectora 22 vulneribus 23 patris 24 ōs 25 tempestātēs 26 eques
27 sōlum 28 legiōnēs 29 leōnēs 30 sēminibus

3 1 No one had seen my sister and tall brothers. 2 The leader placed tired
soldiers into the legion because of the Roman customs. 3 Farmers flee from
the countryside because of the smell of the cattle. 4 Enemies fought with our
soldiers. After the war our men were seeking aid from the sisters of the king
and from the queen. 5 We will throw the blind poet into a dark prison because
of crimes against the honour of the state. 6 The author of letters and of books
made a great work for the state and the common people. 7 A happy boy found
seeds of flowers under a high tree. 8 Why does the work of men break the body?
9 The dogs of the soothsayer drink the blood of a bull. 10 I will say the rumour
to my mother, because I do not understand. 11 The son of the neighbours hates
the crimes of the enemy. 12 The guardians of the altar stand before the soothsayer.
13 The smell of flowers will extend into the small country house. 14 The farmer

bought a new herd for a bull. 15 Because of the custom of the holy island men on journeys sleep in the country house of the king and queen. 16 The sun of the world shines and it removes the darkness from the lands. 17 Happy are men and dogs, because the father of the gods will not make storms. 18 Lions found bulls and killed (them). 19 We give praise to the queen, because she is beautiful. 20 No one of the soldiers was able to see the chief of the legion.

4 1 Soror mātris meae hodiē venit. 2 Gladiōs ferrī in equīs equitēs portāre possunt. 3 Lēge rēx virum interficiet propter/ob scelus sanguinis. 4 Cūr clāram legiōnem rēgis bonī nōn vidētis? 5 Quandō cibum multīs canibus faciēs? 6 Meus pater materque tua, quod nōn in carcere sunt. 7 Virtūte vincere poterimus. 8 Custōdēs carceris hominibus/virīs cibum dant. 9 Tempestās ad oppida īnsulae crās veniet. 10 Capita inimīcōrum sunt in antrō.

5 1 C 2 L 3 K 4 B 5 E 6 H 7 F 8 D 9 I 10 A 11 G 12 J

6 coniūrātiōnem (Unit 2, sentence 2); hominum (2, 3); patris (2, 6); corpore (2, 10); flūmina (3, 4); pāce (3, 9); ōs (3, 11); lustrāmina (3, 12); adūlātiōnem (4, 2); mortis (4, 3); gregibus (4, 4); amōre (4, 5); collem (4, 6); multitūdine (4, 7); generis (4, 7); fontis (4, 10); ratēs (4, 12); virginis (4, 12); urbis (5, 2); ratēs (5, 6); aequora (5, 6); sale (5, 7); parte (5, 11); caecitātem (5, 12); mentis (5, 12); cantiōnem (6, 2); admonitiōne (6, 9); adulēscentis (6, 9); murmure (6, 12); fīnibus (7, 1); flūmine (7, 2); partēs (7, 3); fīnibus (7, 4); tempus (7, 11); inīquitātem (7, 18); ōre (8, 1); morte (8, 5); immortālitātem (8, 5); urbis (8, 6); hominēs (8, 7); virtūte (8, 8); dote (8, 9); magnitūdine (8, 10); pollicis (8, 11); crassitūdine (8, 11); pāce (8, 12); cervīcibus (9, 6); orīgine (9, 8); ratiōne (9, 8); frātrem (9, 10); hērēdem (9, 10); aequoris (10, 5); mentem (10, 7); canibus (10, 9); vicem (11, 4); comitēs (11, 10); auctōritātis (12, 1); mortis (12, 4); caedis (12, 5); hospitem (12, 6); iūdicum (12, 7); lēgis (12, 7); dōtis (12, 8); nōmine (12, 8); temporis (12, 9); suavitate (12, 9); iūra (13, 1); lēgēs (13, 1); lībertātem (13, 1); temporum (13, 3); puppe (13, 5); pede (13, 5); certāminis (13, 10); tempore (14, 2); amōris (14, 8); cōnsulem (14, 9)

Reading: *The Lernean Hydra (Labor II), part 2*

Hercules asked, "What should I do? In this way I will never be able to kill the wild animal." Therefore with his free hand he lit a fire and scorched the nine heads with a burning wood. He was able to do this because they were mortal. But the brave man was not able to kill the tenth head. Therefore he buried it in the ground and placed a large stone upon it. Hercules now had to kill also the body of the monster. He divided into two parts the wild animal with (his) swords. The blood flew from the body of the monster just like a river. Hercules immersed (his) arrows. The poison, which was in the blood, rendered wounds deadly. This was the second labor, which Hercules completed.

UNIT 16

1 [*the* may be dropped in all of these answers] 1 dentibus *to the teeth* 2 cīvī *to the citizen*; cīve *by the citizen* 3 vātis *of the soothsayer* 4 adulēscentēs *young men/women* 5 vestī *for the clothing*; veste *by means of the clothing* 6 cor *heart* 7 serpentis *of the snake* 8 maribus *to the seas*, *by means of the seas* 9 amnēs *streams*; amnium *of the streams* 10 noctibus *by the nights* 11 famēs *hungers*; *hunger*; famem *hunger* 12 urbs *city*; urbem *city* 13 avis *of the bird* 14 animal *animal* 15 sortibus *for luck*

2 1 We throw fish into the stream and river. 2 The offspring of the king of the gods will make peace and he will build great cities. 3 Between the parts of the town there is a long and high bridge. 4 After they had asked for aid from the neighbours, they found (their) sons and daughter. 5 The foreign enemies will come down from the mountains and they will begin to drag our ships to the sea. 6 High walls will touch the clouds. 7 The farmers give the sheep new honey because of hunger. 8 The man was warning the allies by means of red fire. 9 The enemies frighten by fire the inhabitants of the island. 10 The blind poet remembers the death of (his) mother. 11 We do not know the borders of the world. 12 My mind is in my head. 13 We have bodies, ears, teeth, mouths, hair, hearts, and eyes. 14 Animals are standing in the stream, because they seek fish. 15 The guardians of the holy altar begin the fire with branches. 16 We will build a bridge across the river. 17 Water from clouds covers the world, and people are happy. 18 Because a bad serpent had killed the boy, we sought aid from the king. 19 S/he, it fell from the new bridge into the small stream. 20 We are not able to see the stars because of the many clouds.

3 1 Animālia sacra semper adulēscentēs sorte/fortūnā inveniunt. 2 Hostēs pontem novum frēgērunt. 3 Quandō vīnum prōlibus rēgīnae dabis? 4 Nāvēs parvae candidaeque in pontō vēla dabant. 5 Fame vēnimus in silvam et piscēs in amnibus invēnimus. 6 Moenibus barbarī vīllam meōrum parentum oppugnāre nōn poterant. 7 Nōn vendimus vestem mellī. 8 Vātēs verba cīvibus dīcunt prō igne ferō. 9 Rūmōrēs dē montibus altīs sub aequoribus audīvērunt. 10 Cūr circum orbem terrārum/mundum cucurreritis?

4 1 I 2 A 3 B 4 D 5 G 6 H 7 F 8 E 9 J 10 L 11 K 12 C

Reading: *The Fight with the Centaurs (Labor III), part 1*

While Hercules was making a journey to Arcadia, he came into the region of the Centaurs. One of the Centaurs, Pholus by name, kindly welcomed Hercules and prepared dinner for him. After dinner he asked (for) wine from Pholus, because he loved wine. The Centaurs deposited a jar of the best wine into a cave.

"Whose wine is this?" Hercules asked.

Pholus said, "It is the wine of the Centaurs."

"Can I drink it?" he asked.
"You cannot. The Centaurs will kill me, if I will have opened a jar."

UNIT 17

1 1 ācrēs, fortēs, recentēs 2 ācris, fortis, recentis 3 [nom. pl.] ācrēs, fortēs,
recentēs; [gen. sg.] ācris, fortis, recentis 4 ācrī, fortī, recentī 5 ācer, fortis, recēns
6 ācribus, fortibus, recentibus 7 ācrī, fortī, recentī 8 ācrēs, fortēs, recentēs
9 ācria, fortia, recentia 10 [gen. sg.] ācris, fortis, recentis; [dat. sg.] ācrī, fortī,
recentī; [nom. pl.] ācrēs, fortēs, recentēs 11 ācrium, fortium, recentium 12 ācrium,
fortium, recentium 13 ācribus, fortibus, recentibus 14 ācribus, fortibus, recentibus
15 ācrem, fortem, recentem 16 ācrī, fortī, recentī 17 ācrī, fortī, recentī 18 ācre,
forte, recēns 19 [nom. sg.] ācris, fortis, recēns; [nom. pl./acc. pl.] ācrēs, fortes,
recentēs 20 acrēs, fortēs, recentēs 21 ācrī, fortī, recentī

2 1 Happy men see the sun and they leave the sad cave. 2 A wise bird will
find sweet honey in a small tree. 3 After s/he had killed the mother of a noble
man, the disgraceful one ran out of the town. 4 On account of the fierce and cruel
war the parents of many strong soldiers weep. 5 You (pl.) are not able to stand in
a crowded country house. 6 The swift horse was an animal of the immortal god,
(who was) the king of all men and animals. 7 Why does the rich master not
give to the poor people? 8 They were able to build huge country houses for the
happy (people) of the city. 9 The children of the towns of the island always
give honour to our old (people). 10 S/he wrote serious books about the unhappy
things of the queen and king. 11 After a short year, I will not rule and I will
depart. 12 The light wind did not move the ships of the unhappy sailors. 13 A great
number of our allies will carry aid and will build new walls because of the recent
battle. 14 I do not drink mild wine, but my dogs drink (it). 15 The humble slave
does work, but he does not desire money. He desires a new, free life. 16 All (people)
of the city will be present there. 17 The blind, wise, and old poet teaches the
children of the town. 18 We fear a swift and strong wind in a cruel storm. 19 Who
does not remember an immortal life? 20 The smell of a mild flower was filling
the country house *or* A mild scent of flower was filling the country house.

3 1 Fīnēs castrōrum dominī crūdēlēs claudunt. 2 Deus immortālis hominēs/
virōs omnēs orbis terrārum/mundī fēcit. 3 Hominēs/virī turpēs fēminaeque frequentēs
per viās cucurrerant. 4 Pinguēs ovēs et dulce vīnum vulgō dīvīserit vātēs. 5 Auctor
dulcibus dē odōribus flōrum hortī parvī scrībet. 6 Oculīs ācribus pugnāvērunt
animālia. 7 Servī tristēs senēsque auxilium sapientī ā vāte petent. 8 Vīta mīlitis
est brevis. Sagitta per cor potest interficere. 9 Līberī laetī semper canunt pulchrīs
cum avibus in rīpā. 10 Vestrae patriae nōbilī pugnābitis et nostrum rēgem
humilem servābitis.

4 1 E 2 H 3 K 4 B 5 D 6 J 7 A 8 G 9 F 10 L 11 I 12 C

Reading: *The Fight with the Centaurs (Labor III), part 2*

Hercules did not fear the Centaurs. He opened the jar and he drank most (of it). The Centaurs sensed the smell. From all sides they gathered to the cave. There they saw Hercules drinking with a wide (i.e. opened) mouth. Thus angered they made an attack on the strong man. They did not know that Hercules had deadly arrows. Therefore all, whom Hercules wounded with arrows, ended (their) life wretchedly. The remaining Centaurs, when they had seen the death of friends, turned (their) backs and sought safety by flight. Pholus came out of the cave. Whether by chance or by plan of the gods he had wounded (his) foot lightly by an arrow. Immediately he felt a serious pain and he fell dead on the ground. Hercules, who had fled far after the remaining Centaurs, with great sadness found the dead Pholus. With many tears he buried the body of Pholus.

REVIEW OF UNITS 11–17

A   1 possunt 2 poterās 3 sumus 4 poteritis 5 est 6 poterō 7 erō 8 erant

B   1 objective 2 partitive and material 3 with a certain verb and value

C   1 vēnerant 2 docuī 3 cēpit 4 amāveris 5 dūxistis 6 cēperimus 7 amāverant 8 docuistis 9 vēnerat 10 dūxerō

D   1 animālia, flūmina, mīlitēs, noctēs 2 animālī, flūmine, mīlite, nocte 3 animālium, flūminum, mīlitum, noctium 4 animal, flūmen, mīlitem, noctem

E   1 forte 2 fortem 3 fortēs 4 fortium 5 fortibus 6 fortis (gen. sg.), fortī (dat. sg.), fortēs (nom. pl.)

UNIT 18

1   1 adjective 2 ethical; adjective 3 purpose 4 reference 5 adjective 6 possession 7 reference 8 ethical 9 purpose 10 reference 11 possession 12 adjective 13 purpose; reference 14 purpose 15 adjective

2   1 B 2 H 3 K 4 F 5 E 6 I 7 L 8 C 9 D 10 J 11 A 12 G

Reading: *The Running Stag (Labor IV)*

Eurystheus announced the fourth task. There was a stag, whose head had golden horns. The animal had the greatest speed, because (its) feet were strong. Hercules had found the tracks of the stag. When it saw Hercules, he jumped and ran. Hercules ran after the animal in vain. They ran for months and months, but

Hercules was not able to catch the stag. Finally after a year the stag sat, because it was tired. Hercules seized the body and gave it to the king.

UNIT 19

1 1 s/he, it is being killed 2 I am being ordered 3 they will be led 4 I was being heard 5 s/he, it will be ruled 6 you (pl.) will be fed 7 I will be bought 8 it was being fortified 9 you (pl.) are being seen 10 they are being done 11 they are being excited 12 we were being turned 13 I am desired 14 s/he, it is being given 15 it will be drunk 16 you (sg.) will be called 17 you (sg.) were being joined 18 it is (being) written 19 we are being desired 20 they were being closed 21 we will be dragged

2 1 interficiuntur 2 iubēmur 3 dūcētur 4 audiēbāmtur 5 regentur 6 pāscēris 7 emēmur 8 mūniēbantur 9 vidēris 10 facitur 11 excitātur 12 vertēbar 13 optāmur 14 dantur 15 bibentur 16 vocābiminī 17 iungēbāminī 18 scrībuntur 19 cupior 20 claudēbātur 21 trahar

3 1 Strong words are being written by a famous and wise poet. 2 A great rock was being thrown by the soldiers against the walls of the city of the cruel (people). 3 When will dinner be prepared today? 4 The man will be found in the shadows of the black cave. 5 The smell of the flowers of the garden was being carried through the air by the wind. 6 New walls are being built by the old and young. 7 I will not be seized by my enemies for the sake of sweet peace. 8 A small bird is now seen in the high tree. 9 Sweet honey will be given to the states by the prosperous and rich kings. 10 A war will not be begun today, because the leaders will be able to make peace. 11 The left arm of my ally is broken by an arrow. 12 A new ship was being thrown against the waves by strong storms. 13 Soldiers will be ordered by the leaders to fight. 14 A wild bull will be killed by the arrows of an inhabitant. 15 We are forced to flee. 16 The sheep in the fields of the mountain were being divided by the farmers. 17 The words of the author will be sung by the daughters and sons. 18 The country house was being moved by the winds of the storm. 19 You will be touched by the words of the author and poet. 20 The wolf is being dragged out of our fields, because it was killing sheep.

4 1 Ā puerīs epistulae mittēbantur. 2 Rēgnum nymphārum ā deō aequorum regēbātur. 3 Ovis alba ab agricolā interficiētur. 4 Terra umbrā nūbium tegēbātur. 5 Tristibus ab incolīs auxilium petētur. 6 Perīculum urbis nōn vidētur ā līberīs. 7 Cibus bonus capiētur crūdelibus ab hostibus/inimīcīs. 8 Laetīs ā virīs/hominibus fēminīsque vīnum dulce bibētur. 9 Aurum candidum in terrā avibus in āere vidēbātur. 10 Cūr pellēminī ex agrīs vestrīs?

5 1 A 2 C 3 H 4 I 5 F 6 K 7 B 8 E 9 G 10 L 11 D 12 J

6 implentur (Unit 3, sentence 4); tenēbātur (4, 8); vibrātur (4, 11); compelluntur
(5, 1); tangitur (8, 4); nārrābitur (10, 3); dīcēris (10, 11); terrētur (11, 10);
dētinēbantur (15, 4); sequitur (16, 2); reperiētur (17, 7); accipitur (18, 11).
Sequitur is the deponent verb.

Reading: *The Augean Stables (Labor V), part 1*

Eurystheus ordered now the fifth difficult labor. At that time there was a king,
Augeas by name, who had three thousand cows. The animals were enclosed in
a stable of enormous size. The stable was of terrible dirtiness because it was
not being cleaned. Eurystheus sent Hercules to King Augeas. The king did not
know Hercules. The reason of (his) arrival was not known by the king.

"What will you give, if the stable will be cleaned within twenty hours?"
asked Hercules.

The king did not believe. The task will not be completed so quickly.

"Well," he said, "I will give a tenth part of all the cows, which are in the stable."

UNIT 20

1 1 amāta erat 2 urbs dīvīsa erit 3 rēgēs tāctī erant 4 territī erimus 5 corōnae
positae erant 6 bellum inceptum est 7 cibus noster parātus est 8 populus pulsus
erat 9 mūrus aedificātus erit 10 fābulae scrīptae sunt

2 1 The ships had been driven by the cruel storms. 2 The happy boy was loved
by (his) mother and father. 3 Where had you (sg. f.) been seen? 4 The wine
will have been drunk through the night by the soldiers. 5 Love between the
daughter of the king and the son of the farmer has been felt. 6 The slave had
always been called by the master. 7 The rumour about the immortals was
announced to the world. 8 The smell of flowers had been desired. 9 Rocks and
arrows were thrown against the ramparts of our enemies. 10 The sun has been
covered by the clouds. 11 The country houses have been built by means of
branches of trees. 12 The letter of the poet had been written for the queen. 13 A
wolf will have been killed by the arrows of the boys. 14 Before the war the towns
of the island were fortified by the inhabitants. 15 A number of joyful farmers
had been warned by the son of the sailor about great storms. 16 The old dog
has been bought by a new master. 17 The branches were carried by the water.
18 We (m.) have been forced to go. 19 The words of the famous author will have
been heard. 20 The gold had been found in the dark cave by beautiful women.

3 1 Agrī pulchrōrum flōrum āb hostibus/ab inimīcīs optati/cupītī erant. 2 Iuvenēs
ā senibus rogātī erunt. 3 Puer terrītus ā mātre tentus est. 4 Carmen cantum est
ab omnibus. 5 Quandō vīsī erātis?

4 1 H 2 J 3 E 4 B 5 C 6 K 7 A 8 I 9 D 10 L 11 G 12 F

Reading: *The Augean Stables (Labor V), part 2*

Hercules undertook the task, although he knew it to be difficult. He saw the stable, which had never been cleaned. Indeed not far off from the royal home a river of copious water flowed. Hercules at first with much effort led a ditch to the wall of the stable. Then he broke through the wall and let the water into the stable. There was a horrible noise. The water was rushing within the walls with incredible speed and was carrying all the filth. Hercules, just like a chief, was standing by as a victor after war. He was greatly rejoicing because he had completed the difficult task according to plan against the opinion of all. But he was not happy, because the king gave nothing, which had been promised.

UNIT 21

1 1 Fīlia illīus virī/hominis eum amat. 2 Fīlia eius vēnerat. 3 Haec fīlia illōrum virōrum/hominum laeta est. 4 Hanc fīliam hōrum virōrum/hominum sciō/nōvī. 5 Quandō fīliam eōrum/eārum vīdistī? 6 Fortūnā/sorte suā aurum invenient. 7 Fortūnā/sorte illā bellum gerēmus. 8 Hōrum omnium meministī. 9 Rēx ille hanc īnsulam rēxit. 10 Illī deī gladiōs eīs dant.

2 1 The moon shines and its light covers this land. 2 Those sailors were on that deep sea. 3 His father is silent because he sleeps. 4 We will drink that wine of their (f.) garden. 5 This reward was given to this soothsayer by that god. 6 This blind poet had written that letter to her/him. 7 When did you (pl.) find these places? 8 The country houses of this town will be built by them by means of those rocks. 9 Their (m.) children ran in the forest and there they sang to those animals. 10 That one (m.) was killed by this arrow. 11 He says his own story to (his) son. 12 He says his (someone else's) story to (his) son. 13 Through these high gates those soldiers of that city will come. 14 This smell of those flowers is in the air. 15 That soldier will have been killed by his own wounds. 16 Those ones (m.) had not been able to sail because of those serious storms. 17 In that crowded city there is neither food nor water. 18 The queen gave to his wife this sweet honey. 19 His sister reads the books of those famous authors. 20 They do not hear their own words.

3 1 T 2 S 3 F 4 J 5 L 6 O 7 E 8 G 9 B 10 I 11 H 12 Q 13 R 14 P 15 N 16 D 17 K 18 M 19 C 20 A

Reading: *The Stymphalian Birds (Labor VI), part 1*

After a few days Hercules made a journey to the town Stymphalus. Birds were living in a neighboring lake. They were rendering the entire region dangerous. These birds were horrible. They were able to pierce through all things with (their) sharp beaks. Many men were living in that region. Many had been killed by them. Hercules came to the lake. He had to conquer great difficulty. Indeed the lake consisted not of water, but of mud. The birds were sitting in high trees in the middle of the lake.

UNIT 22

1 1 Ipse istō leōne interfectus erat. 2 Nautae eīdem vīdērunt rēgīnam ipsam. 3 In aetāte equitum ipsī rēgēs pugnāvērunt eōsdem hostēs/inimīcōs. 4 Bibēmus vīnum īnsulae istīus. 5 Eīsdem ā fīnitimīs vīsa erit. 6 Quandō sēnsistī ventum ipsum? 7 In idem aurum iaciēbam meōs oculōs. 8 Templum istud aedificātur inter nostrōs agrōs. 9 Virī/hominēs caecī eīdem eōsdem librōs poētārum eōrundem lēgerant. 10 Istī deī immortālēs nihil agricolīs pauperibus dant.

2 1 The wicked deeds of that damn man make (his) mother unhappy. 2 I myself loves children. 3 A new storm had forced the men and animals to flee away from the same towns. 4 What does that damn king order? 5 The same farmers killed a herd of sheep, but it does not belong to them. 6 The girl herself of that wretched sailor was similar to that damn woman of yours. 7 We are not able to go into the city itself because of the walls. 8 We heard nothing through the long night from that high mountain itself. 9 Soldiers will have set sail with the loot of that damn province of yours. 10 All night the boy has the same dream. 11 We are tired, because we ran around the wide garden of the master. 12 The crowd of barbarians was near the gate itself. 13 The same letter is being written by him himself. 14 The same moon shone in the time of the ancients, it itself shines today, and it itself will shine for our children. 15 The happy girls saw the same sword of iron of the strong soldier. 16 Because of the strong wind that branch of that damn tree of yours broke my head. 17 You ought to sing to the crowd yourself (nom. fem. sg.). 18 We did not remember the words of the author himself. 19 The beautiful nymph herself will move those rocks of the mountain for the tired sailors. 20 Our allies had carried the bulls into the same caves.

3 1 D 2 G 3 I 4 M 5 T 6 Q 7 O 8 H 9 S 10 E 11 F 12 J 13 C 14 P 15 L 16 K 17 A 18 B 19 R 20 N

Reading: *The Stymphalian Birds (Labor VI), part 2*

Hercules examined the place. "How am I able to drive away the birds? They sit in those trees. How am I able to approach them?" A goddess touched him at the back. She was standing by and was holding two rattles. The rattles had been made by Vulcan out of bronze. She handed them to Hercules, then she vanished. Hercules now climbed a nearby hill and made a fierce noise with the rattles. The birds, thoroughly scared, flew away. Hercules pierced a great part of the birds with arrows. The citizens of that city were freed from danger. They brought great thanks to Hercules.

REVIEW OF UNITS 18–22

A 1 purpose 2 possession and reference 3 ethical

B 1 he will have been taught 2 s/he, it was being heard 3 we will be seized 4 they (f.) have been loved 5 they are being led 6 doctī erātis 7 audiar 8 capta erunt 9 amābāris 10 dūcēmur

C 1 Hic hanc amat. Puer ipse mātrem ipsam amat. 2 Hic huic hās mittit. Poēta ipse rēgīnae ipsī litterās ipsās mittit. *Or if rēgīnae is taken as genitive:* Hic huius hās mittit. Poēta ipse rēgīna ipsīus litterās ipsās mittit. 3 Hīs hunc interficiam. Sagittīs ipsīs virum ipsum interficiam. 4 Huic hī sunt. Rēgī ipsī līberī ipsī sunt.

UNIT 23

1 1 The sailors were wishing to set sail, but the ships were small and the storm was strong. 2 What do you (sg.) prefer? To go onto the island with the mothers of the children or to remain in the country house? 3 We carried away the cruel enemies from the town. 4 You (pl.) go now to the field. There you will feed the animals. 5 The poet, ally of the king, will carry words of the queen to the happy inhabitants. 6 S/he wanted to fight with the neighbours concerning the borders, because he had nothing. 7 This sword was being carried by a solider into that damn battle. 8 They wanted to place a branch of peace onto the altar of the temple, because the gods frightened them in a dream. 9 The country house of the wise man is overtaken by the weapons of the wrathful mob. 10 Food has been collected in the wide forest by the tired son. 11 What does s/he have? S/he wants to offer a fat sheep to the queen. 12 The strong will go into the crowded city, because there they will have good things. 13 In that age the wise had preferred to write, but they did not say words for all people. 14 Why is your daughter carried across the bridge? Because she is not able to run. 15 I had found a beautiful crown. I wanted to give it to the servant of the queen. 16 Where are they going to and what are they carrying? They run to the bank of the stream, because they wish to catch fish by means of branches. 17 The light of the radiant moon and stars had shone onto the water, but the black clouds carried the light away. 18 Even the eyes of men will want to see light in the caves, but they will not be able. 19 The friends of the poet prefer to hear about ancient times. 20 They carry iron and trees into the city for the temple of the goddess.

2 1 Quandō verba illōrum poētārum clārōrum canere volēs? 2 Odōre sanguinis non terrēre māluit frāter meus canēs iūcundōs. 3 Ventus odōrem flōrum fert trāns agrōs lātōs. 4 Nōluerat bellum gerere cīvitās contrā fīnitimōs suōs. 5 Cūr nōluistis manēre hīc apud vīllam, postquam vīnum biberātis? 6 Prosperus fīlius eius in tenebrīs equīs ferīs nōn praeterībātur. 7 Lacrimīs meīs cibum aquamque sapientī ā deā quaerere volō (. . . sapientem deam rogāre . . .). 8 Propter/ob somnium meī sorōris, īvimus/iimus ad patriam nostrī patris. 9 Cūr fert gladium? Eō pācem nōn invenīre potest. 10 Mūrum novum/moenia nova vīllae aedificāre nōlent, quod eum/ea fortis tempestās franget.

3 1 D 2 H 3 A 4 J 5 L 6 K 7 G 8 B 9 C 10 F 11 E 12 I

Reading: *The Cretan Bull (Labor VII), part 1*

Hercules had to complete another labor. Eurystheus now sent him to Crete, where a wild bull was laying waste to the island. Hercules had to carry the bull alive to Greece. He climbed (his) ship and immediately loosened (it), for the wind was greatly suitable. When the ship was approaching the island, a huge storm almost carried the end of his life. A great terror occupied the spirits of sailors. They deposited all hope of safety. But Hercules alone was not frightened. He did not know fear, because he had conquered so many difficulties.

UNIT 24

1 1 Which of the two books will you (sg.) read? 2 The whole world praised a single woman, a beautiful and noble queen. 3 My friend had denied any word in front of the king. There he stood and was silent. 4 Another camp was built by a single man. 5 Some slaves see some masters, other slaves see other masters. 6 You (pl.) will do either one. 7 The farmers seek in all the mountain the wine of the other god. 8 No one will make a long journey, because wild storms harmed the whole town of the neighbours. 9 After the ships had left from the island, the light of neither was seen and neither was found. 10 The ears of these wise animals hear all men. No man knows this. 11 Out of fear of hunger we ask aid from each goddess. 12 By means of which of the harms will the inhabitants of that island be forced to flee? 13 In the bad forest I saw a single beautiful nymph. 14 One soldier was killed by one sword, another soldier was killed by another. 15 You (sg. m.) alone are worthy of money. 16 The branches of this huge tree had fallen onto the land by all the strong winds of the entire world. 17 They do not wish to go into any temple, because they have no money. 18 Which of the fat bulls did the man prepare for his blind ally? 19 You (pl.) hasten to the other city, where their happy friends are. 20 Citizens know the other name of that (damn) city (of yours).

2 1 Utrum scelerum iste (m.)/ista (f.) fēcit? 2 Erat nūllus sanguis post scelus. 3 Dēns ūnus puerī in flūmen cecidit. 4 Volunt illī nautae circum tōtum mundum/ orbem terrārum nāvigāre. 5 Virtūs ūnīus pācem ferre potest. 6 Inimīcī/hostēs neutrum oppidum cēperant. 7 Quod sōlī sunt, timent hī līberī. 8 Ipse lēgit nūllās litterās gravēs. 9 Aliī ad oppidum vēnērunt, aliī ad īnsulam īvērunt/iērunt. 10 Utram amphoram bibēs?

3 1 B 2 A 3 I 4 F 5 E 6 K 7 J 8 C 9 H 10 D 11 G 12 L

Reading: *The Cretan Bull (Labor VII), part 2*

The sea was tranquil, when the sailors drove the ship safe to land. Hercules immediately hastened to the king of Crete and taught him the reason of (his) arrival.

He promised the king, "I will free the island from danger."

The king was affected by great joy. After all had been prepared, Hercules hastened to that region, where the monster was living. He saw the bull. He ran to it and snatched its horns. The monster was strong, but the hands of Hercules held it firmly. Thus Hercules dragged the bull with great effort to the ship and happy, he returned to Greece with the booty.

UNIT 25

1 1 masculine singular genitive – cuius 2 masculine singular nominative – quī 3 masculine plural accusative – quōs 4 feminine singular nominative – quae 5 neuter plural nominative – quae 6 feminine singular dative – cui 7 masculine singular accusative – quem 8 masculine singular ablative – quō 9 feminine plural accusative – quās 10 feminine plural ablative – quibus 11 neuter singular nominative – quod 12 masculine plural genitive – quōrum 13 masculine plural dative – quibus 14 masculine plural ablative – quibus 15 neuter plural genitive – quōrum

2 1 The son, whose father was king, sees the great fields. 2 The slaves killed their master with stones, which they had found in the fields. 3 The poet, whom every one praises, says that that man is bad. 4 The wounds, by which the soldiers had been killed, were serious. 5 The consuls, who have power, write laws for the people. 6 The strong storm, which the farmers saw, was terrifying the sailors. 7 Why do the stars, which sit in the sky, shine? 8 The prison of darkness, into which our enemy has been thrown, is silent. 9 The children, whose father had set sail, were alone. 10 The barbarians carry a battle, which excites the animals through the whole forest.

3 1 Fīliī, quōrum patrēs rēgēs fuērunt, agrum magnum vident. 2 Servus dominōs suōs saxō interfēcit, quod in agrō invēnerat. 3 Poētae, quōs omnis laudat, dīcunt istōs hominēs malōs esse. 4 Vulnus, quō mīles interfectus erat, grave erat. 5 Cōnsul, cui potestātēs sunt, lēgem populō scrībit. 6 Tempestātēs fortēs, quās agricola vīdit, nautam terrēbant. 7 Cūr sīdus, quod in caelīs sedet, fulget? 8 Carcerēs tenebrārum, in quōs sunt iactī inimīcī nostrī, tacent. 9 Līberī, quōrum patrēs vēla dederant, sōlī fuērunt. 10 Pugnās recentēs, quae animal per tōtās silvās excitant, barbarus portat.

4 1 Fīlia poētae quī canem invēnerat bene canit. 2 Tempestās, quae advēnerit, oppida dēlēbit, quae in lītoribus aedificāta sunt. 3 Fēminae, quārum līberī deōs laudant, laetae sunt. 4 Pecūniam dare dēbēs auctōrī, cuius librī omnibus scrīptī sunt. 5 Petīverāmus auxilium ā rēge, quī animōs laetōs nostrōs et somnia nōn frēgit.

5 1 L 2 A 3 H 4 B 5 D 6 F 7 C 8 J 9 K 10 E 11 I 12 G

Reading: *The Man-Eating Horses of Diomedes (Labor VIII), part 1*

After Hercules returned from the island Crete, he was sent to Thrace. The task, which was remaining there for him, was again greatly dangerous. Indeed he had to lead back horses of King Diomedes into this own country. These horses were wild: they were eating the flesh of men. Diomedes threw all foreigners, who entered into his kingdom, to the horses. Therefore Eurystheus said to himself, "Hercules will also be a victim of the horses." The brave man ran into Thrace with great speed. He wanted to complete the task as quickly as possible.

UNIT 26

1 1 Whose wine is this? 2 Did you (pl.) come with him? 3 What kind of weapons had been found? 4 How many soldiers do not wish to fight against the barbarians? 5 From where did the sad boys run? Where are they now? 6 Why do you (sg.) give a reward and praise to the parents? 7 To where does the river go? 8 Why do they drink the blood of that sheep? 9 When will the huge gates of the city be closed? 10 The poet, who had written the many letters is wise, isn't he? 11 Who is not able to hear the words of the holy gods? 12 How will he build new walls? 13 In which dream had he seen the place, in whose temple there was gold and money? 14 How many books will the wretched author have written? 15 Why was I not able to sing to the crowd? 16 Whose mother do you (pl.) know? 17 Does the sun shine today? 18 Why are you (pl.) tired? When will you (pl.) sleep? 19 Will you (sg.) remain with the ones in the town or will you (pl.) go with the others into the city? 20 For what did he sell the wide field?

2 1 Quid līberōs parvōs terret? 2 Quandō dabis nautae pecūniam nostram? 3 Quis agrum dīvīsit? 4 A quō portae mūrī/moenium frāctae sunt? 5 Oppidumne suum mīlitēs mūnient? 6 Cūr/Quam ob rem nōn adestis? Abestis! 7 Quō (modō) fulget sōl per nūbēs obscūrās? 8 Quot fābulās vulgō poēta leget? 9 In cuius memoriā hīc aedificābātur rēgnum pācis? 10 Quō nauta vēla dabat?

3 1 K 2 J 3 F 4 C 5 G 6 L 7 I 8 H 9 A 10 D 11 B 12 E

Reading: *The Man-Eating Horses of Diomedes (Labor VIII), part 2*

Hercules met the king, but Hercules was not able to persuade him with kind words. Then the strong man was moved by anger. He killed the king and threw him to the horses. In this way the cruel king died in the same manner, by which he himself had killed many innocent men. Hercules did not remain long in Thrace. Those who inhabited that region, wanted to create him king. But Hercules was not able to undertake a kingdom, for he had to hand the horses to Eurystheus. Without delay he loosened from the harbor and after a little while he put the safe horses onto the shore of Agos.

UNIT 27

1 1 sē, nostram 2 ego, nōs, tuum 3 vōs, mihi, meum 4 ego, mihi 5 nostrum 6 tū, mē, tū, mē 7 sibi, suum, nōs 8 vestra, nōs vōbīs, 9 tū, tē, mihi 10 nōs, vestrā 11 sibi, nostrī 12 tū, ego, nōs 13 nōbīs, nostram 14 nōs, tē, nostrā 15 suam/suās

2 1 eī/eae 7 is, ipsī/ipsae, eī 10 is 11 eī/eae 13 is, eius 14 ipsum/ipsam 15 is, eōrum/eārum

3 1 You (sg.) were teaching many of us. 2 S/he found him/herself in our temple. 3 The queen will give us a punishment. 4 The poet had written about love of you (pl.) in a joyful letter. 5 My sister saw me, but I was not seen by my brother. 6 Young people were not able to hear themselves but they had been able to hear you. 7 You (pl.) always order us. 8 We announce to you (sg.) the words of that (damn) king (of yours). 9 Why do you (sg.)/are you (sg.) calling me and my sister? 10 The sun sees itself in the river.

4 1 F 2 J 3 C 4 I 5 D 6 H 7 E 8 G 9 K 10 L 11 A 12 B

Reading: *The Battle with the Amazons (Labor IX), part 1*

A race of Amazons consisted entirely of women. They feared no one. They even dared to engage in battle with men. Hippolyta, their queen, had a most famous belt which she had received from Mars. The daughter of King Eurystheus vigorously desired to possess this belt. Eurystheus therefore sent Hercules with soldiers to Asia, where the Amazons lived. "Queen," Hercules said, "You don't know me, do you? From where I have come? Hercules is my name. My master, King Eurystheus, wants your belt. I will carry it with me."

Hippolyta, because she was an Amazon, responded gently: "Now I know the reason of your arrival. If I am able to make the daughter of your master happy, I will willingly do it."

UNIT 28

1 1 Bring the food here! 2 Tell the words of this queen to the king! 3 Do not fear the gods! 4 Doors, be opened! 5 Sing and be happy! 6 Hold the wild wolf! 7 Be ruled by me! 8 Cover the sun with trees! 9 Body be excited, because I am still now tired! 10 See the huge rocks, which have fallen from the high mountain!

2 1a. Be present faithful ones! 1b. Come, come into Bethlehem! 1c. See the born king of angels! 2a. Come, come Emmanuel! 2b. Free the captive Israel, who groans in exile! 2c. Rejoice, rejoice Emmanuel! 2d. Dispel the clouds of night and the fearful dark of night! 2e. Open up the heavenly kingdoms! 2f. Make a safe path above! 2g. And close the ways below!

3 1 C 2 E 3 B 4 K 5 D 6 G 7 J 8 H 9 A 10 L 11 F 12 I

4 īte (Unit 4, sentence 12); frangite (4, 12); cave (5, 5); pellite (5, 9); redde (6, 2); face (15, 1); quaerite (19, 3); pulsāte (19, 3); date (20, 3); cōnsulite (27, 4). **Face** is an archaic form of expected **fac**.

Reading: *The Battle with the Amazons (Labor IX), part 2*

When she heard this, Juno assumed the form of the Amazons and aroused them against the Greeks. "You are wise! Do not believe these men! They have come to you, because they wish to seize your queen and to lead her with them into Greece."

The women were stirred up and immediately they formed a battle line and made an attack on the Greeks. Hercules asked himself, "Why are the Amazons doing this? I ought to resist."

They bitterly fought for a long time. When the queen had been seized, the Amazons sought safety by flight. Hercules said, "Soldiers, we, Greeks, never fight against women. Now, because this battle has ended, we will dare freedom to all the captives." All the Greeks sent the Amazons to (their) homes.

REVIEW OF UNITS 23–28

A 1 ībimus 2 ferunt 3 mālēbam 4 fertur 5 nōn vult 6 vīs

B 1 sōlōrum 2 sōlīs 3 solī (dative), solo (ablative) 4 solīus 5 solum 6 solīus (genitive sg.), solī (dative sg.), solae (nominative pl.)

C 1 cuius 2 quem 3 quōrum (because the verb *to remember* takes the genitive!)

D 1 cūr ~ quam ob rem, quandō, quō modō ~ ut ~ quō 2 –ne suffixed to the first word of the sentence 3 quam 4 quot

E 1 ego, tē 2 nostrum, tuum 3 nōs, vōs

F 1 amā 2 audīre 3 nōlīte capere 4 dūc

UNIT 29

1 1 Boy, where is your brother? 2 Soldiers, come to me! 3 My slave, why have you done nothing? 4 His/her country house is in the country. 5 We will build a new temple in Rome. 6 Girls, carry to me the sweet food, which I wish. 7 At Carthage one is able to see many stars, which shine in the heavens. 8 Brothers, drive the herd of sheep onto the boat! 9 We seek aid in peace and in war from the beautiful goddess. 10 We will come to the servant of the god, who is in Rhodes. 11 We found an eagle, which was on the ground. 12 We have wide fields in Athens. 13 Ally, why do you not want me? 14 At my home (my) friends had remained. 15 Lead the barbarians into the prison, men! 16 Touch, son, the gate of the holy temple! 17 Poet, write a new book! 18 Hear me, animals! 19 Crowded towns are found on Rhodes. 20 Wife, because of danger go with me to that cave!

2 1 K 2 G 3 C 4 A 5 H 6 L 7 J 8 I 9 B 10 D 11 F 12 E

Reading: *Cacus Steals the Oxen (Labor X), part 1*

Hercules drove the cows of Geryon through Spain and Italy. He came with them to the Tiber. "I am tired from the journey," he said. "Peaceful days are given to me. Here I will remain." Not too far at all from a river there was a cave in which Cacus, a horrible monster, lived. He blew fire from (his) mouth. This monster snatched away four cows, while Hercules was sleeping. He dragged them by (their) tails into the cave. The next day as soon as he was stirred from sleep, Hercules noticed the theft. Hercules was not able to know (i.e. find) their tracks. He sought the cows in vain, but he was deceived by false tracks.

UNIT 30

1 1 exclamation 2 adverbial 3 extent of space 4 limit of motion 5 Greek 6 duration of time 7 duration of time 8 adverbial 9 Greek 10 exclamation 11 limit of motion 12 extent of space 13 adverbial 14 Greek 15 extent of space

2 1 G 2 L 3 K 4 A 5 H 6 B 7 E 8 F 9 I 10 J 11 C 12 D

Reading: *Cacus Steals the Oxen (Labor X), part 2*

When he decided to leave, one of his own cows began to bellow. Suddenly four (cows) enclosed in a cave replied the bellow. Thus Hercules knew the place, where the four cows were being hidden. He, angered very much, ran to the cave. But he was not able to enter, because a huge rock was placed in the entrance by Cacus. "What must I do?" he asked himself. After a short time he moved the rock away with great strength. Because the cave was filled with smoke, Hercules was not able to see. Thus he rushed into the cave and snatched the neck of the monster. That one was not able to free himself by any means and soon dead he fell to the ground.

UNIT 31

1 1 Whatever you (sg.) see, do not be afraid! 2 Someone gave me something, but I do not know who. 3 Each one has someone, who loves him. 4 No one had money. The queen alone was rich. 5 I drank nothing. I will drink anything. 6 Those ones run from each thing/Those ones run from each one. 7 Whoever sees that (damn) man, she knows him to be a god. 8 I send nothing to nobody, because a certain (man) found my money. 9 The country houses in Carthage have been thrown into light by the moon, because there was no cloud in the sky. Each (man) was blind. 10 I know no one, who lives here. 11 Each thing frightens my friend. 12 My friend was frightened by something. 13 Divide each thing and give something to each! 14 Beware of the dog! Beware of all animals! Beware of each! 15 Someone wrote me a letter. Whoever wrote it, that one is a good author. 16 When the enemies fight us, no one is strong. 17 Why do you (sg.) do nothing? You ought to do something for us. 18 When will a certain woman, who had been seized by the barbarians come? 19 Who did this? We will ask a certain man, who was here. 20 Whatever, which serves as a harm, we are able to kill.

2 1 Aliquis illam portam clausit. 2 Quidquam nōn poterāmus cernere. 3 Interficite quidcumque vidētis! 4 Aliquis altā dē arbore cecidit. 5 Quaedam meī meminit. 6 Quandō aliquid tangit, quidque in aurum vertit. 7 Rēx lupum cuique dīvīsit. 8 Quidcumque vīnum bonum facit, dēbēmus discere. 9 Nēmō animālia pāverat. 10 Nihil/nīl vīdit, quandō mēcum hīc stetit.

3 1 I 2 L 3 K 4 E 5 C 6 D 7 H 8 B 9 F 10 A 11 G 12 J

Reading: *The Golden Apples of Hesperides (Labor XI), part 1*

Hercules was sent by Eurystheus to the farthest part of the world. He had to snatch away the golden apples of the Hesperides. He did not know the garden, in which the apples were being guarded. He made a journey through many lands and came to the place where Atlas was holding the Earth on (his) shoulder. This place was near to the ocean. "I seek the garden," Hercules said, "I traversed many lands, beloved old man. I have come to this place because I will be helped by you. You indeed alone are able to help me. I know that you to be the father of the Hesperides. Willingly they will do whatever you ask from them, because the Hesperides are your daughters. Help me!"

"Friend," the old man responds, "it is true that the Hesperides are my daughters. I alone am a mortal who knows the place of the garden. Willingly I will help you, if you will hold the Earth for me."

UNIT 32

1 1 aliquī 2 quandam 3 quamcumque 4 ūlla 5 quemque 6 nūllum 7 quibusdam 8 aliquam 9 quōcumque 10 aliquā, alicuius

2 1 quidquam, sibi 2 tū, quae, sē 3 eam 4 vōs 5 nōs, quī, nōs 6 mē 7 quī, sē 8 eī/eae 9 is, tibi

3 1 A certain storm will come. 2 Do you (pl.) know any dangers, which the enemies will make for us? 3 Each rock fell from some mountain. 4 A certain gate had been opened by an unhappy slave. 5 The old do not desire any immortal dream. 6 Common words were being heard in some city. 7 I have no honours. 8 The boy of some woman ran away from the holy temple. 9 Whichever wine you (sg.) drink, I will drink it also. 10 Will you (sg.) bring a reward to him or will you (sg.) lead him into some cave of darkness? 11 Do not weep! There is no harm. 12 Whichever serious wicked deeds those ones did, we ought not be afraid. 13 The king of each city rules with joy. 14 We do not believe certain ancient ones. 15 Some wretched man broke my right arm. 16 S/he does not wish to remain here, because s/he does not have any good fortune. 17 Do you (pl.) send whichever bull to them, which had been seized by you? 18 Certain neighbours sell their own swords, because there is no battle. 19 Each citizen of each city ought to read this book of that author. 20 When will some soldiers save us?

4 1 G 2 E 3 C 4 A 5 K 6 F 7 D 8 I 9 H 10 J 11 L 12 B

Reading: *The Golden Apples of Hesperides (Labor XI), part 2*

Hercules heard this and was affected with great joy. Not in vain had he come to the farthest part of the world.

"Place the Earth," he said, "on my shoulder! Hasten to your daughters! Do not return without the apples!" After Hercules had said these (things), Atlas placed the Earth on his shoulder. The old man immediately ran to the garden.

He persuaded (his) daughters. But the girls do not want to violate the will of
the goddess Juno. They resisted for a long time. But at last they handed the
apples to (their) father. Now Atlas returned without delay to Hercules, because
he wanted to hand the apples over to him. With great joy Hercules saw the old
man. But Hercules was a cunning man. "Beloved old man," he said, "I will
willingly hold the Earth. But hold it for a short time. I want to place something
on my shoulder, because the Earth is so heavy."

Hercules handed the Earth to Atlas. The old man held it. Hercules seized the
apples and with a happy face said: "Old man, I thank you. Unfortunately, I have
to return to Greece. Farewell!"

UNIT 33

1 1 present, active, masculine/feminine, plural, nominative/accusative 2 perfect
participle, passive, masculine, singular, genitive *or* perfect participle, passive,
masculine, plural, nominative 3 future, active, masculine, singular, accusative *or*
future, active, neuter, singular, nominative/accusative 4 perfect participle, passive,
masculine/neuter, plural, genitive 5 perfect participle, passive, masculine/neuter,
singular, dative/ablative 6 future, active, feminine, singular, genitive/dative *or*
future, active, feminine, plural, nominative 7 perfect participle, passive, feminine,
singular, ablative 8 present, active, masculine/feminine/neuter, singular, ablative
9 perfect participle, passive, feminine, singular, accusative 10 present, active,
masculine/feminine, singular, accusative

flente (8) cannot be used with a noun. It would need to be *flentī* when modifying a noun.

2 1 amātūrō frātre 2 mānsā nāvī 3 trāctum caput 4 iactōrum sēminum 5 flentēs
virī 6 ventae tempestātēs 7 rēctārum urbium 8 fulgentia sīdera 9 scrīptō rūmōre
10 fugientem ovem

3 1 Who, drinking the wine, carried nothing to us? 2 I see a man holding his
own daughter. 3 The storm which is going to come frightens us. 4 The god,
praised by the citizens, will give all things to them. 5 The soldiers had stood
there, closing the gate of the walls. 6 The famous poet was killed by a broken
branch. 7 The author will write the words, which had been heard. 8 The laughing
friend begins this work. 9 The boys are about to run into the cave. 10 The
queens will give aid to the seeking girl.

4 1 L 2 I 3 B 4 E 5 F 6 K 7 J 8 H 9 C 10 A 11 G 12 D

Reading: *Bringing Cerberus out of the Underworld (Labor XII), part 1*

After the golden apples had been returned to Eurystheus, only one of the twelve
labors remained. The king greatly feared Hercules. Therefore he wanted to send

him to a dangerous place. It was the place from which he will never able to return. He ordered him to drag the dog Cerberus from Hades into the light. This task was very difficult. No one had been able to complete it. With Mercury as leader Hercules descended into Hades. At first he came to the bank of the river Styx, by which the kingdom of Pluto was confined. It was necessary to cross it. There was no bridge on this river. The shadows of the dead were led across by Charon to the further bank by a boat. This old man was so terrified by Hercules. In no way did he want to lead Hercules across. But Hercules forced him to do it.

UNIT 34

1 (Any of the subordinate conjunctions mentioned in the unit could be used for these answers. To simplify things, only one was chosen for each of the following). 1 The words of the poet having been heard, the boys were happy. 2 Since the storm was serious, the ship was carried to the island. 3 The queen seeing the danger, the soldiers destroyed her temple. 4 Because the rocks are not small, a rampart is being built today. 5 Although s/he was crying, there was nothing, which we had been able to do. 6 The book having been written for the people, all the nobles praise the author. 7 Since time is short, you (pl.) ought to live in peace. 8 With unknown people running, the danger of wolves is announced. 9 The enemies going with their own king through the streets of the land, the people of the towns and cities were silent. 10 Since I am strong, my boys are not afraid of darkness. 11 Someone will lead us to the altar of the temple, because aid was sought from the gods. 12 The loot of that farmer found, you (sg.) will have fields. 13 We believe whatever the king tells us, our town being beautiful and not crowded. 14 The task done, we are home now. 15 The children fleeing from the lion, the feet had been heard in the peace of the night. 16 Since there is no light in the prison, s/he will be able to see no one. 17 What will be done, with the worthy sons of the fatherland having been killed? 18 They drinking good wine, everyone fell into sleep. 19 Soldiers fortifying the camp, we will be saved. 20 I desire many things with a new year having been begun.

2 1 Portā apertā mīlitēs in vīllam īvērunt/iērunt. 2 Quandō ad oppidum miserum ībitis, nūllō ibi vīvente? 3 Cibō ā eius mātre parātō, frātrēs rāmōs portābant. 4 Ignī fortī/valentī dormiunt. 5 Incolīs īnsulae sagittīs interfectīs, est nēmō, quī animālia servāre potest. 6 Eius nōmine malō, nēmō quidquam eī dīcit. 7 Ovibus rūrī stantibus, nūbēs nigrae caelum implēvērunt. 8 Nostrā patriā pulchrā, multī virī/hominēs hūc venīre volunt. 9 Crūdēlibus īnsidiīs imperātīs, legiō nōluit manēre apud inimīcōs/hostēs. 10 Odōre sanguinis sēnsō, parentēs hortum nōn relinquunt.

3 1 A 2 E 3 G 4 L 5 J 6 I 7 O 8 B 9 M 10 C 11 N 12 F 13 H 14 D 15 K

Reading: *Bringing Cerberus out of the Underworld (Labor XII), part 2*

Thus led to the farther [i.e. other] bank Hercules hastened to the seat of Pluto himself. The king, standing at the gates of the city prohibited the strong man. Hercules was not able to enter the kingdom by the will of the king. But wounded by an arrow of Hercules, he changed his opinion and gladly heard the words of Hercules. He found Cerberus and asked Pluto, "Is it permitted for me to carry Cerberus away?" The king of the dead responded, "I will allow this willingly, but after your labor Cerberus will be led back to Hades." Hercules agreed. Then he dragged Cerberus, seized not without great danger, to the city of Eurystheus. When the monster was seen, a great fear seized the soul of the king. Hercules asked with many tears, "Do not keep the monster in the city." Hercules therefore led Cerberus back to Hades. Thus against the opinion of all, the twelve labors, which Eurystheus had commanded, were completed within twelve years. Hercules, freed from the servitude of the king, returned to Thebes with great joy. Now he lived there without cares.

REVIEW OF UNITS 29–34

A   1 Rōmae 2 Carthāgine ~ Carthāginī 3 domī

B   1 fīliī 2 rēx 3 deus 4 socī

C   1 extent of space, duration of time 2 Greek 3 exclamation, adverbial

D   1 Aliquis aliquem amat. Aliquī puer aliquam mātrem amat. 2 Aliquis alicui aliquem mittit. Poēta aliquī rēgīnae alicui litterās aliquās mittit. *Or if rēgīnae is taken as genitive:* Aliquis alicuius aliquem mittit. Poēta aliquī rēgīnae alicuius litterās aliquās mittit. 3 Aliquibus aliquem interficiam. Aliquibus sagittīs aliquem virum interficiam. 4 Alicui aliquī sunt. Alicui rēgī aliquī līberī sunt.

E   1 amantem 2 audīta 3 dūctūrō 4 Capta

F   1 virō audītō 2 adulēscentibus castra aedificantibus 3 antrō flammīs vīsō

UNIT 35

1   1 Whom do you (pl.) believe? 2 Children do not want to please their parents. 3 The god of storms harmed the ships of some sailors. 4 The senate will put a young man in command of the legion. 5 Whoever serves a master, that one is not free. 6 The mother favours not one of her own daughters. 7 The king having been killed by arrows, the queen had not able to forgive the man standing there.

8 The cruel neighbours ordered me to carry gold into the town. 9 They ordered me to remain in the country. 10 The unhappy man envied his happy wife. 11 Spare us serious work! 12 The wild dog does not obey the soldiers. 13 The king of barbarians does not trust us, because we killed his friend. 14 No one will run to help the poet, who was writing beautiful words to each (person). 15 You (pl.) ought to resist their battle with your hands themselves. 16 The horns of the bull will harm no one who will be in the field. 17 The soothsayer ordered them to carry gifts to the goddesses. 18 Who was at the head of all the gods? 19 S/he prefers war to immortal peace. 20 We threw fire into the enemy camp.

2 1 Quandō nymphae pontī nautīs favēbunt? 2 Rēx nōbīs imperat pārēre mātribus nōstrīs. 3 Corōnam ipsam laetitiae antepōnit. 4 Ea nautīs ventōs fortēs indulgēbit. 5 Deī virō/hominī, quī bona mundī/orbī terrārum facit, favent. 6 Puerī invīdērunt agricolae fīliō, quī praemium invēnerat. 7 Quem imperātor vulgō populī praeficiet? 8 Serviam nōn tibi, quī omnia ā mē cēpistī. 9 Quīcumque pācī studet, ille eam inveniet. 10 Cūr alicui fīditis, quem nōn scītis?

3 1 L 2 K 3 G 4 F 5 I 6 C 7 B 8 A 9 D 10 H 11 J 12 E

Reading: *Hercules and His Friend Admetus, part 1*

The brave man making a journey to Thessaly, Hercules entered the house of the king Admetus on a certain day. The king and the guest were good friends. With Ademtus welcoming him with hospitality, the strong man noticed that the king was greatly sad.

"What has happened?"

"Nothing," Admetus responded. "A certain stranger woman has died."

"I do not wish to disturb you, friend. I will spend the night in the house of another friend. I give you the greatest thanks."

"Not in this way, dear friend. I will never allow you to do this. You will remain with me. In the last part of the villa our grief will disturb you minimally."

Because Hercules did not want to offend (his) good friend, he remained in his house.

UNIT 36

1 1 nt. nom/acc. sg. **cornū** 2 dat. and abl. pl. of all genders **domibus, fidēbus, cornibus, senātibus, diēbus, faciēbus** 3 dat. and abl. pl. of all genders **domibus, fidēbus, cornibus, senātibus, diēbus, faciēbus** 4 fem. or masc. nom. sg. **domus, fidēs, senātus, diēs, faciēs**; gen. sg. of all genders **domūs, fideī, cornūs, senātūs, diēī, facieī** 5 fem. acc. pl. **domūs, fidēs, faciēs** 6 masc. and nt. dat. sg. **cornū, senātuī, dieī**; masc. and nt. abl. sg. **cornū, senātū, diē** 7 masc. acc. pl. **senātūs, diēs** 8 fem. and masc. nom. or acc. pl. **domūs, fidēs, senātūs, diēs, faciēs** 9 nt.

nom. and acc. sg. **cornū** 10 gen. pl. all genders **domuum, fidērum, cornuum, senātuum, diērum, faciērum**

2 1 The armies were led out of the camp to some town by the king. 2 The arrows leaving from his bow will begin an attack. 3 Which animals live in this lake? 4 No one was able to do anything, after the queen had been filled by grief. 5 The noble and blind poet will have written the beautiful verses. 6 The senate and kings fight against each other and they will always fight. 7 The trust of the people having been broken, the queen no longer has power. 8 Each remained the entire day in prison. 9 Seize the horns of that wild bull! 10 I will carry by means of my small hands the gift to the temple of the soothsayer. 11 Did you (sg.) see the face of that damn queen, to whom we will give no honour? 12 The farmer does not wish to feed the herd and flock today. 13 Every house of the crowded city had been destroyed by the army. 14 His knees are stronger than mine. 15 The walls having been built, hope of safety will grow. 16 Why is an attack being carried by the hostile barbarians against you? 17 Hasten home, since the thing has begun. 18 Clouds have many faces. 19 The poet writing verses, the nymph gives aid to the author. 20 The eagle of the gods obeys the senate.

3 1 Arcuī mīlitis fortis invideram. 2 Nostrī lūctūs meminisse nōlumus. 3 Fidēs eius erat similis speī illīus. 4 Exercitus proximus contrā miserum senātum impetum fēcit. 5 Ea fortis genibus est. 6 Ante bellum pecūs inter domum oppidumque stetērunt. 7 Sōle altō in caelō fulgente diēs longī sunt. 8 Quaecumque rēs invenīs, eās tenēre dēbēs. 9 Cornibus taurī tāctīs animal cucurrit. 10 Lacus ille manibus sōlīs aedificātus est.

4 1 B 2 E 3 I 4 G 5 D 6 F 7 L 8 K 9 A 10 C 11 J 12 H

Reading: *Hercules and His Friend Admetus, part 2*

He was sitting alone at the table. The servants had to work diligently. Their guest had consumed a great abundance of food and wine. Suddenly Hercules began to sing. The servants, thoroughly terrified, looked at the singing guest.

"What are you looking at? Come and drink with me!"

"We are not able to drink," the servants said.

"Why are you not able to drink?," Hercules asked. "Because a stranger woman has died?"

"Stranger woman? Who said this to you?"

"Admetus himself. The king is not able to be a liar."

"It is so. But Admetus wanted to be hospitable."

"Why are you all so sad? Respond! Tell me. Who is that woman?"

"Alcestis, our queen."

UNIT 37

1 1 difficilius 2 longiōribus 3 terribiliōribus 4 brevior; breviōris 5 cōpiōsiōrēs 6 pulchriōrum 7 iūcundiōrēs 8 sacriōrēs; sacriōris 9 fēlīcior, fēlīcius 10 sapientiōrum

2 1 The more serious the war, the more frightened are the people of the town. 2 A rather strong man will not be seized and killed. 3 The rather huge animals ran through the forest at night. 4 The legions of the army are more gentle than rocks in the street. 5 Our neighbours are more friendly than yours (pl.). 6 A journey having been made we drank rather sweet wine, which the wife of the host had given to us. 7 Whose face seems prettier? 8 I saw a rather white cloud, which shone in the sky. 9 This field of this farmer is not wider than that field of that man. 10 The tired men having been seized by sleep, the legion had no power. 11 The more famous the poet is, the more beautiful the verses he writes. 12 Wolves are swifter than dogs. 13 The king of the island wants to build walls higher than the temple by means of the hands of the people. 14 Around the river the more cruel goddess seizes horses, which drink water near the riverbank. 15 The city is more crowded than the countryside. 16 Food, which was made by an old man, was sweeter than the food of a young man. 17 We are eager for the flesh of a wilder and fatter animal. 18 The more serious the wounds of the sailor, the more unhappy are his friends. 19 We had to read the rather beautiful works of the more famous author. 20 Is the goddess more cruel than that one?

3 1 Quandō accipiēs vītam līberiōrem? 2 Nūbēs nigrior est . . . quam tenebrae antrī *or* tenebrīs antrī. 3 Quantō miserior es, tantō īnfēlīcior est vīta, quam dūcis. Lūctus omnis mundī/orbis terrārum tibi erit. 4 Vēlīs datīs nautae animal sacrius petēbant. 5 Quī custōs perīculum crūdēlius inveniet? 6 Lentiōrēs mīlitēs in castrīs mānsērunt. 7 Ovem pinguiōrem optāmus/cupīmus. 8 Bracchia sua fortiōra sunt . . . quam suum caput *or* suō capite. 9 Undae multō asperiōrēs arborēs īnsulae et rāmōs eōrum dēlēbunt. 10 Gladium fortiōrem antepōnimus sagittae noviōrī.

4 1 L 2 B 3 J 4 K 5 A 6 C 7 G 8 E 9 F 10 H 11 I 12 D

Reading: *Hercules and His Friend Admetus, part 3*

"O wretched me! I, guest, sand in this home of sadness. What am I am able to do for my faithful friend?"

In a deep silence he thought for a long time. Then suddenly he stood up.

"I will force Death. I will return to Ademtus (his) queen."

Dinner having been removed, he ran to the tomb. Death resisted strongly. Finally Hercules conquered it. Alcestis was freed. Sad Admetus returned home. Hercules greeted (his) friend entering. Alcestis stood with a man of a great body in the doorway.

"Do you know this woman, Admetus?"

"This is deceit," Admetus exclaimed.

This is not deceit. She is your wife, who died. She lives again. I received her from death by a battle. Lo Alcestis, your dear wife."

Thus Hercules offered himself as a faithful friend.

UNIT 38

1 1 dulcissimō, dulcissimae 2 immortālissimōrum, immortālissimārum 3 optimam 4 longissimō 5 sacerrimīs 6 minimārum 7 lātissimī 8 sapientissimus, a, um 9 facillimīs 10 senissimum, senissimam

2 1 The most beautiful daughter of the king will be captured by enemy sailors. 2 At my parents' I drink the sweetest wine. 3 The leader of the senate ought to be as noble as possible. 4 Many days of this year we have done nothing. 5 They will have sought greater praise and immortal peace from the soothsayer of the gods. 6 The best legion, which had saved the towns of the island, believed the emperor. 7 In the forest no one saw the very radiant and very swift horse. 8 The army having been most disgraceful, the soldiers ran from the city without victory. 9 Is the temple the greatest, which you (sg.) have ever seen? 10 Because of the worst attacks the citizens had no food. 11 The farmer threw seeds into the most firm land. 12 The most famous poet wrote verses as beautiful as possible. 13 The old slaves are not able to please the very new man. 14 The weeping boy will be placed onto the most sacred altar. 15 We do not trust this one, who lives in the highest mountain. 16 Do you (pl.) fear a very wretched death? 17 Honey is always the sweetest of all foods, which are in the country house. 18 We heard the very sad voice of the horseman. 19 You (pl.) came to the greatest city of the whole world. 20 The wildest animals of the forest are able to harm the men and women of that town.

3 1 Quid faciēs, postquam tempestās fortissima vēnerit? 2 Nēmō improbissimum scelus facit. 3 Quaecumque arbor melior est, eam inveniēmus. 4 Agricolā pecū ovium agente, nūbēs lentissimae in caelō stetērunt. 5 Cūr rogātis auxilium plūrimum servōs celerrimī deī? *or* Cūr quaeritis auxilium plūrimum dē servīs celerimī deī? 6 Nēmō est dīgnior quam is. Est dīgnissimus cīvis Rōmae. 7 Nōlī indulgēre laetissimīs/fēlīcissimīs et iūcundissimīs līberīs! 8 Miserrima rēgīna persuāsit nōbīs īre. 9 Moenibus/mūrīs altissimīs dēlētīs, inimīcī/hostēs iēcērunt in castra mīlitēs. 10 Fulgente in caelō sōle, antrum est quam obscūrissimum.

4 1 K 2 D 3 E 4 F 5 I 6 H 7 G 8 J 9 B 10 C 11 A 12 L

Reading: *The Death of Hercules, part 1*

On a certain day Hercules had to make a sacrifice. He put on white clothing.
Nessus, whom Hercules had killed at one time, while dying gave his own blood
to the wife of Hercules. Nessus had said that the blood was sacred. The blood
grew the love, which men have for their own wives. The wife of Hercules, who
wanted to save the love of her husband for herself, wet the clothing with the
deadly blood of Nessus. Hercules, after the clothing had been wet, shortly felt
a very sharp pain in (his) entire body. He was not able to take it off, so there
was no hope for him. Hercules, as if driven by fury, collected himself (i.e.
hastened) to Mount Oetas. Prepared to meet death, he constructed a funeral pyre
with the greatest speed.

UNIT 39

1 1 amīcē, amīcius, amīcissimē 2 celeriter, celerius, celerrimē 3 pulchrē, pulchrius,
pulcherrimē 4 iūcundē, iūcundius, iūcundissimē 5 breviter, brevius, brevissimē
6 leviter, levius, levissimē 7 asperē, asperius, asperrimē 8 lātē, lātius, lātissimē
9 difficiliter, difficilius, difficillimē 10 dignē, dignius, dignissimē

2 1 S/he sings more beautifully than I. 2 They set sail as quickly as possible.
3 The queen cruelly killed the men, who were in prison. 4 (His/her) mouth
having been wounded, s/he responds more slowly now. 5 We happily remained
at home. 6 The soldiers were throwing arrows wildly. 7 The legion disgracefully
destroyed the city for the sake of the senate. 8 The dog, taught well, saved the
captured boy in the cave. 9 Here we have lived for a long time. 10 Do not do
worse than them! 11 First you (pl.) ought to sail to the island with the ships.
12 Which animal works the most in the fields? 13 The hostile armies will come
nearer to the camp. 14 No one thinks more wisely than that one. 15 The storm
fights us more mildly than the gods. 16 My father forgives me in a friendly
manner. 17 I will obey my parents as easily as possible. 18 The cruel king
persuaded him more easily than the wise queen. 19 Secretly and gradually the
blind author goes to the country house of that damn rich man. 20 The war having
been begun the leader of the enemies stands humbly before the king.

3 1 Iūcundē bibimus, quod līberī suum canem servāvērunt. 2 Equus rāmōs
magnōs arboris firmē capit lātō ōre. 3 Dēbuī trahere modo taurum, quī interfectus
erat. 4 Cūr omnia [*or* omnēs rēs] clam fēcit? 5 Ventī tempestātis oppidum
parvum quam ācerrimē pellent. 6 Nymphae sacrae pulchrius agricolīs [quam
agricolae] canunt. 7 Senēs lēgēs sapientius faciunt iuvenibus [quam iuvenēs].
8 Arcus et sagittae recenter inventae/inventa sunt in silvā. 9 In somnium quam
celerrimē cadit. 10 Sōl in caelō fulgēbat quam candidissimē.

4 1 C 2 E 3 G 4 J 5 B 6 I 7 A 8 D 9 H 10 F 11 K 12 L

Reading: *The Death of Hercules, part 2*

Then seeing those, who were standing around, he asked, "Can you ignite the funeral pyre?"

But all refused, "Such a crime we will never commit."

At last a certain shepherd put a fire under the funeral pyre. Immediately smoke filled everything and Hercules, covered by a dense cloud, was snatched away into Olympus by Jupiter. This was the end of the life of Hercules, of one of the most famous men of Greece. He was a man of many virtues and faults. He had wanted to atone for (his) faults. Twelve difficult labors were given to him. But the gods thought him worthy for great virtues. He was lifted up into heaven.

UNIT 40

1 1 comparison 2 place from which 3 verb (fruor) 4 source 5 degree of difference 6 means 7 personal agent 8 time within which 9 separation 10 absolute 11 time when 12 separation/place from which 13 personal agent 14 source/place from which 15 absolute; place from which

2 1 G 2 D 3 H 4 I 5 C 6 E 7 J 8 B 9 A 10 F 11 K 12 L

Reading: *Excerpt from Caesar's Gallic Wars*

All Gaul is divided into three parts, of which one the Belgians inhabit, another the Aquitani, a third those who are called in their own language Celts, in our Gauls.

They all differ between each other in language, customs, and laws.

The river Garumn divides the Gauls from the Aquitani, the rivers Matrona and Sequana divide the Gauls from the Belgians.

Of them all the Belgians are the strongest, because they are far removed from the culture and civilization of the Province, and are nearest to the Germans, who live across the Rhine and with whom they are constantly fighting.

REVIEW OF UNITS 35–40

A 1 intransitive 2 does not take dative 3 intransitive 4 prefix 5 prefix 6 intransitive

B 1 dative plural, ablative plural 2 nominative singular, nominative plural, accusative plural 3 genitive singular 4 genitive plural 5 nominative plural, accusative plural 6 dative singular

C 1 pulchrius, pulcherrimum 2 pulchriōrem, pulcherrimum 3 pulchriōrēs, pulcherrimās 4 pulchriōrum, pulcherrimōrum 5 pulchriōribus, pulcherrimīs 6 pulchriōris (genitive sg.), pulchriōrī (dative sg.), pulchriōrēs (nominative pl.), pulcherrimae (all three possibilities)

D 1 laetē 2 laetius 3 laetissimē 4 ācriter 5 ācrius 6 ācerimē

E 1 degree of difference 2 absolute 3 source 4 time

DICTIONARIES

Latin–English

ā/ab [+ abl.] *away from*
abdūcō, -ere, abdūxī, abductus *to lead away*
abiciō, -icere, -iēcī, -iectus *to throw away*
abripiō, -ere, -ripuī, -reptus *to snatch away*
abscindō, -ere, -scidī, -scissus *to cut off*
absum, abesse, āfuī *to be absent*
ac *and*
accendō, -ere, -ccendī, -cēnsus *to light up*
accidō, -ere, accidī *to happen*
accipiō, -ere, -cēpī, -ceptus *to receive, accept*
accūsō (1) *to accuse*
ācer, ācris, ācre *sharp, keen, fierce*
aciēs, -ēī (f.) *line of troops*
ācriter *fiercely*
ad [+ acc.] *to*
addō, -ere, -didī, -ditus *to increase*
adeō *so*
adeō, adīre, adīvī/iī, aditus *to approach*
adferō see **afferō**
adimō, -ere, -ēmī, -emptus *to take away from*
adiungō, -ere, -iūnxī, -ūnctus *to attach*
Admētus, -ī *Admetus* (king)
admonitiō, admonitiōnis (f.)
   admonition, reprimand
adspergō, -ere, -spersī, -spersus *to sprinkle*
adstō, -stāre, -stitī *to stand by*
adsum, adesse, adfuī *to be present*
adulātiō, adulātiōnis (f.) *flattery, adulation*
adulēscēns, adulēscentis (m./f.)
   young man, young woman
adūrō, -ere, -ūssī, -ūstus *to scorch, singe*
adveniō, -īre, -vēnī, -ventus *to arrive*
adventus, -ūs *arrival*
aedificō (1) *to build*
aeger, aegra, aegrum *sick*
aequor, aequoris (nt.) *sea; water*
āēr, āeris (m.) *air*

aes, aeris (nt.) *copper, brass*
aestās, aestātis (f.) *summer*
aestimō (1) *to judge*
aestuōsus, -a, -um *agitated*
aetās, aetātis (f.) *age, time*
aeternus, -a, -um *eternal*
aethēr, aetheris (m.) *sky, upper air*
afferō, afferre, attulī, allātus
   to bring to, present
afficiō, -ere, -fēcī, -fectus *to affect; afflict with*
ager, agrī *field*
agger, aggeris (m.) *rampart*
aggredior, -ī, aggressus sum *to attack*
agō, -ere, ēgī, āctus *to drive, do*
agricola, -ae (m.) *farmer*
āit *s/he says*
alacer, alacris, alacre *quick, ready*
albus, -a, -um *white*
Alcestis, Alcestidis (f.) *Alcestis*
Alcmēna, -ae *Alcmena* (mother of Hercules)
alimentum, -ī *food, nourishment*
aliquī, aliqua, aliquod *some, any*
aliquis, aliquid *someone, something*
alius, alia, aliud [gen.: -īus, dat.: -ī]
   other, another
alō, -ere, aluī, altus *to nourish; support*
altē *high*
alter, -a, -um *the other*
altum, -ī *deep sea*
altus, -a, -um *high, tall; deep*
alveus, -ī *riverbed*
Amāzōn, Amāzonis (f.) *Amazon*
ambiguus, -a, -um *doubtful*
ambō, ambae, ambō *both*
ambulō (1) *to walk*
amīcitia, -ae *friendship*
amīculus, -ī *close friend*

amīcus, -a, -um *friendly*
amnis, amnis (m.) *stream*
amō (1) *to love*
amor, amōris (m.) *love, yearning*
āmoveō, -ēre, -mōvī, -mōtus *to remove*
amphora, -ae *jar*
amplus, -a, -um *great, distinguished*
an *or*
ancilla, -ae *female servant*
ancora, -ae *anchor*
angelus, -ī *angel*
angustus, -a, -um *narrow*
anima, -ae *breath, life, soul, spirit*
animadvertō, -ere, -vertī, -versus *to notice*
animal, animālis (nt.) *animal*
animus, -ī *mind, spirit, courage*
annus, -ī *year*
antepōnō, -ere, anteposuī, antepositus *to prefer*
antequam *before*
antīquus, -a, -um *ancient*
antrum, -ī *cave*
aperiō, -īre, aperuī, apertus *to open, uncover*
Apollō, Apollinis (m.) *Apollo* (god)
appāreō, -ēre, appāruī, apparatus *to appear*
appellō (1) *to call, name*
appellō, -ere, -pulī, -pulsus *to drive to*
appropinquō (1) *to approach*
apud *at the house of, among*
aqua, -ae *water*
aquila, -ae *eagle*
Aquitānī, -ōrum *Aquitani* (in SW Gaul)
āra, -ae *altar*
arāneum, -ī *spider web*
arbitror (1) *to think*
arbor, arboris (f.) *tree*
Arcadia, -ae *Arcadia* (part of Greece)
arcus, -ūs *bow*
ārdeō, -ēre, ārsī, ārsus *to burn, glow*
argentum, -ī *silver*
Argolicus, -a, -um *of Argos*
arma, -ōrum *weapons*
armentum, -ī *cattle, herd*
ars, artis (f.) *art, skill*
ascendō, -ere, -scendī, -scēnsus *to rise*
Asia, -ae *Asia*
asper, aspera, asperum *rough, harsh*
assūmō, -ere, -sumpsī, -sumptus *to take up*
asȳlum, -ī *sanctuary*
at *but*
āter, ātra, ātrum *black, gloomy*
Athēnae, -ārum *Athens*
Atlās, Atlantis (m.) *Atlas*
atque *and*

attineō, -ēre, attinuī, attentus *to concern, pertain*
auctor, auctōris (m.) *author, authority*
auctoritās, auctoritātis (f.) *power, authority*
audeō, -ēre, ausus sum *to dare*
audiō, -īre, audīvī, audītus *to hear*
auferō, auferre, abstulī, ablātus *to carry away*
Augēās, Augēae (m.) *Augeas* (king)
aura, -ae *breeze, air*
aureus, -a, -um *golden*
auris, auris (f.) *ear*
aurum, -ī *gold*
aut *or*
autem *moreover*
auxilium, -ī *aid, help*
avis, avis (f.) *bird*
āvolō (1) *to fly away*
balteus, -ī *belt*
barbarus, -ī *foreigner, barbarian*
bāsiō (1) *to kiss*
beātus, -a, -um *happy, prosperous*
Belgae, -ārum (m) *Belgae* (in North. Gaul)
bellum, -ī *war, battle*
bene *well*
benīgnē *kindly, friendly*
bēstia, -ae *wild animal*
bibō, -ere, bibī, bibitus *to drink*
bīnī, -ae, -a *two each*
bonus, -a, -um *good*
bōs, bovis (m./f.) [gen. pl. *boum*] *bull, ox*
bracchium, -ī *arm*
brevis, breve *short*
brevitās, brevitātis (f.) *brevity, conciseness*
cachinnus, -ī *laugh*
Cācus, -ī *Cacus* (giant)
cadō, -ere, cecidī, cāsus *to fall*
caecitās, caecitātis (f.) *blindness*
caecus, -a, -um *blind*
caedēs, caedis (f.) *murder, slaughter*
caedō, -ere, cecīdī, caesus *to kill*
caelicus, -a, -um *heavenly, celestial*
caelitēs, caelitum (m. pl.) *gods*
caelum, -ī *sky*
callidus, -a, -um *sly, cunning*
calor, calōris (m.) *heat*
campus, -ī *plain, field*
candēns, candentis *shining white*
candidātus, -ī *candidate for office*
candidus, -a, -um *shining white, radiant*
canis, canis (m./f.) *dog*
canō, -ere, cecinī, cantus *to sing*
cantiō, cantiōnis (f.) *song*
cantō (1) *to sing*

capiō, -ere, cēpī, captus *to take, seize*
captīvus, -a, -um *captive, captured*
caput, capitis (nt.) *head*
carcer, carceris (m.) *prison*
careō, -ēre, caruī, caritus [+ abl.] *to lack*
carmen, carminis (nt.) *poem, song*
carō, carnis (f.) *flesh*
carrus, -ī *cart, wagon*
Carthāgō, Carthāginis (f.) *Carthage*
cārus, -a, -um *dear, beloved*
castra, -ōrum *camp*
cāsus, -ūs *misfortune*
catēna, -ae *chain*
cauda, -ae *tail*
causā [+ preceding gen.] *for the sake of*
causa, -ae *cause, reason*
caveō, -ēre, cāvī, cautus *to beware*
cavus, -a, -um *hollow*
cecid- see **cadō**
cecin- see **canō**
cēdō, -ere, cessī, cessus *to move, step; yield*
celeber, celebris, celebre *famous*
celeberrimus, -a, -um *most famous*
celer, celeris, celere *swift*
celeritās, celeritātis (f.) *speed*
celeriter *quickly*
cēlō (1) *to conceal, hide*
Celtae, -ārum (m.) *Celts* (in Central Gaul)
cēna, -ae *dinner*
Centaurus, -ī *Centaur*
cēp- see **capiō**
Cerberus, -ī *Cerberus* (dog)
cernō, -ere, crēvī, crētus *to decide, discern*
certāmen, certāminis (nt.) *contest*
certē *certainly*
certus, -a, -um *resolved*
cervīx, cervīcis (f.) *neck*
cervus, -ī *stag*
cessō (1) *to stop*
cēterī, -ae, -a *the rest, others*
Charōn, Charontis (m.) *Charon* (ferryman)
cibāria, -ōrum *provisions*
cibus, -ī *food*
circum [+ acc.] *around*
circumplector, -ī, -plexus sum *to surround*
circus, -ī *racecourse, Circus Maximus*
cīvīlis, cīvīle *civil*
cīvis, cīvis (m./f.) *citizen*
cīvitās, cīvitātis (f.) *state*
clam *secretly*
clāmor, clāmōris (m.) *shout, cry*
clārus, -a, -um *famous*
claudō, -ere, clausī, clausus *to close*

clāvus, -ī *nail*
clēmēns, clēmentis *merciful*
cochlea, -ae *snail*
coēg- see **cōgō**
coepiō, -ere, coepī, coeptus *to begin*
cōgitō (1) *to think*
cognōscō, -ere, -nōvī, -nitus *to learn;*
  (perfect) *to know*
cōgō, -ere, coēgī, coāctus *to force, compel*
cohors, cohortis (f.) *cohort*
collis, collis (m.) *hill*
collum, -ī *neck*
color, colōris (m.) *color*
columba, -ae *dove*
coma, -ae *hair*
comes, comitis (m./f.) *companion*
commendō (1) *to entrust*
commisceō, -ēre, commiscuī, commīxtus
  to mix together
committō, -ere, commīsī, commissus *to join,*
  engage; commit
commodus, -a, -um *proper*
commoveō, -ēre, -mōvī, -mōtus *to influence*
commūnis, commūne *common*
comparō (1) *to prepare, purchase*
compellō (1) *to address*
compellō, -ere, compulī, compulsus
  to drive together, compel
compendium, -ī *shortcut*
comperiō, -īre, -perī, -pertus *to learn*
complūrēs, complūra *several, many*
comprimō, -ere, -pressī, -pressus *to squeeze*
concēdō, -ere, -cessī, -cessus *to grant, allow*
concordia, -ae *harmony*
concors, concordis *harmonious*
concubius, -a, -um *lying in sleep*
  nox concubia, noctis concubiae *early*
    night, bedtime
condō, -ere, condidī, conditus *to found*
cōnferō, -ferre, contulī, collātus *to collect*
cōnficiō, -ere, -fēcī, -fectus *to accomplish*
cōnflīgō, -ere, cōnflīxī, cōnflīctus
  to fight, engage
coniungō, -ere, coniūnxī, coniūnctus
  to join together
coniūrātiō, -ōnis (f.) *conspiracy*
cōnor, -ārī, -ātus sum *to try*
cōnscendō, -ere, -scendī, -scēnsus *to climb*
cōnsentiō, -īre, -sēnsī, -sēnsus *to agree*
cōnsīdō, -ere, cōnsēdī, cōnsessus *to sit down*
cōnsilium, -ī *plan, decision*
cōnsōlor (1) *to console*
cōnspectus, -ūs *view*

cōnspiciō, -ere, -spēxī, -spectus *to observe*
cōnspicuus, -a, -um *noticeable, visible*
cōnstituō, -ere, -stituī, -stitūtus *to establish, decide*
cōnstō (1), -stitī *to consist of*
cōnsuēscō, -ere, cōnsuēvī, cōnsuētus *to get accustomed; (perfect) to be accustomed*
cōnsuētūdō, cōnsuētūdinis (f.) *habit*
cōnsul, cōnsulis (m.) *consul*
cōnsulāris, cōnsulāris (m.) *ex-consul*
cōnsulō, -ere, -suluī, -sultus *to reflect; look out for*
cōnsūmō, -ere, -sūmpsī, -sūmptus *to spend*
contendō, -ere, -ī, -tentus *to hurry, hasten; to entreat*
conterminus, -a, -um *neighbouring, bordering*
continēns, continentis *bordering, adjacent*
continenter *continuously*
continuō *immediately*
contrā [+ acc.] *against*
convellō, -ere, -vellī, -vulsus *to shatter*
conveniō, -īre, -vēnī, -ventus *to meet*
convertō, -ere, convertī, conversus *to change*
convīvium, -ī *banquet*
coorior, -īrī, -ortus sum *to arise*
cōpia, -ae *supply*
cōpiōsus, -a, -um *rich, abundant*
coquō, -ere, coxī, coctus *to cook*
cor, cordis (nt.) *heart, feelings*
cornū, -ūs *horn*
corōna, -ae *crown*
corpus, corporis (nt.) *body*
corripiō, -ere, -ripuī, -reptus *to seize*
crās *tomorrow*
crassitūdō, crassitūdinis (f.) *thickness*
crēdō, -ere, crēdidī, crēditus [+ dat.] *to believe, trust*
cremō (1) *to burn*
creō (1) *to create*
crepitus, -ūs *noise*
crepundia, -ōrum *rattle*
crēscō, -ere, crēvī, crētus *to grow*
Crēta, -ae *Crete* (island)
crēv- see **cernō**, **crescō**
crūdēlis, crūdēle *cruel*
crūdēlitās, crūdēlitātis (f.) *cruelty*
cubiculum, -ī *bedroom*
cucurr- see **currō**
culpa, -ae *blame, fault*
culpō (1) *to blame*
cultus, -ūs *culture*
cum [+ abl.] *with; [conj.] when, since, because*

cūnctus, -a, -um *all, whole, entire*
cupidus, -a, -um *desirous*
cupiō, -ere, cupīvī, cupītus *to desire*
cūr *why*
cūra, -ae *care, concern*
cūrō (1) *to care*
currō, -ere, cucurrī, cursus *to run*
cūstōdiō, -īre *to guard, watch over*
custōs, custōdis (m./f.) *guardian*
damma, -ae (m.) *deer*
damnātiō, damnātiōnis (f.) *condemnation*
damnō (1) *to condemn*
dē [+ abl.] *down from, about, concerning*
dea, -ae *goddess*
dēbeō, -ēre, dēbuī, dēbitus *to owe, ought*
dēcernō, -ere, dēcrēvī, dēcrētus *to decree*
decimus, -a, -um *tenth*
dēcipiō, -ere, -cēpī, -ceptus *to deceive*
decorō (1) *to adorn*
ded- see **dō**
dēdūcō, -ere, -dūxī, -ductus *to lead away*
dēfendō, -ere, -fendī, -fēnsus *to defend*
dēfēnsor, dēfēnsōris (m.) *defender*
dēferō, -ferre, -tulī, -lātus *to convey*
dēfessus, -a, -um *tired*
dēficiō, -ere, -fēcī, -fectus *to be lacking*
dēfōrmis, dēfōrme *disfigured*
dēiciō, -ere, -iēcī, -iectus *to throw down*
dein *then*
deinde *then, next*
dēleō, -ēre, dēlēvī, dēlētus *to destroy*
Delphicus, -a, -um *Delphic*
dēmum *at last*
dēnique *finally*
dēns, dentis (m.) *tooth*
dēnsus, -a, -um *dense, thick*
dēpellō, -ere, dēpulī, dēpulsus *to remove, dispel*
dēpōnō, -ere, -posuī, -positus *to deposit*
dēscendō, -ere, dēscendī, dēscēnsus *to descend*
dēsīderium, -ī *longing*
dēspondeō, -ēre, dēspondī, dēspōnsus *to pledge*
dētineō, -ēre, dētinuī, dētentus *to detain, keep back*
dētrahō, -ere, -trāxī, -trāctus *to take away/off*
deus, -ī *god*
dēvastō (1) *to lay waste*
dēvolvō, -ere, dēvolvī, dēvolūtus *to roll down*
dēvorō (1) *to devour*
dexter, dextra, dextrum *right*
dīcō, -ere, dīxī, dictus *to say*
dictiō, -ōnis (f.) *speaking*
dictum, -ī *word*
diēs, -ēī (m.) *day*

differō, -ferre, distulī, dīlātus *to differ*
difficilis, difficile *difficult*
difficultās, difficultātis (f.) *difficulty*
digitus, -ī *finger*
dīgnus, -a, -um *worthy*
dīligenter *diligently*
dīmittō, -ere, -mīsī, -missus *to let go*
Diomēdēs, Diomēdis (m.) *Diomedes (king)*
dīrus, -a, -um *fearful, terrible*
discēdō, -ere, discessī, discessus *to depart*
discō, -ere, didicī *to learn*
discurrō, -ere, discurrī, discursus *to run by*
discutiō, -ere, -cussī, -cussus *to dash to pieces*
disiciō, -ere, disiēcī, disiectus *to scatter*
disputō (1) *to discuss*
dissimilis, dissimile *dissimilar*
dissolvō, -ere, -solvī, -solūtus *to pay up*
dīstō (1) *to be apart*
diū *for a long time*
diūtissimē *for a very long time*
dīves, dīvitis *rich*
dīvidō, -ere, dīvīsī, dīvīsus *to divide, separate*
dīx- see **dīcō**
dō, dare, dedī, datus *to give*
doceō, -ēre, docuī, doctus *to teach*
doleō, -ēre, doluī *to grieve, pain*
dolor, dolōris (m.) *pain, sorrow*
domesticus, -a, -um *domestic, of the house*
domina, -ae *mistress*
dominus, -ī *master*
domus, -ūs (f.) *home*
dōnum, -ī *gift*
dormiō, -īre, dormīvī, dormītus *to sleep*
dōs, dōtis (f.) *dowry*
dubitō (1) *to doubt; hesitate*
dūcō, -ere, dūxī, ductus *to lead; consider*
dūdum *just now*
dulcis, dulce *sweet*
dum *while*
duo, duae, duo *two*
duodecim *twelve*
dūrus, -a, -um *hard, rough*
dux, ducis (m.) *chief, leader*
dux- see **dūcō**
ē/ex [+ abl.] *out of, from*
ecce *lo, look*
efferō, efferre, extulī, ēlātus *to carry out*
efficiō, -ere, -fēcī, -fectus *to accomplish, make*
ēg- see **agō**
ego *I*
ēgregius, -a, -um *extraordinary, distinguished*
ēloquentia, -ae *eloquence*
emō, -ere, ēmī, emptus *to buy*

enim *indeed*
eō *to there, there*
eō, īre, īvī, itus *to go*
epistula, -ae *letter, epistle*
eques, equitis (m.) *horseman, knight;* (pl.) *cavalry*
equidem *indeed, certainly*
equus, -ī *horse*
ergō *therefore*
ērigō, -ere, -rēxī, -rēctus *to raise up*
ēripiō, -ere, ēripuī, ēreptus *to snatch away*
ērudītus, -a, -um *accomplished*
ērumpō, -ere, -rūpī, -ruptus *to burst*
ēsuriō, -īre, ēsurīvī, ēsurītus *to be hungry*
et *and*
etiam *also, even, again, still*
Eurystheus, -ī *Eurystheus (king)*
ēvānēscō, -ere, -vānuī *to vanish*
ēveniō, -īre, ēvēnī, ēventus *to turn out, come to pass*
ēvertō, -ere, ēvertī, ēversus *to overturn*
ēvocō (1) *to call forth, summon*
ex/ē [+ abl.] *out of, from*
exāminō (1) *to examine*
excellō, -ere *to excel*
excidō, -ere, -cidī *to fail*
excipiō, -ere, -cēpī, -ceptus *to welcome*
excitō (1) *to excite, arouse*
exclāmō (1) *to shout out*
exclūdō, -ere, -clūsī, -clūsus *to shut out*
exemplum, -ī *example, sample*
exeō, exīre, exīvī/exiī, exitus *to go out*
exercitus, -ūs *army*
exhērēdō (1) *to disinherit*
exigō, -ere, exēgī, exāctus *to pass*
exilium, -ī *exile, banishment*
expiō (1) *to atone for*
expolītus, -a, -um *polished*
expōnō, -ere, -posuī, -positus *to put out*
exstruō, -ere, -strūxī, -strūctus *to construct*
extrēmus, -a, -um *farthest, last*
fabricō (1) *to make, forge*
fābula, -ae *story*
faciēs, -ēī *form, shape; face*
facinus, -oris (nt.) *crime*
faciō, -ere, fēcī, factus *to do, make*
factum, -ī *deed*
facultās, facultātis (f.) *opportunity*
falsus, -a, -um *false*
fāma, -ae *report, fame, story*
famēs, famis (f.) *hunger*
familia, -ae *family*
fātum, -ī *fate, destiny*
faucēs, faucium (f. pl.) *throat*

faveō, -ēre, fāvī, fautus   [+ dat.] *to favour*
fēc- see **faciō**
fēlīx, fēlīcis *happy*
fēmina, -ae *woman*
ferculum, -ī *litter*
ferē *almost*
ferō, ferre, tulī, lātus   *to carry, bear*
ferōx, ferōcis *wild*
ferreus, -a, -um *of iron*
ferrum, -ī *iron*
ferus, -a, -um *wild*
fessus, -a, -um *tired*
fidēlis, fidēle *faithful*
fidēs, -eī *faith, trust*
fīdō, -ere, fīsus sum   [+ dat.] *to trust*
fīlia, -ae *daughter*
fīlius, -ī *son*
fingō, -ere, finxī, fictus   *to imagine*
fīniō, -īre, -īvī, -ītus   *to limit, bound, determine*
fīnis, fīnis (m.)   *end, boundary*
fīnitimī, -ōrum *neighbours*
fīō, fierī, factus sum   *to be made, to be done*
firmē *firmly*
firmiter *firmly*
firmus, -a, -um   *firm, strong*
flagrō (1)   *to blaze, burn*
flamma, -ae *flame*
fleō, -ēre, flēvī, flētus   *to weep, cry*
flētus, -ūs *weeping*
flōs, flōris (m.)   *flower*
fluidus, -a, -um   *flowing*
flūmen, flūminis (nt.)   *river*
fluō, -ere, flūxī, flūxus   *to flow*
fōns, fontis (m.)   *spring, source*
foris, foris (f.)   *door*
fōrma, -ae   *form, shape*
formīdō, formīdinis (f.)   *terror*
formīdolōsus, -a, -um   *terrifying*
fōrmō (1)   *to form, shape*
fors, fortis (f.)   *chance*
fortis, forte   *strong, brave*
fortiter *strongly*
fortūna, -ae   *luck, fortune, fate*
fossa, -ae   *ditch, trench*
fragor, fragōris (m.)   *crash, uproar*
frangō, -ere, frēgī, frāctus   *to break*
frāter, frātris (m.)   *brother*
fraus, fraudis (f.)   *deceit*
frēg- see **frangō**
frequēns, frequentis *crowded*
fretum, -ī *strait*
frōns, frondis (f.)   *leaf*
frōns, frontis (f.)   *forehead, appearance*

frūctus, -ūs   *fruit*
fruor, -ī, frūctus sum [+ abl.]   *to enjoy*
frūstrā   *in vain*
fu- see **sum**
fuga, -ae   *flight, refuge*
fugiō, -ere, fūgī, fugitus   *to flee*
fugō (1)   *to put to flight*
fulgeō, -ēre, fulsī,   *to shine*
fūmifer, fūmifera, fūmiferum   *smoky*
fūmus, -ī   *smoke*
fundō, -ere, fūdī, fūsus   *to pour out, lay low*
furor, furōris (m.)   *fury, rage*
fūrtum, -ī   *theft; trick*
fūstis, fūstis (m.)   *club*
Gallī, -ōrum   *Gauls*
Gallia, -ae   *Gaul*
Gallicus, -a, -um   *Gallic*
Garumna, -ae   *Garonne river*
gaudeō, -ēre, gāvīsus sum   *to rejoice*
gaudium, -ī   *joy*
gemō, -ere, gemuī, gemitus   *to groan*
gēns, gentis (f.)   *race, tribe*
genū, -ūs   *knee*
genus, generis (nt.)   *race, birth, kind*
Germānī, -ōrum   *Germans*
gerō, -ere, gessī, gestus   *to wage,*
   conduct, manage
Gēryōn, Gēryonis (m.)   *Geryon* (king)
gess- see **gerō**
gladius, -ī   *sword*
glomerō (1)   *to form into a ball*
glōria, -ae   *glory*
gradus, -ūs   *step*
Graecia, -ae   *Greece*
grātia, -ae   *thanks*
grātus, -a, -um   *pleasing*
gravis, grave   *harsh, serious*
gremium, -ī   *bosom, lap*
grex, gregis (m.)   *herd*
habeō, -ēre, habuī, habitus   *to have*
habitō (1)   *to live*
haud   *not at all*
herbārius, -ī   *skilled in plants, herbalist*
Herculēs, Herculis (m.)   *Hercules*
hērēs, hērēdis (m./f.)   *heir*
Hesperidēs, Hesperidum (f.)   *Hesperides*
hesternus, -a, -um   *of yesterday*
hīc   *here*
hic, haec, hoc   *this, these*
hiems, hiemis (f.)   *winter*
hinc   *from here*
Hippolyta, -ae   *Hippolyta*
Hispānia, -ae   *Spain*

historia, -ae *history, story*
hodiē *today*
homō, hominis (m.) *man, human being*
honestās, honestātis (f.) *integrity*
honestum, -ī *virtue, goodness*
honor, honōris (m.) *honour*
hōra, -ae *hour*
horribilis, horribile *terrifying*
hortus, -ī *garden*
hospes, hospitis (m.) *guest, host*
hospitālis, hospitāle *hospitable*
hospitāliter *with hospitality*
hostis, hostis (m./f.) *enemy*
hūc *to here*
hūmānitās, -tātis (f.) *refinement; civilization*
humilis, humile *low, humble*
humus, -ī (f.) *ground*
Hydra, -ae *Hydra*
iaciō, -ere, iēcī, iactus *to throw*
iactō (1) *to fling*
iam *now, already*
ibi *there*
ictus, -ūs *blow*
īdem, eadem, idem *same*
idōneus, -a, -um *suitable*
iēc- see **iaciō**
igitur *therefore*
īgnāvus, -a, -um *lazy*
ignis, ignis (m.) *fire*
ignōrō (1) *to not be acquainted*
īgnōscō, -ere, īgnōvī, īgnōtus [+ dat.] *to forgive*
ignōtus, -a, -um *unknown*
ille, illa, illud *that, those*
illīc *over there*
illinc *from there*
imāgō, imāginis (f.) *likeness*
imbuō, -ere, -buī, -būtus *to wet*
immergō, -ere, -mersī, -mersus *to immerse*
immineō, -ēre *to threaten*
immittō, -ere, -mīsī, -missus *to let in*
immō *no, rather*
immortālis, immortāle *immortal*
immortālitās, immortālitātis (f.) *immortality*
immūtō (1) *to change*
impedīmentum, -ī *obstacle; (pl.) baggage*
impedītus, -a, -um *impassable*
impellō, -ere, -pulī, -pulsus *to strike*
imperātor, imperātōris (m.) *emperor*
imperium, -ī *command*
imperō (1) [+ dat.] *to command*
impetrō (1) *to obtain*
impetus, -ūs *attack*
impleō, -ēre, implēvī, implētus *to fill*

impōnō, -ere, -posuī, -positus *to put upon*
impotēns, impotentis *powerless; violent*
improbitās, improbitātis (f.) *wickedness*
improbus, -a, -um *wicked*
imprōvīsō *unexpectedly*
imprōvīsus, -a, -um *unexpected*
impūbēs, impūberis *youthful*
in [+ acc.] *into, onto;* [+ abl.] *in, on*
inānis, inane *empty, vacant*
incēdō, -ere, -cēssī, -cēssus *to advance*
incidō, -ere, -cidī, -cāsus *to occur, happen*
incipiō, -ere, incēpī, inceptus *to begin*
incitō (1) *to urge on, rouse*
inclūdō, -ere, -clūsī, -clūsus *to enclose*
incola, -ae (m.) *inhabitant*
incolō, -ere, -coluī, -cultus *to inhabit*
incolumis, incolume *uninjured, safe*
incrēdibilis, incrēdibile *incredible*
inde *from there*
indīgnus, -a, -um *unworthy*
indulgeō, -ēre, indulsī, indultus [+ dat.]
    to indulge, grant
induō, -ere, -duī, -dūtus *to put on*
īnfēlīx, īnfēlicis *unhappy*
īnferior, īnferius *lower*
īnferus, -a, -um *lower, below*
īnfringō, -ere, īnfrēgī, īnfrāctus *to break, weaken*
ingēns, ingentis *huge*
ingravēscō, -ere *to increase*
inhūmānus, -a, -um *savage*
iniciō, -ere, iniēcī, iniectus *to throw in*
inimīcus, -a, -um *unfriendly, enemy*
inīquitās, inīquitātis (f.) *difficulty, unevenness*
iniūria, -ae *injustice, injury*
inliciō, -ere, -lexī, -lectus *to mislead*
innocēns, innocentis *innocent*
inquam *I say* [defective verb]
inquit *s/he said* [defective verb]
īnscius, -a, -um *ignorant*
īnscrībō, -ere, -scrīpsī, -scrīptus *to record*
īnsidiae, -ārum *ambush, treachery*
īnsidior (1) *to wait in ambush*
īnsignis, īnsigne *distinguished*
īnstituō, -ere, īnstituī, īnstitūtus *to resolve,*
    undertake
institūtum, -ī *custom, habit*
īnstruō, -ere, -strūxī, -strūctus *to equip*
īnsula, -ae *island*
īnsuō, -ere, īnsuī, īnsūtus *to sew in*
integer, integra, integrum *complete, sound*
intellegō, -ere, intellēxī, intellēctus *to understand*
inter [+ acc.] *between*
interficiō, -ere, interfēcī, interfectus *to kill*

interrogō (1)   *to ask*
intersum, interesse, interfuī   *to be amongst*
intexō, -ere, -texuī, -textus   *to interweave*
intrā [+ acc.]   *within*
intrepidus, -a, -um   *brave*
intrō (1)   *to enter*
introitus, -ūs   *entrance*
inūsitātus, -a, -um   *unusual*
inveniō, -īre, invēnī, inventus   *to find*
invideō, -ēre, invīdī, invīsus [+ dat.]   *to envy*
invīsus, -a, -um   *hated*
invītus, -a, -um   *unwilling*
Iovis   [see **Iuppiter**]
ipse, ipsa, ipsud   *very, self*
īra, -ae   *anger, rage*
īrātus, -a, -um   *angry*
irruō, -ere, irruī   *to rush in*
is, ea, id   *this, that, he, she it, they*
īscītus, -a, -um   *ignorant, stupid*
ita   *thus, so*
Ītalia, -ae   *Italy*
itaque   *therefore, and so*
iter, itineris (nt.)   *journey*
iubeō, -ēre, iussī, iussus   *to order*
iūcundus, -a, -um   *joyful*
iūdex, iūdicis (m.)   *judge*
iūdicō (1)   *to judge*
iugum, -ī   *yoke*
iungō, -ere, iūnxī, iūnctus   *to join*
iūnior, iūnius   *younger*
Iūnō, Iūnōnis (f.)   *Juno (goddess)*
Iuppiter, Iovis (m.)   *Jupiter (god)*
iūrō (1)   *to take an oath*
iūs, iūris (nt.)   *right, law*
iūs iūrandum, iūris iūrandī (nt.)   *oath*
iuss-   see **iubeō**
iussum, -ī   *command*
iuvenis, iuvenis   *young*
iuvō (1) iūvī, iūtus   *to help*
labor, labōris (m.)   *work*
labōrō (1)   *to work*
lac, lactis (nt.)   *milk*
lacerō (1)   *to tear to pieces*
lacessō, -ere, lacessīvī, lacessītus   *to exasperate*
lacrima, -ae   *tear*
lactūca, -ae   *lettuce*
lacus, -ūs   *lake*
laetitia, -ae   *joy*
laetus, -a, -um   *happy*
laevus, -a, -um   *left*
laniō (1)   *to mangle*
lapis, lapidis (m.)   *stone*
lātrō (1)   *to bark*

lātus, -a, -um   *broad, wide*
latus, lateris (nt.)   *side*
laus, laudis (f.)   *praise*
lectus, -ī   *bed*
lēgātus, -ī   *delegate; lieutenant*
legiō, legiōnis (f.)   *legion*
legō, -ere, lēgī, lēctus   *to read, gather*
lenis, lēne   *gentle*
lēniter   *gently*
lentus, -a, -um   *slow*
leō, leōnis (m.)   *lion*
Lerna, -ae   *Lerna (city)*
lētālis, lētāle   *deadly*
levis, leve   *light*
leviter   *lightly*
lēx, lēgis (f.)   *law*
libenter   *willingly*
līber, lībera, līberum   *free*
liber, librī   *book*
līberī, -ōrum   *children*
līberō (1) [+ abl.]   *to free*
lībertās, lībertātis (f.)   *freedom*
licet, -ēre, licuit   *it is allowed*
līgnum, -ī   *wood*
līmen, līminis (nt.)   *doorway*
līmus, -ī   *mud*
lingua, -ae   *language, tongue*
linteum, -ī   *sail*
liquidus, -a, -um   *clear*
littera, -ae   *letter (of alphabet)*; (pl.) *letter, epistle*
lītus, lītoris (nt.)   *coast*
locus, -ī [pl. is neuter: loca, -ōrum]   *place*
longē   *by far*
longinquus, -a, -um   *long, lasting*
longus, -a, -um   *long*
loquor, loquī, locūtus sum   *to speak*
lūctus, -ūs   *grief*
lūdibrium, -ī   *laughing stock, mockery*
lūdicer, lūdicra, lūdicrum   *playful*
lūdō, -ere, lūsī, lūsus   *to ridicule, mock*
lūdus, -ī   *game*
lūgeō, -ēre, lūxī   *to mourn*
lūmen, lūminis (nt.)   *light*
lūna, -ae   *moon*
lupus, -ī   *wolf*
lustrāmen, lustrāminis (nt.)   *purifying offerings*
lūstrō (1)   *to illuminate*
lūx, lūcis (f.)   *light*
macula, -ae   *spot, stain*
maestus, -a, -um   *sad, gloomy*
magister, magistrī   *teacher, master*
magistrātus, -ūs   *magistrate*
magnificus, -a, -um   *grand*

289

magnitūdō, magnitūdinis (f.) *size, greatness*
magnopere *greatly*
magnus, -a, -um *great, big*
māior, māius *greater*
māiōrēs, māiōrum (m. pl.) *ancestors*
mālō, mālle, māluī *to prefer*
malus, -a, -um *bad, evil*
maneō, -ēre, mānsī, mānsus *to remain*
manus, -ūs (f.) *hand*
mare, maris (nt.) *sea*
marīnus, -a, -um *related to the sea*
marītus, -ī *husband*
marmoreus, -a, -um *marble-like*
Mars, Martis (m.) *Mars (god)*
mās, maris *male*
mārītus, -ī *husband*
māter, mātris (m.) *mother*
mātrimōnium, -ī *marriage*
Matrona, -ae *Marne river*
maximē *especially*
maximus, -a, -um *greatest*
medius, -a, -um *middle (of)*
mel, mellis (nt.) *honey*
meminī, meminisse *to remember*
memoria, -ae *memory*
mendāx, mendācis *lying*
mēns, mentis (f.) *mind*
mēnsa, -ae *table*
mēnsis, mēnsis (m.) *month*
mentiō, mentiōnis (f.) *mention*
Mercurius, -ī *Mercury (god)*
mēta, -ae *goal, limit*
metuō, -ere, metuī, metūtus *to fear*
metus, -ūs *fear*
meus, -a, -um *my*
micō (1) *to flicker, sparkle*
mīles, mīlitis (m.) *soldier*
mīlle [indeclinable in singular; pl.: mīlia, -um]
  (nt.) *thousand*
minimē *at least, minimally*
minor (1) *to threaten*
minus *less*
mīs- see **mittō**
misceō, -ēre, miscuī, mīxtus *to mix*
miser, misera, miserum *wretched*
miserē *wretchedly*
mītis, mīte *mild*
mittō, -ere, mīsī, missus *to send*
modo *only, just*
modus, -ī *way*
moenia, moenium (nt. pl.) *walls, ramparts*
mōlēs, mōlis (f.) *effort*
molō, -ere, moluī, molitus *to grind*

moneō, -ēre, monuī, monitus *to warn*
mōns, montis (m.) *mountain*
mōnstrō (1) *to show*
mōnstrum, -ī *monster*
mora, -ae *delay*
morbus, -ī *disease, illness*
morior, -īrī, mortuus sum *to die*
moror (1) *to delay*
mors, mortis (f.) *death*
mortālis, mortāle *mortal*
mortifer, -a, -um *deadly*
mortuus, -a, -um *dead*
mōs, mōris (m.) *custom*
moveo, -ēre, mōvī, mōtus *to move*
mox *soon*
mūgiō, -īre *to bellow*
mulier, mulieris (f.) *woman*
multitūdō, multitūdinis (f.) *great number, multitude*
multus, -a, -um *much, many*
mundus, -ī *world*
mūniceps, mūnicipis (m./f.) *citizen*
mūniō, -īre, mūnīvī, mūnītus *to fortify*
mūnītiō, mūnītiōnis (f.) *fortification*
mūnus, mūneris (nt.) *gift*
murmur, murmuris (nt.) *murmur, roaring*
mūrus, -ī *wall*
mūtō (1) *to change, exchange*
nam *indeed, for*
nārrō (1) *to narrate, tell*
nāscor, nāscī, nātus sum *to be born*
nāsus, -ī *nose*
nātūra, -ae *nature*
nātus, -a, -um *born*
nauta, -ae (m.) *sailor*
nāvigō (1) *to sail*
nāvis, nāvis (f.) *ship*
nebula, -ae *cloud*
nec *and not*
nec . . . nec *neither . . . nor*
necessārius, -ī *male relative*
necesse est *it is necessary*
necessitās, necessitātis (f.)
  necessity, compulsion
necō (1) *to kill*
nefārius, -a, -um *criminal*
negō (1) *to deny, say no*
negōtium, -ī *business, task*
Nemea, -ae *Nemea (city)*
nēmō, nēminis (m./f.) *no one, nobody*
neque *and not, nor*
nequeō, nequīre, nequīvī, nequītus *to be unable*
nēquīquam *in vain*
nescio, -īre, nescīvī, nescītus *to not know*

Nessus, -ī   *Nessus* (a Centaur)
neuter, neutra, neutrum   *neither*
niger, nigra, nigrum   *black*
nihil   *nothing*
nīl   *nothing*
nisī   *lest, unless*
nōbilis, nōbile   *noble*
nōbilitās, nōbilitātis (f.)   *nobility*
noceō, -ēre, nocuī, nocitus   [+ dat.] *to harm*
nōlō, nōlle, nōluī   *to not want*
nōmen, nōminis (nt.)   *name*
nōn   *not*
nōndum   *yet*
nōs   *we*
nōscō, -ere, nōvī, nōtus   *to learn;* (perf.) *know*
noster, nostra, nostrum   *our*
nōtēscō, -ere, nōtuī   *to become known*
nōv-   see **nōscō**
novem   *nine*
novus, -a, -um   *new*
nox concubia, noctis concubiae   *early night, bedtime*
nox, noctis (f.)   *night*
noxa, -ae   *harm*
nūbēs, nūbis (f.)   *cloud*
nūdō (1)   *to bare, expose*
nūdus, -a, -um   *bare, naked*
nūllus, -a, -um   [gen.: -īus, dat.: -ī] *none, no*
num   *really* [introduces question whose answer is anticipated to be *no*]
numerus, -ī   *number*
numquam   *never*
nunc   *now*
nūntiō (1)   *to announce*
nympha, -ae   *nymph*
obiciō, -ere, -iēcī, -iectus (+ dat.)   *to throw before*
oblīvīscor, -ī, oblītus sum   *to forget*
obmūtēscō, -ere, -mūtēscuī   *to cease*
obscūrus, -a, -um   *dark*
obsidiō, -ōnis (f.)   *siege*
occīdō, -ere, -cīdī, -cīsus   *to strike down; kill*
occupō (1)   *to seize, occupy*
occurrō, -ere, occurrī, occursus   *to occur*
Ōceanus, -ī   *Ocean*
octōgintā   *80*
oculus, ī   *eye*
ōdī, -isse   *to hate* [perfect forms are translated as present]
odium, -ī   *hatred*
odor, odōris (m.)   *smell*
Oeta, -ae   *Oeta* (mountain)
offendō, -ere, -fendī, -fēnsus   *to offend*
offēnsus, -a, -um   *offended, displeased*

offerō, offerre, obtulī, oblātus   *to offer, expose*
officium, -ī   *duty*
ōlim   *once, formerly*
Olympus, -ī   *Mt. Olympus*
omnīnō   *entirely*
omnis, omne   *all, every*
onerō (1)   *to load, oppress*
operātiō, operātiōnis (f.)   *working, operation*
opertus, -a, -um   *covered*
opīniō, opīniōnis (f.)   *opinion*
oppidum, -ī   *town*
opprimō, -ere, -pressī, -pressus   *to overwhelm*
oppugnō (1)   *to attack*
ops, opis (f.)   *power*
optimus, -a, -um   *best*
optō (1)   *to desire*
opus est   *it is necessary*
opus, operis (nt.)   *work*
ōrāculum, -ī   *oracle*
ōrātiō, ōrātiōnis (f.)   *speech*
orbis, orbis (m.)   *circle, world*
   orbis terrārum   *world*
Orcus, -ī   *Lower World*
orīgō, orīginis (f.)   *origin, source*
ōrnō (1)   *to adorn*
ōrō (1)   *to beg, ask*
ōs, ōris (nt.)   *mouth*
ostendō, -ere, -ī, -tentus   *to show*
ōtium, -ī   *leisure*
ovis, ovis (f.)   *sheep*
ōvum, -ī   *egg*
pānis, pānis (m.)   *bread*
pār, paris   *equal*
parasītus, -ī   *parasite*
parcō, -ere, pepercī, parsus   [+ dat.] *to spare*
parēns, parentis (m./f.)   *parent* [not an *i*-stem]
pāreō, -ēre, pāruī, pāritus [+ dat.]   *to obey*
pariēs, parietis (m.)   *wall*
parō (1)   *to prepare*
pars, partis (f.)   *part, some; side*
particeps, participis (m.)   *partner*
partior, -ī, partītus sum   *to divide, distribute*
parum   *too little*
parvus, -a, -um   *small, little*
pāscō, -ere, pāvī, pāstus   *to feed, eat*
passus, -ūs   *step, pace*
pāstor, pāstōris (m.)   *shepherd*
pāstōrius, -a, -um   *of a shepherd*
pateō, -ēre, patuī,   *to be open, extend*
pater, patris (m.)   *father*
patria, -ae   *country, fatherland*
paucus, -a, -um   *few, scarce*
paulātim   *gradually*

291

paulisper *for a short time*
paulō *a little*
paulum *a little*
pauper, pauperis *poor*
pāv- see **pāscō**
pāx, pācis (f.) *peace*
peccātum, -ī *fault*
peccō (1) *to make a mistake, sin*
pectus, pectoris (nt.) *chest*
pecū, -ūs *flock; (pl.) pastures*
pecūnia, -ae *money*
pecus, pecoris (nt.) *cattle*
pelagus, -ī (nt.) *sea*
pellis, pellis (f.) *skin, hide*
pellō, -ere, pupulī, pulsus *to drive (away),
   strike*
penetrō (1) *to enter into*
per [+ acc.] *through*
peragrō (1) *to traverse*
percutiō, -ere, -cussī, -cussus *to strike*
perditus, -a, -um *destitute*
perdūcō, -ere, -dūxī, -ductus *to bring, induce*
peregrīnus, -ī *stranger, foreigner*
pereō, perīre, perīvī, peritus *to die, perish*
perficiō, -ere, -fēcī, -fectus *to complete*
perīculōsus, -a, -um *dangerous*
perīculum, -ī *danger*
permittō, -ere, -mīsī, -missus *to give up*
pernoctō (1) *to spend the night*
perpetuus, -a, -um *continuous, unbroken*
perrumpō, -ere, -rūpī, -ruptus *to break through*
persequor, -ī, -secūtus sum *to pursue*
persōna, -ae *character*
persuādeō, -ēre, persuāsī, persuāsus
   [+ dat.] *to persuade*
perterritus, -a, -um *scared thoroughly*
perveniō, -īre, -vēnī, ventus *to come to*
pēs, pedis (m.) *foot*
petō, -ere, petīvī, petītus *to seek, ask*
philosophia, -ae *philosophy*
Pholus, -ī *Pholus* (a Centaur)
pinguis, pingue *fat*
piscis, piscis (m.) *fish*
placeō, -ēre, placuī, placitus [+ dat.]
   to please
plausus, -ūs *applause*
plēbs, plebis (f.) *common people*
plumbum, -ī *lead*
plūrimum *very much*
plūrimus, -a, -um *most*
plūs, plūris *more*
Plūtō, Plūtōnis (m.) *Pluto* (god)
pōculum, -ī *cup, drink*

poena, -ae *punishment, penalty*
poēta, -ae *poet*
pollex, pollicis (m.) *thumb*
pompa, -ae *procession*
pōmum, -ī *apple*
pōmus, -ī (f.) *fruit tree*
pōne *behind*
pōnō, -ere, posuī, positus *to put, place*
pōns, pontis (m.) *bridge*
pontus, -ī *(deep) sea*
populāris, populāre *popular*
populus, -ī *people*
porrō *in turn*
porta, -ae *gate*
portō (1) *to carry*
portus, -ūs *port, harbor*
possideō, -ēre, -sēdī, -sessus *to possess*
post [+ acc.] *after*
posteā *afterwards*
posterus, -a, -um *next*
postquam *after*
postrēmō *finally*
postulō (1) *to demand*
posu- see **pōnō**
potēns, potentis *powerful*
potentia, -ae *power*
potestās, potestātis (f.) *power*
potius *rather*
praebeō, -ēre, -buī, -bitus *to offer, show*
praecipiō, -ere, -cēpī, -cēptus *to command,
   order*
praecipuus, -a, -um *special, particular*
praeclārē *excellently*
praeclūdō, -ere, -clūsī, -clūsus *to close*
praeda, -ae *booty, loot*
praeferō, praeferre, praetulī, praelātus *to
   carry before*
praeficiō, -ere, praefēcī, praefectus
   to put in command of
praemittō, -ere, -mīsī, -missus *to send forth*
praemium, -ī *reward*
praesēns, praesentis *present*
praesidium, -ī *support, assistance*
praestō, -āre, praestitī, praestitus *to be
   superior, excel*
praesum, praeesse, praefuī, *to be at
   the head*
praeter [+ acc.] *beyond, except*
praetereā *besides, moreover*
praetor, -tōris (m.) *praetor*
praetrepidus, -a, -um *very nervous*
prātum, -ī *meadow*
prehendō, -ere, -hendī, -hēnsus *to seize*

premō, -ere, pressī, pressus *to press*
press- see **premō**
pretium, -ī *price*
prīmum *at first, to begin with*
prīmus, -a, -um *first*
prīnceps, prīncipis (m.) *chief, leader*
prīncipium, -ī *beginning*
prius *before*
prīvō (1) [+ abl.] *to deprive*
prō [+ abl.] *for, in front of*
procāx, procācis *bold, insolent*
prōcēdō, -ere, -cessī, -cessus *to advance*
procul *at a distance*
prōdeō, prōdīre, prōdīvī/prōdiī, prōditus
  to advance
proelium, -ī *battle*
profectiō, -ōnis (f.) *departure*
profectō *really*
prōferō, prōferre, prōtulī, prōlātus *to bring
  forth, mention*
proficīscor, -ī, profectus sum *to set out*
profundus, -a, -um *deep*
prōh dolor *I am sorry; unfortunately*
prohibeō, -ēre, prohibuī, prohibitus *to prevent*
prōlēs, prōlis (f.) *offspring*
prōmeritum, -ī *merit*
prōmittō, -ere, -mīsī, -missus *to promise*
prōnūntiō (1) *to announce*
prope [+ acc.] *near; (as adverb) nearly*
properō (1) *to hasten*
propinquus, -ī *kinsman*
propinquus, -a, -um *neighbouring*
propior, propius *shorter, closer*
proprius, -a, -um *one's own*
propter [+ acc.] *on account of*
proptereā *therefore*
proptereā quod *because*
prōsequor, prōsequī, prōsecūtus sum *to pursue*
prosperus, -a, -um *prosperous, fortunate*
prōspiciō, -ere, -spexī, -spectus *to watch*
prōsum, prōdesse, prōfuī [+ dat.] *to benefit*
prōvectus, -a, -um *advanced*
prōvincia, -ae *province*
proximus, -a, -um *nearest*
prūdēns, prūdentis *prudent*
pūblicus, -a, -um *public*
  rēs pūblica *republic*
puella, -ae *girl*
puer, puerī *boy*
pugna, -ae *battle*
pugnō (1) *to fight*
pulcher, pulchra, pulchrum *beautiful*
pulsō (1) *to knock*

puppis, puppis (f.) *ship*
pupul- see **pellō**
pūrgō (1) *to clean*
pūrus, -a, -um *pure*
putō (1) *to think*
pyra, -ae *pyre*
Pȳthia, -ae *Pythia*
quā *where*
quadrīga, -ae *chariot*
quaerō, -ere, quaesīvī, quaesītus *to ask,
  inquire, seek*
quaestūra, -ae *quaestorship*
quaestus, -ūs *advantage, profit*
quālis, quāle *what kind*
quam *how; than*
quamquam *although*
quamvīs *although*
quandō *when; since*
quantus, -a, -um *how much, how great*
quartus, -a, -um *fourth*
quasi *as if*
quattuor *four*
-que *and* (attaches to the second of a pair)
queror, -ī, questus sum *to complain*
questus, -ūs *lament*
quī *who*
quī, quae, quod *which*
quia *because*
quīcumque, quaecumque, quidcumque
  whoever, whatever
quīcumque, quaecumque,
  quodcumque *whichever*
quid *what*
quīdam, quaedam, quiddam
  certain [pronoun]
quīdam, quaedam, quoddam
  certain [adjective]
quidem *indeed*
quiēscō, -ere, quiēvī, quiētus *to keep silent*
quiētus, -a, -um *peaceful, still*
quīn *that*
quīntus *fifth*
quīque, quaeque, quodque *each* [adjective]
Quirīs, Quirītis (m.) *Roman citizen*
quis *who?*
quisquam, quidquam *anyone, anything*
quisque, quidque *each one, each thing*
quisquis, quidquid *whoever, whatever*
quō *to where*
quod *because; as*
quōmodo *how?*
quōnam *where?*
quoniam *since*

quoque *also*
quotiēns *how often*
rabiēs, rabiēī *rage, fury*
rāmus, -ī *branch*
rapiō, -ere, rapuī, raptus *to snatch*
ratiō, ratiōnis (f.) *account, reasoning*
ratis, ratis (f.) *raft, ship, vessel*
recēns, recentis *recent*
recessus, -ūs *retreat*
recipiō, -ere, recēpī, receptus *to receive*
reclūdō, -ere, reclūsī, reclūsus *to open up*
rēctē *correctly*
recūsō (1) *to refuse*
reddō, -ere, reddidī, redditus *to give back, repay; render*
redeō, redīre, redīvī/rediī, reditus *to return*
redūcō, -ere, -dūxī, -ductus *to lead back*
referō, -ferre, rettulī, relātus *to bring back*
rēgīna, -ae *queen*
regiō, -ōnis (f.) *region, country*
rēgius, -a, -um *royal*
rēgnum, -ī *kingdom*
regō, -ere, rēxī, rēctus *to rule*
relinquō, -ere, relīquī, relictus *to leave, abandon*
reliquus, -a, -um *remaining*
remaneō, -ēre, -mānsī, -mānsus *to remain*
removeō, -ēre, -ōvī, -ōtus *to remove*
repentē *suddenly*
repentīnus, -a, -um *hasty*
reperiō, -īre, repperī, repertus *to find*
repleō, -ēre, -plēvī, -plētus *to refill*
rēs, reī (f.) *thing, matter; state*
  rēs pūblica *republic*
resistō, -ere, restitī, [+ dat.] *to resist*
resolvō, -ere, resolvī, resolūtus *to relax*
resorbeō, -ēre *to suck back*
respondeō, -ēre, respondī, respōnsus *to respond*
retineō, -ēre, -tinuī, -tentus *to restrain*
rēx- see **regō**
rēx, rēgis (m.) *king*
Rhēnus, -ī *Rhine River*
Rhodanus, -ī *Rhone River*
Rhodus, -ī (f.) *Rhodes*
rīdeō, -ēre, rīsī, rīsus *to laugh*
rīdiculus, -a, -um *funny*
rigeō, -ēre, riguī *to be rigid*
rīpa, -ae *riverbank*
rīs- see **rīdeō**
rīte *properly*
rōbustus, -a, -um *strong*
rogō (1) *to ask, request*
rogus, -ī *funeral pyre*
Rōma, -ae *Rome*

Rōmānus, -a, -um *Roman*
rostrum, -ī *beak*
ruber, rubra, rubrum *red*
rūmor, rūmōris (m) *rumour*
ruō, -ere, ruī *to go to ruin*
rūrsus *again*
rūs, rūris (nt.) *country, countryside*
sacer, sacra, sacrum *holy, sacred*
sacrificium, -ī *sacrifice*
saepe *often*
saevus, -a, -um *wrathful, cruel*
sagitta, -ae *arrow*
sāl, salis (m.) *salt; humour, wit*
saliō, -īre, salui, saltus *to jump*
salsē *humorously*
salūs, salūtis (f.) *safety; health; greeting*
salūtō (1) *to greet*
salvus, -a, -um *intact, safe, well*
sanguis, sanguinis (m.) *blood*
sānus, -a, -um *sane*
sapiēns, sapientis *wise*
sapienter *wisely*
sapientia, -ae *wisdom*
satis *enough, sufficient* [indeclinable adj.]
saxum, -ī *rock*
scapulae, -ārum *shoulder blades*
scelerātus, -a, -um *wicked*
scelus, sceleris (nt.) *crime, wickedness*
scientia, -ae *knowledge*
sciō, -īre, scīvī, scītus *to know*
scrībō, -ere, scrīpsī, scrīptus *to write*
scrīptor, scrīptōris (m.) *writer*
scrīptum, -ī *writing, written work*
scūtum, -ī *shield*
sēcrētus, -a, -um *private, secret*
secundus, -a, -um *second; next; prosperous*
sed *but*
sedeō, -ēre, sēdī, sessus *to sit*
sēdēs, sēdis (f.) *seat*
sēditiō, sēditiōnis (f.) *insurrection*
sēmen, sēminis (nt.) *seed*
semper *always*
senātor, senātōris (m.) *senator*
senātus, -ūs *senate*
senecta, -ae *old age*
senex, senis *old*
sēns- see **sentiō**
sēnsus, -ūs *sense*
sententia, -ae *opinion*
sentiō, -īre, sēnsī, sēnsus *to feel*
sepeliō, -īre, sepelīvī, sepultus *to bury*
septem *seven*
sepulcrum, -ī *tomb*

Sēquanī, -ōrum *Sequani* (between Saone River and Jura Mts.)

sequor, sequī, secūtus sum *to follow*

serpēns, serpentis (m./f.) *snake*

serpō, -ere, serpsī, serptus *to crawl*

serta, -ōrum *garlands*

serva, -ae *servant, female slave*

serviō, -īre, servīvī, servītus [+ dat.] *to serve*

servitūs, servitūtis (f.) *slavery*

servō (1) *to save*

servus, -ī *male servant, slave*

seu *or, whether*

sevēritās, sevēritātis (f.) *strictness*

sī *if*

sībila, -ōrum *whistling*

sīc *in this way*

sīcut *likewise*

sīdus, sīderis (nt.) *star, constellation*

silentium, -ī *silence*

silva, -ae *forest*

similis, simile *similar*

simul *at once*

simul atque *as soon as*

sine [+ abl.] *without*

singulārius, -a, -um *single*

singulī, -ae, -a *one each*

sinus, -ūs *love*

sitis, sitis (f.) *thirst*

sīve . . . sīve *either . . . or*

societās, societātis (f.) *fellowship, alliance*

socius, -ī *ally, comrade*

sōl, sōlis (m.) *sun*

soleō, -ēre, solitus sum *to be in the habit*

sollicitō (1) *to trouble, disturb*

sōlum *only*

solum, -ī *ground, land*

sōlus, -a, -um *alone, sole*

solvō, -ere, solvī, solūtus *to loosen, free*

somniō (1) *to dream*

somnium, -ī *dream*

somnus, -ī *sleep*

sonus, -ī *noise, sound*

sopor, sopōris (m.) *slumber*

sordidus, -a, -um *dirty*

soror, sorōris (f.) *sister*

sors, sortis (f.) *lot, luck*

spatium, -ī *space; period (of time)*

speciēs, -ēī *appearance*

spectātor, spectātōris (m.) *spectator*

spectō (1) *to observe*

spērō (1) *to hope*

spēs, -eī *hope*

spīrō (1) *to breathe, blow*

splendor, splendōris (m.) *lustre*

spoliō (1) *to rob, plunder*

squālor, squālōris (m.) *filth, dirtiness*

stabulum, -ī *stable, stall*

statim *immediately*

statua, -ae *statue*

status, -ūs *position, standing*

stēlla, -ae *star*

stet- see **stō**

stō, stāre, stetī, status *to stand*

struō, -ere, strūxī, strūctus *to heap up*

studeō, -ēre, studuī *to be eager (for), to be zealous*

studium, -ī *zeal, enthusiasm; spirit*

stultē *foolishly*

stupor, stupōris (m.) *bewilderment*

Stymphālus, -ī *Stymphalus* (city)

Styx, Stygis (f.) *Styx* (river)

suāvis, suave *sweet, pleasant, kind*

suāvitās, suāvitātis (f.) *sweetness*

subdō, -ere, -didī, -ditus (+ dat.) *to put under*

subigō, -ere, subēgī, subāctus *to impel, compel*

subitō *suddenly*

sublica, -ae *pile*

subscrīptiō, subscrīptiōnis (f.) *note of a censor*

subsidium, -ī *relief*

succurrō, -ere, succurrī, succursus [+ dat.] *to run to help*

sum, esse, fuī, futūrus *to be*

summa, -ae *chief part*

summus, -a, -um *highest, greatest*

sūmō, -ere, sumpsī, sūmptus *to assume*

sūmptus, -ūs *cost, expense*

superior, superius *higher; preceding*

superō (1) *to outlive*

superstitiō, superstitiōnis (f.) *superstition*

superus, -a, -um *upper, above*

supplēmentum, -ī *reinforcements*

supplicātiō, supplicātiōnis (f.) *thanksgiving*

supplicium, -ī *punishment*

surgō, -ere, surrēxī, surrēctus *to stand up, rise*

suscipiō, -ere, -cēpī, -ceptus *to undertake*

suspīciō, suspīciōnis (f.) *suspicion, mistrust*

suus, -a, -um *his own, her own, its own, their own, one's own*

symbola, -ae *contribution (for a common meal)*

tābēscō, -ere, tābēscuī *to decay*

taceō, -ēre, tacuī, tacitus *to be silent*

tālis, tāle *such*

tam *so*

tamen *nevertheless, all the same*

tamquam *just as, as if*

tandem *finally; (in questions) just*

tangō, -ere, tetigī, tāctus   *to touch*
tantum   *only*
tantus, -a, -um   *so great*
taurus, -ī   *bull*
tēctum, -ī   *roof, house*
tegō, -ere, tēxī, tēctus   *to cover*
tēlum, -ī   *javelin, weapon*
tempestās, tempestātis (f.)   *weather, storm*
templum, -ī   *temple*
tempus, temporis (nt.)   *time*
tendō, -ere, tetendī, tentus   *to stretch out; aim*
tenebrae, -ārum   *darkness*
teneō, -ēre, tenuī, tentus   *to hold*
tergum, -ī   *hide*
ternī, -ōrum   *three each*
terra, -ae   *land*
terreō, -ēre, terruī, territus   *to frighten, terrify*
terribilis, terribile   *terrifying*
terror, terrōris (m.)   *fright, terror*
tertius, -a, -um   *third*
tetig-   see **tangō**
tēx-   see **tegō**
theātrum, -ī   *theatre*
Thēbae, -ārum   *Thebes*
Thessalia, -ae   *Thessaly*
Thrācia, -ae   *Thrace*
Tiberis, Tiberis (m.)   *Tiber River*
timeō, -ēre, timuī   *to be afraid, fear*
timidē   *timidly*
timidus, -a, -um   *shy*
timor, timōris (m.)   *fear*
Tīrȳns, Tīrynthis (acc. -ntha)   *Tiryns* (city)
titulus, -ī   *inscription*
tolerō (1)   *to endure*
tollō, -ere, sustulī, sublātus   *to lift*
torus, -ī   *couch, bed*
tot   *so many*
tōtus, -a, -um   [gen. sg.: -īus, dat. sg.: -ī]
   whole, entire, all
trabs, trabis (f.)   *beam*
trādō, -ere, trādidī, trāditus   *to hand down*
trādūcō, -ere, -dūxī, -ductus   *to lead across*
trahō, -ere, trāxī, trāctus   *to drag, take*
tranquillus, -a, -um   *calm*
trāns [+ acc.]   *through*
trānsfīgō, -ere, -fīxī, -fīxus   *to pierce through*
trānseō, -īre, -īvī, -itus   *to cross over*
trānsitus, -ūs   *passage*
trāx-   see **trahō**
trecentī, -ae, -a   *300*
trēs, tria   *three*
trīgintā   *30*
tristis, triste   *sad*

tristitia, -ae   *sadness*
tū   *you* (sg.)
tul-   see **ferō**
tum   *then*
tumeō, -ēre, tumuī   *to swell*
tumultus, -ūs   *confusion*
tumulus, -ī   *mound*
tunica, -ae   *undergarment, tunic*
turba, -ae   *mob; riot*
turbō (1)   *to disturb*
turpiculus, -a, -um   *somewhat ugly*
turpis, turpe   *disgraceful*
tūtus, -a, -um   *safe*
tuus, -a, -um   *your* (sg.)
tyrannus, -ī   *tyrant*
ubi   *when, where*
ubique   *everywhere*
ūllus, -a, -um   [gen. sg.: -īus, dat. sg. –ī] *any*
ulterior, ulteriōris   *farther*
ultimus, -a, -um   *last, edge of*
ultrō   *of one's own accord, voluntarily*
umbra, -ae   *shadow, shade*
umerus, -ī   *shoulder*
ūmor, ūmōris (m.)   *moisture*
umquam   *ever*
unda, -ae   *wave, water*
unde   *from where*
undique   *from all sides, everywhere*
ūnus, -a, -um   [gen.: -īus, dat.: -ī]
   one, alone, single, sole
urbs, urbis (f.)   *city*
ūrō, -ere, ūssī, ūstus   *to burn*
ursa, -ae   *bear*
ūsus, -ūs   *use*
ut(ī)   *that, as*
uter, utra, utrum   *which?*
uterque, utraque, utrumque   *each of two*
utervīs, utravīs, utrumvīs   *either one,*
   whichever of the two you please
ūtor, -ī, ūsus sum [+ abl.]   *to use*
utrum . . . an   [double question]
uxor, uxōris (f.)   *wife*
vacca, -ae   *cow*
valdē   *greatly*
valē   *farewell!*
valeō, -ēre, valuī   *to be strong*
validius   *more strongly*
vallum, -ī   *rampart*
vānus, -a, -um   *empty*
vastō (1)   *to devastate*
vātēs, vātis (m./f.)   *soothsayer*
vector, vectōris (m.)   *passenger*
vehementer   *vehemently, very much*

vel *or, rather*

vēlum, -ī *sail*; vēla (pl.) dare *to set sail*

velut *just as*

vendō, -ere, vendidī, venditus *to sell*

venēnum, -ī *poison*

veniō, -īre, vēnī, ventus *to come*

ventus, -ī *wind*

venustus, -a, -um *charming*

verbum, -ī *word*

vērē *truly*

vērnus, -a, -um *vernal, of spring*

vērō *in truth, in fact*

versus, -ūs *verse, line of poetry*

vertō, -ere, vertī, versus *to turn*

vērum *in truth, to be sure*

vērus, -a, -um *true*

vervēx, vervēcis (m.) *wether; stupid person*

vescor, -ī [+ abl.] *to eat*

vester, vestra, vestrum *your (pl.)*

vestīgium, -ī *footstep, track*

vestis, vestis (f.) *clothing*

vestītus, -ūs *clothing*

vetitus, -a, -um *forbidden*

vetus, veteris *old*

vexō (1) *to trouble*

via, -ae *road, way*

vibrō (1) *to sparkle*

vīcīnus, -a, -um *neighbouring*

vicis (f.) (no nom.) *change, turn*; in vicem *in turn*

victima, -ae *victim*

victor, victōris *victorious*

victōria, -ae *victory*

videō, -ēre, vīdī, vīsus *to see*; [passive] *seem*

vigil, vigilis *awake*

vīgintī *twenty*

vīlla, -ae *country house*

vincō, -ere, vīcī, victus *to conquer*

vinculum, -ī *chain*

vindicō (1) *to liberate, protect*

vīnum, -ī *wine*

violō (1) *to violate*

vir, -ī *man*

virgō, virginis (f.) *maiden, virgin*

virtūs, virtūtis (f.) *courage, virtue*

vīs, (pl.) vīrēs, vīrium (f.) *force, power, strength*; (pl.) *strength*

viscera, viscerum (nt. pl.) *entrails, flesh*

vīta, -ae *life*

vitium, -ī *fault*

vītō (1) *to avoid, shun*

vīvō, -ere, vīxī, vīctus *to live*

vīvus, -a, -um *alive*

vīx- see **vīvō**

vocō (1) *to call*

volō, velle, voluī *to want, wish*

volturius ~ vulturius, -ī *vulture*

voltus, -ūs (m.) *face*

voluntās, voluntātis (f.) *will*

voluptās, voluptātis (f.) *pleasure*

vōs *you* (pl.)

vōx, vōcis (f.) *voice*

Vulcānus, -ī *Vulcan* (god)

vulgus, -ī *crowd*

vulnerō (1) *to wound*

vulnus, vulneris (nt.) *wound*

vultus, -ūs *face, expression*

English–Latin

abandon relinquō, -ere, relīquī, relictus

about dē [+ abl.]

across trāns [+ acc.]

after post [+ acc.]; postquam [+ verbal clause]

age aetās, aetātis (f.)

against contrā [+ acc.]

aid auxilium, -ī

air āēr, āeris (m.)

all omnis, omne

ally socius, -ī

alone sōlus, -a, -um

altar āra, -ae

always semper

ambush īnsidiae, -ārum

ancient antīquus, -a, -um

anger īra, -ae

animal animal, animālis (nt.)

announce nūntiō (1)

anyone, anything quisquam, quidquam

arm bracchium, -ī

army exercitus, -ūs

around circum [+ acc.]

arrive adveniō, -īre, -vēnī, -ventus

arrow sagitta, -ae

ask rogō (1); quaerō, -ere, quaesīvī, quaesītus [dē *from*]

attack [noun] impetus, -ūs; [verb] oppugnō (1)

author auctor, auctōris (m.)

bad　malus, -a, -um
barbarian　barbarus, -ī
battle　pugna, -ae
be　sum, esse, fuī
be able　possum, posse, potuī
be absent　absum, abesse, āfuī
be afraid　timeō, -ēre, timuī
be eager　studeō, -ēre, studuī [+ dat.]
be open　pateō, -ēre, patuī
be present　adsum, adesse, adfuī
be strong　valeō, -ēre, valuī
bear　ursa, -ae
beautiful　pulcher, pulchra, pulchrum
because　quod
before　ante [+ acc.]
begin　incipiō, -ere, incēpī, inceptus
believe　crēdō, -ere, crēdidī, crēditus [+ dat.]
between　inter [+ acc.]
bird　avis, avis (f.)
black　niger, nigra, nigrum
blind　caecus, -a, -um
blood　sanguis, sanguinis (m.)
book　liber, librī
border　fīnis, fīnis (m.)
bow　arcus, -ūs
boy　puer, -ī
branch　rāmus, -ī
break　frangō, -ere, frēgī, frāctus
bridge　pōns, pontis (m.)
bring　ferō, ferre, tulī, lātus
broad　lātus, -a, -um
brother　frāter, frātris (m.)
build　aedificō (1)
bull　taurus, -ī
burn　ārdeō, -ēre, ārsī, ārsus
buy　emō, -ere, ēmī, ēmptus
camp　castra, -ōrum
can　possum, posse, potuī
carry　portō (1); ferō, ferre, tulī, lātus
cave　antrum, -ī
certain　quīdam, quaedam, quiddam
children　līberī, -ōrum
citizen　cīvis, cīvis (m./f.)
city　urbs, urbis (f.)
close　claudō, -ere, clausī, clausus
clothing　vestis, vestis (f.)
cloud　nūbēs, nūbis (f.)
coast　lītus, lītoris (nt.)
come　veniō, -īre, vēnī, ventus
command　imperō (1) [+ dat.]
conquer　vincō, -ere, vīcī, victus
country　patria, -ae
country house　vīlla, -ae

countryside　rūs, rūris (nt.)
courage　virtūs, virtūtis (f.)
cover　tegō, -ere, tēxī, tēctus
crime　scelus, sceleris (nt.)
crowd　vulgus, -ī
crowded　frequēns, frequentis
crown　corōna, -ae
cruel　crūdēlis, crūdēle
damn (that damn)　iste, ista, istud
danger　perīculum, -ī
dark　obscūrus, -a, -um
darkness　tenebrae, -ārum
daughter　fīlia, -ae
day　diēs, -ēī (m.)
decide　cernō, -ere, crēvī, crētus
deep　altus, -a, -um
deep sea　pontus, -ī
deny　negō (1)
depart　discēdō, -ere, discessī, discessus
descend　dēscendō, -ere, dēscendī, dēscēnsus
desire　optō (1); cupiō, -ere, cupīvī, cupītus
destroy　dēleō, -ēre, dēlēvī, dēlētus
dinner　cēna, -ae
disgraceful　turpis, turpe
divide　dīvidō, -ere, dīvīsī, dīvīsus
do　faciō, -ere, fēcī, factus
dog　canis, canis (m./f.)
down from　dē [+ abl.]
drag　trahō, -ere, trāxī, trāctus
dream　somnium, -ī
drink　bibō, -ere, bibī, bibitus
drive　agō, -ere, ēgī, āctus
drive away　pellō, -ere, pupulī, pulsus
eagle　aquila, -ae
emperor　imperātor, imperātōris (m.)
enemy　inimīcus, ī; hostis, hostis (m./f.)
envy　invideō, -ēre, invīdī, invīsus [+ dat.]
evil　malus, -a, -um
everyone, everything　quisque, quidque
extend　pateō, -ēre, patuī
eye　oculus, -ī
faith　fidēs, -eī
fall　cadō, -ere, cecidī, cāsus
family　familia, -ae
famous　clārus, -a, -um
farmer　agricola, -ae (m.)
fat　pinguis, pingue
father　pater, patris (m.)
fatherland　patria, -ae
favour　faveō, -ēre, fāvī, fautus [+ dat.]
feed　pāscō, -āre, pāvī, pāstus
feel　sentiō, -īre, sēnsī, sēnsus
field　ager, agrī

fierce ācer, ācra, ācrum
fight pugnō (1)
fill impleō, -ēre, implēvī, implētus
find inveniō, -īre, invēnī, inventus
fire ignis, ignis (m.)
firm firmus, -a, -um
fish piscis, piscis (m.)
flame flamma, -ae
flock pecū, pecūs
flower flōs, flōris (m.)
food cibus, -ī
force cōgō, -ere, coēgī, coāctus
forest silva, -ae
fortify mūniō, -īre, mūnīvī, mūnītus
fortunate prosperus, a, -um
free līber, lībera, līberum
friendly amīcus, -a, -um
frighten terreō, -ēre, terruī, territus
from ā [+ abl.]; *(down) from* dē [+ abl.]
garden hortus, -ī
gate porta, -ae
girl puella, -ae
give dō, dare, dedī, datus
go eō, īre, īvī/iī, itus
god deus, -ī
goddess dea, -ae
gold aurum, -ī
golden aureus, -a, -um
good bonus, -a, -um
grant indulgeō, -ēre, indulsī [+ dat.]
great magnus, -a, -um
grief lūctus, -ūs
grow crēscō, -ere, crēvī, crētus
guardian custōs, custōdis (m./f.)
hand manus, -ūs (f.)
happy laetus, -a, -um; fēlīx, fēlīcis
harm [noun] noxa, -ae; [verb] noceō, -ēre, nocuī, nocitus
harsh asper, aspera, asperum
hasten properō (1)
hate ōdī, ōdisse [perfect forms are translated as present]
hatred odium, -ī
have habeō, -ēre, habuī, habitus
head caput, capitis (nt.)
hear audiō, -īre, audīvī, audītus
heart cor, cordis (nt.)
help auxilium, -ī
here hīc; *(to) here* hūc
high altus, -a, -um
hold teneō, -ēre, tenuī, tentus
holy sacer, sacra, sacrum
honey mel, mellis (nt.)

hope spēs, -eī
horn cornū, -ūs
horse equus, -ī
horseman eques, equitis (m.)
house domus, -ūs (f.)
how many quot
humble humilis, humile
hunger famēs, famis (f.)
immortal immortālis, immortāle
in in [+ abl.]
in front of prō [+ abl.]
indulge indulgeō, -ēre, indulsī [+ dat.]
inhabitant incola, -ae (m.)
injustice iniūria, -ae
into in [+ acc.]
iron ferrum, -ī
island īnsula, -ae
jar (2-handled) amphora, -ae
joy laetitia, -ae
joyful iūcundus, -a, -um
keen ācer, ācris, ācre
keep teneō, -ēre, tenuī, tentus
kill interficiō, -ere, interfēcī, interfectus
king rēx, rēgis (m.)
kingdom rēgnum, -ī
knee genū, -ūs
knight eques, equitis (m.)
know sciō, -īre, scīvī, scītus; *perfect*, nōvī, nōtus (its non-perfect forms **nōscō, -ere** mean *learn*)
   not know nesciō, -īre, nescīvī, nescītus
lake lacus, -ūs
land terra, -ae
language lingua, -ae
laugh rīdeō, -ēre, rīsī, rīsus
law lēx, lēgis (f.)
lead dūcō, -ere, dūxī, ductus
learn discō, -ere, didicī
leave relinquō, -ere, relīquī, relictus
legion legiō legiōnis (f.)
letter litterae, -ārum; epistula, -ae
life vīta, -ae
lion leō, leōnis (m.)
live vīvō, -ere, vīxī, vīctus
long longus, -a, -um
loot praeda, -ae
love amō (1)
luck fortūna, -ae; sors, sortis (f.)
make faciō, -ere, fēcī, factus
male slave servus, -ī
man vir, -ī; homō, hominis (m.)
many multus, -a, -um
master dominus, -ī

memory   memoria, -ae
mind   animus, -ī
mob   turba, -ae
money   pecūnia, -ae
moon   lūna, -ae
mother   māter, mātris (m.)
mountain   mōns, montis (m.)
mouth   ōs, ōris (nt.)
my   meus, -a, -um
name   nōmen, nōminis (nt.)
near   apud [+ acc.]
nearest   proximus, -a, -um
neighbours   fīnitimī, -ōrum
neither   neuter, neutra, neutrum
new   novus, -a, -um
no   nūllus, -a, -um
no one   nēmō, nēminis (m./f.)
noble   nōbilis, nōbile
not   nōn
not know   nesciō, -īre, nescīvī, nescītus
not want   nōlō, nōlle, nōluī
nothing   nihil, nīl
nymph   nympha, -ae
obey   pāreō, -ēre, pāruī, pāritus [+ dat.]
offspring   prōlēs, prōlis (f.)
old   senex, senis
on   in [+ abl.]
on account of   propter [+ acc.]; ob [+ acc.]
one   ūnus, -a, -um
only   modum
open   aperiō, -īre, aperuī, apertus
ought   dēbeō, -ēre, dēbuī, dēbitus
our   noster, nostra, nostrum
out of   ē/ex [+ abl.]
overtake   praetereō, praeterīre,
   praeteriī, praeteritus
pastures   pecūs, pecuum
parent   parēns, parentis (m./f.)
   [not an *i*-stem]
peace   pāx, pācis (f.)
peaceful   quiētus, -a, -um
people   populus, -ī
persuade   persuādeō, -ēre, persuāsī,
   persuāsus [+ dat.]
place [noun]   locus, -ī (pl. is neuter: loca,
   -ōrum); [verb] pōnō, -ere, posuī, positus
plain   campus, -ī
poet   poēta, -ae
poor   pauper, pauperis
praise   laudō (1)
prefer   mālō, mālle, māluī; antepōnō, -ere,
   anteposuī, antepositus
prepare   parō (1)

press   premō, -ere, pressī, pressus
price   pretium, -ī
prison   carcer, carceris (m.)
prosperous   prosperus, -a, -um
province   prōvincia, -ae
punishment   poena, -ae
put in command   praeficiō, -ere, -fēcī, -fectus
queen   rēgīna, -ae
quick   celer, celeris, celere
radiant   candidus, -a, -um
ramparts   moenia, moenium (nt. pl.)
read   legō, -ere, lēgī, lēctus
receive   accipiō, -ere, -cēpī, -ceptus
recent   recēns, recentis
remain   maneō, -ēre, mānsī, mānsus
remember   meminī, meminisse [+ gen.]
respond   respondeō, -ēre, respondī,
   respōnsus
reward   praemium, -ī
river   flūmen, flūminis (nt.)
riverbank   rīpa, -ae
road   via, -ae
Rome   Rōma, -ae
rule   regō, -ere, rēxī, -rēctus
rumor   rūmor, rūmōris (m.)
run   currō, -ere, cucurrī, cursus
sacred   sacer, sacra, sacrum
sad   tristis, triste
sail   nāvigō (1); set sail   vēla (pl) dare
sailor   nauta, -ae (m.)
same   īdem, eadem, idem
save   servō (1)
say   dīcō, -ere, dīxī, dictus
sea   aequor, aequoris (nt.); deep sea   pontus, -ī
secretly   clam
see   videō, -ēre, vīdī, vīsus
seek   petō, -ere, petīvī, petītus
seek from   petere ā [+ abl.]
seize   capiō, -ere, cēpī, captus
-self   ipse, ipsa, ipsud
sell   vendō, -ere, vendidī, venditus
senate   senātus, -ūs
send   mittō, -ere, mīsī, missus
sense   sentiō, -īre, sēnsī, sēnsus
serious   gravis, grave
servant (female)   serva, -ae; (male) servus, -ī
serve   serviō, -īre, servīvī, servītus [+ dat.]
set sail   vēlum, -ī; [verb] vēla (pl) dare
shade   umbra, -ae
shadow   umbra, -ae
sheep   ovis, ovis (f.)
shine   fulgeō, -ēre, fulsī,
shining white   candidus, -a, -um

ship nāvis, nāvis (f.)
short brevis, breve
similar similis, simile [+ dat.]
sing canō, -ere, cecinī, cantus
sister soror, sorōris (f.)
sky caelum, -ī
sleep [noun] somnus, -ī; [verb] dormiō, -īre, dormīvī, dormītus
slow lentus, -a, -um
small parvus, -a, -um
smell odor, odōris (m.)
soldier mīles, mīlitis (m.)
some alius, alia, aliud
some . . . other alius . . . alius
someone aliquis, aliquid
son fīlius, -ī
song carmen, carminis (nt.)
soothsayer vātēs, vātis (m./f.)
soul anima, -ae
spirit animus, -ī
stand stō, stāre, stetī, status
star stēlla, -ae
state cīvitās, cīvitātis (f.)
storm tempestās, tempestātis (f.)
story fābula, -ae
stream amnis, amnis (m.)
street via, -ae
strike pellō, -ere, pupulī, pulsus
strong fortis, forte; *be strong* valeō, -ēre, valuī
sun sōl, sōlis (m.)
sweet dulcis, dulce
swift celer, celeris, celere
sword gladius, -ī
take capiō, -ere, cēpī, captus
teach doceō, -ēre, docuī, doctus
teacher magister, magistrī
tear lacrima, -ae
temple templum, -ī
than quam
that, those ille, illa, illud
their own suus, -a, -um
there ibi
thing rēs, -eī
think putō (1)
this, these hic, haec, hoc
through per [+ acc.]
throw iaciō, -ere, iēcī, iactus
tired dēfessus, -a, -um
to ad [+ acc.]
today hodiē

tomorrow crās
tooth dēns, dentis (m.)
touch tangō, -ere, tetigī, tāctus
town oppidum, -ī
tree arbor, arboris (f.)
trust fīdō, -ere, fīsus sum [+ dat.]
turn vertō, -ere, vertī, versus
under sub [+ acc. ~ abl.]
unfriendly inimīcus, -a, -um
unhappy īnfēlīx, īnfēlicis
unknown ignōtus, -a, -um
victory victōria, -ae
wage gerō, -ere, gessī, gestus
wall mūrus, -ī; moenia, -ium (nt. pl.)
want volō, velle, voluī;
    not want nōlō, nōlle, nōluī
war bellum, -ī
warn moneō, -ēre, monuī, monitus
water aqua, -ae
wave unda, -ae
weapons arma, -ōrum
weep fleō, -ēre, flēvī, flētus
well bene
whichever quīcumque, quaecumque, quidcumque
whoever, whatever quīcumque, quaecumque, quidcumque
when quandō
where ubi; *to where* quō
which of two uter, utra, utrum
white albus, -a, -um
who quis
whole tōtus, -a, -um
why cūr; quam ob rem
wicked improbus, -a, -um
wide lātus, -a, -um
wild ferus, -a, -um
wind ventus, -ī
wine vīnum, -ī
wise sapiēns, sapientis
with cum [+ abl.]
wolf lupus, -ī
woman fēmina, -ae
word verbum, -ī
world mundus, -ī; orbis (m.) terrārum
worthy dīgnus, -a, -um
wretched miser, misera, miserum
write scrībō, -ere, scrīpsī, scrīptus
young iuvenis, iuvenis
young man adulēscēns, adulēscentis
your vester, vestra, vestrum

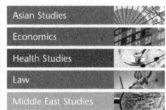

Made in the USA
Las Vegas, NV
20 February 2021